The Lady Jane Grey's Prayer Book

British Library Harley Manuscript 2342,
Fully Illustrated and Transcribed

Introduction by
J. Stephan Edwards

Copyright © 2016 J. Stephan Edwards

All rights reserved. No part of this publication may be reproduced, stored in a retrieval system, or transmitted, in any form or by any means, electronic, mechanical, photocopying, recording or otherwise, without the prior written permission of the author.

J. Stephan Edwards asserts the moral right to be identified as the author of this work.

Publisher's Cataloguing-in-Publication data

Names: Edwards, J. Stephan (John Stephan), 1958–
Title: The Lady Jane Grey's Prayer Book: British Library Harley Manuscript 2342 | by J. Stephan Edwards
Description: Palm Springs, CA: Old John Publishing, 2016 | Includes bibliographical references and index.
Identifiers: LCCN 2016909134 (print) |
 ISBN 978-0-9976809-0-4 (hardcover) |
 ISBN 978-0-9976809-1-1 (paperback).
Subjects: LCSH: Prayers and devotions—Early works to 1800. | Christian life—reformed authors.| Grey, Jane, Lady, 1537-1554. |
 BISAC: RELIGION | Prayerbooks | Christian.
Classification: LCC BV245.E39 2016 (print) | DDC 242.8
LC record available at https://lccn.loc.gov/2016909134

References to Internet Web sites (URLs) were accurate at the time of writing. Neither the author nor the publisher is responsible for URLs that may have expired or changed since the manuscript was prepared.

*For Miles Burton Cousar,
on his first birthday*

Also from this Author:

*A Queen of a New Invention:
Portraits of Lady Jane Grey Dudley,
England's Nine Days Queen*

Contents

List of Illustrations, with credits	vi
Introduction	1
A Brief History of Lady Jane Grey Dudley	21
Notes on the Transcriptions	29
The Prayer Book	31
Bibliography	319
Index	323

List of Illustrations, with Credits

Figure 1:   Spine of the modern binding of British Library Harley Manuscript 2342, *The Lady Jane Grey's Prayer Book.*
© The British Library Board, Harley 2342

Figure 2:   Detail of a letter written by Katherine Parr to Henry VIII in her own hand, dated at Hampton Court, 31 July 1544.
National Archives (Kew), State Papers 1/190, f. 220

Figure 3:   Decorated incipit W from folio 74 verso.
© The British Library Board, Harley 2342

Figure 4:   A Latin pocket Book of Hours, circa 1480, showing rich illlumination. Newberry Library (Chicago), Vault Case MS 131.
© The Newberry Library

Figure 5:   A book of psalms with cover of calf leather tooled in gold and painted, sixteenth century.
© The British Library Board, Shelfmark c17a20

Figure 6:   Book of prayers with embroidered cover showing combined cypher of King Henry VIII and Queen Katherine Parr, called "The Prayerbook of Princess Elizabeth."
© The British Library Board, Royal 7DX

Figure 7:   Enameled gold cover of pendant prayerbook, British Museum, 1894,0729.1.
© The British Museum

Figure 8:   Unknown woman with prayerbook suspended by gold chain from unseen girdle at waist, England, 1550s, Fitzwilliam Museum, PD.1-1963.
© Fitzwilliam Museum, Cambridge

Figure 9:   Unknown woman with small prayerbook open in her hands, England, 1550s, Minneapolis Institute of Art, MIA 87.6.
© Minneapolis Institue of Art

The Lady Jane Grey's Prayer Book: An Introduction*

At about noon on 12 February 1554, the Lady Jane Grey Dudley walked solemnly across the frozen ground of the Tower of London, moving slowly toward the iconic White Tower. For the past seven months, since 19 July 1553, she had been held as a prisoner in an upstairs room of the home of Nathaniel Partridge, the Gentleman Gaoler, in the southwest corner of the Tower's inner curtain wall. But on this day, the Lady Jane was to be executed for treason, despite being just seventeen years old.[1] A scaffold had been newly erected in the preceding days, positioned against the north wall of the White Tower itself, and it was toward that scaffold that Jane walked. The Lieutenant of the Tower Sir John Brydges led the way, accompanied by a handful of other officials. Two gentlewomen walked with Jane, and while they wept at the prospect of what was to come, Jane remained dry-eyed

---

* Jane Grey is commonly referred to in the modern era using simply 'Lady Jane Grey.' The modern style 'Lady' is not consistent with the style used by her own contemporaries, however. She was instead usually identified as 'the Lady Jane.' Inclusion of the definite article 'the' before the honorific 'Lord' or 'Lady' served in sixteenth-century usage to denote a person of highest rank and status, especially those of royal blood. The modern equivalent 'His/Her Royal Highness' did not come into use in England until the following century. Mary and Elizabeth Tudor, for example, were each correctly referred to as 'the Lady Mary' or 'the Lady Elizabeth' until they came to the throne as Queen (see the Third Act for the Succession, in which Edward is styled 'Prince', but his half-sisters are each styled 'the Lady' despite restoration to the royal succession). The honorific 'Princess' could not properly be used in connection with either Mary or Elizabeth since both had been declared illegitimate. And Jane's mother Frances was usually styled 'the Lady Frances' owing to her status as the daughter of a Queen of France. Jane was accorded the same honor as her mother. Additionally, after her marriage in May 1553, Jane signed her own name as "Jane Dudley," not "Jane Grey." And it is by "Jane Dudley" that she should more properly be known today. The title of this essay, however, repeats the pre-existing title of the prayer book itself.

[1] On the question of Jane's date of birth and her resulting age at the time of her execution, see J. Stephan Edwards, "On the Birth Date of Lady Jane Grey," *Notes and Queries* 54, no. 3 (Sept. 2007), 240–242; "A Further Note on the Date of Birth of Lady Jane Grey," *Notes and Queries* 55, no. 2 (June 2008), 146–148.

and calm. An executioner waited patiently on the scaffold, his axe concealed beneath the straw that covered the floor in anticipation of rivers of blood.[2]

Jane had been tried by the Court of King's Bench on 13 November 1553 and found guilty of treason, for which the only punishment was death. Her conviction stemmed from having, in what were very probably her own words, "accepted that of which I was not worthy," the Crown of England.[3] She had allowed herself to be proclaimed Queen of England on 10 July 1553 following the death of her cousin Edward VI. Her reign had lasted just nine short days. The people had risen in favor of Edward's half-sister Mary, and Jane had been deposed on 19 July. But even after Jane had been sentenced to death, Queen Mary had initially stayed the sentence in the belief that her young cousin was entirely a victim of plots hatched and carried out by others. The reprieve had been short-lived, however, for in the last week of January 1554 Sir Thomas Wyatt and others had staged a revolt in opposition to Mary's planned marriage to Prince Philip of Spain. Simultaneously, Jane's own father had rebelled against Mary in his home county of Leicestershire, calling there for the restoration of Queen Jane to the throne. Wyatt and his army succeeded in reaching the gates of London, but a public plea by Queen Mary herself saved the day. Mary realized in the aftermath of the two risings that Jane posed a potential threat to her own throne and marriage, and she therefore reluctantly allowed the execution to go forward.[4]

Earlier on that cold February morning, Jane had watched as the headless body of her husband Guildford Dudley had been wheeled back into the Tower precincts on a cart for burial in the Chapel of St Peter-ad-Vincula.[5] Like Jane, Guildford had been found guilty of treason some months earlier and sentenced to die, though Mary had briefly stayed his sentence as well. When it finally came, Guildford's execution had been a public spectacle conducted on Tower Hill, immediately outside the walls of the Tower. Jane did not witness the execution of her husband, but having seen its bloody aftermath she was all too aware of the fate that awaited her. She did at

---

[2] *The Chronicle of Queen Jane and of Two Years of Queen Mary*, edited by John Gough Nichols (London: J.B. Nichols and Son for the Camden Society, 1850), 56.

[3] Giovanni Francesco Commendone, "Il Successi d'Inghilterra" in *The Accession, Coronation, and Marriage of Mary Tudor, as related in four manuscripts of the Escorial*, translated by Cesare V. Malfatti (Barcelona, 1956), 45.

[4] On the rebellions of late January 1554 known collectively as Wyatt's Rebellion, see David Loades, *Two Tudor Conspiracies* (Cambridge: Cambridge University Press, 1965), *The Wyatt Rebellion* (Oxford: Davenant Press, 2000).

[5] *Chronicle of Queen Jane*, 54–55.

least have the small comfort of knowing that her own end would come within the walls of the Tower and out of view of the common people. There would be no crowds of curious onlookers or jeering mob. Only a small audience of workers and residents of the Tower would witness her death.

To console herself in her final moments, Jane carried in her hands a miniature prayer book no bigger than the palm of her own hand.[6] She recited the prayers from its pages as she walked.[7] Prior to leaving the Gentleman Gaoler's house, she had very carefully inscribed the little book with a message to the Lieutenant of the Tower, Sir John Brydges (see folios 74v–77r). At some unknown earlier point, and despite having been held apart throughout their incarceration, Jane and Guildford had each also written in the book messages addressed to Jane's father, Henry Grey, Duke of Suffolk (see folios 59v–60r and 78r–80r).[8] It is doubtful that Grey ever saw the messages, however. He had been captured following his rising in Leicestershire and brought to the Tower just two days before Jane's execution. Eleven days later, Henry Grey would suffer the same fate as his daughter and son-in-law.

Having arrived at the scaffold and climbed the steps to where the executioner stood, Jane turned to address the small assemblage, as was customary. Eye-witnesses to the executions of prominent persons in the sixteenth century sometimes transcribed the last words of the deceased for purposes of remembrance and dissemination, and just such an account of Jane's execution survives to detail her own final statement.

> When she mounted upon the scaffold, she said to the people standing thereabout, "Good people, I come hither to die, and by a law I am condemned to the same. The fact in deed against the Queen's highness was unlawful, and the consenting thereunto by me. But touching the procurement and desire thereof by me or on my behalf, I do wash my hands thereof in innocency, before God and the face of you good Christian people this day." And therewith she wrung her hands in which she had her book. Then she said, "I pray you all good Christian people to bear me witness that I die a true Christian woman, and that

---

[6] The pages of the prayer book measure just 85 x 70 millimeters, or 3.3 x 2.75 inches.
[7] *Chronicle of Queen Jane*, 56.
[8] The Lady Jane Grey Dudley had been held in the upstairs rooms of Gentleman Gaoler's personal quarters, as noted. Her husband Guildford Dudley and Guildford's brothers John, Ambrose, and Robert were all held in an upstairs chamber of the Beauchamp Tower about fifty yards away and incorporated into the inner curtain wall on the west side of the Tower of London. John Dudley was held in St. Thomas's Tower.

I look to be saved by none other means than by the mercy of God, in the merits of the blood of His only son Jesus Christ. And I confess when I did know the Word of God, I neglected the same and loved myself and the world and therefore this plague or punishment is happily and worthily happened unto me for my sins. And yet I thank God of His goodness that He has thus given me a time and respite to repent. And now good people, while I am alive I pray you to assist me with your prayers."

And then she kneeling down, she turned to Feckenham, saying, "Shall I say this Psalm?"[9] And he said, "Yes." Then she said the Psalm of Miserere Mei Deus in English in most devout manner to the end. Then she stood up and gave her maid Mistress Tylney her gloves and handkerchief, and her book to Master Thomas Brydges, the Lieutenant's brother.[10] Forthwith she untied her gown. The hangman went to her to have helped her off therewith, then she desired him to let her alone.[11] Turning towards her two gentlewomen who helped her off therewith, and also her frose paste and neckercher, giving to her a fair handkercher to knit about her eyes.[12] Then the hangman kneeled down and asked her forgiveness, whom she forgave most willingly. Then he willed her to stand upon the straw, which doing she saw the block. Then she said, "I pray thee dispatch me quickly." Then she kneeled down saying, "Will you take it off before I lay me down?" And the hangman answered her "No, Madame." She tied the kercher about her eyes, then feeling for the block said, "What shall I do? Where is it?" One of the standersby guiding her thereunto, she laid her head down upon the block and stretched out her body and said, "Lord, into thy hands I commend my spirit." And so she ended.[13]

---

[9] John Howman de Feckenham (c.1510–1584), Roman Catholic abbot of Westminster and chaplain-confessor to Queen Mary.

[10] Thomas Brydges (alternatively Bridges, Bruges) served first as Deputy Lieutenant of the Tower under his elder brother, eventually succeeding him briefly in the office of Lieutenant. Thomas Brydges died in 1559.

[11] The executioner was in fact an axeman. Since hangings were far more common than beheadings, the term 'hangman' was often used generically to describe all executioners.

[12] Costume historians have never adequately identified the meaning of 'frose paste,' though it is generally thought to have been a type of headdress. See Valerie Cumming, C.W. Cunnington, and P.E. Cunnington, *The Dictionary of Fashion History* (New York: Berg, 2010), s.v. 'frose paste.' A neckercher, or neckerchief, was a large square of white linen folded into a triangle and draped across the shoulders like a shawl, often with two of the three corners tucked into the bodice at the front of the shoulders. Handkercher is synonymous with handkerchief.

[13] *Here in this booke ye haue a godly epistle made by a faithful Christian A comunication*

Jane's intended eventual recipient of the prayer book, Thomas Brydges's elder brother Sir John Brydges, had been an early supporter of Mary's claim to the throne and had helped to defeat the rebellion of Thomas Wyatt in the days before Jane's execution. Mary rewarded Brydges by creating him Baron Chandos of Sudeley and by granting him possession of Sudeley Castle, former Gloucestershire home of Queen Katherine Parr. It is not known precisely why the Lady Jane gave her book to the Sir John, since he was Roman Catholic, but her inscription to him (discussed below) suggests the possibility of proselytism. Jane's prayer book remained with the Brydges of Sudeley Castle until late in the seventeenth century. The book then passed out of the Brydges family to the Reverend Robert Burscough, an official of the Church of England. His interest in Jane's prayer book stemmed no doubt from his other interests as a priest and the book's status as a historical curiosity. Burscough was otherwise a collector primarily of medieval medical manuscripts, despite having no medical training himself.[14] Following Burscough's death in 1709, his widow sold or donated portions of his collection of books, and many of the medical texts were acquired by the Library of Exeter Cathedral.

The Lady Jane's prayer book was sold separately some years later, however, in 1715. It was purchased by Robert Harley, 1st Earl of Oxford, one his era's pre-eminent collectors of books and manuscripts. The volume must have been a prized acquisition, since England was at that time in the midst of a decade-long popular obsession with the Lady Jane Grey Dudley, and her prayer book was a historical artifact imbued with a uniquely confirmable association with her.[15] Tales of the Lady Jane were at that time being deployed in multiple cultural formats as propaganda against the escalating efforts of James Stuart, the exiled Roman Catholic eldest son of King James II and VII (deposed 1688), to reclaim the thrones of England, Scotland, and Ireland following the death in 1714 of Stuart's

---

betwene Feckna[sic] and the Lady Iane Dudley. A letter that she wrote to her syster Lady Katherin. The ende of the Ladye Iane vpon the scaffolde. Ye shal haue also herein a godly prayer made by maister Iohn Knokes. (London: Successor of A. Scoloker?, 1554?), f.11r-v. This pamphlet was published just weeks after Jane's death for use as pro-reformist propaganda.

[14] Laura Nuvoloni, "The Harleian Medical Manuscripts," *The Electronic British Library Journal* 2008: Article 7, 12.
< http://www.bl.uk/eblj/2008articles/article7.html>, accessed 2 October 2015.

[15] Jean I. Marsden, Fatal Desire: Women, Sexuality, and the English Stage, 1660-1720 (Ithaca: Cornell University Press, 2006), 171.

Protestant half-sister Queen Anne.[16] The first book-length biography of the Lady Jane was published in 1714, for example.[17] The playwright Nicholas Rowe wrote *Lady Jane Grey: A Tragedy in Five Acts* early in 1715 in unambiguous support of the accession in the previous year by George of Hanover to the late Queen Anne's throne in accordance with the Act of Settlement of 1701.[18] Though commercially unsuccessful, Rowe's play nonetheless stimulated a pamphlet war on the subject of the royal succession that continued for several years thereafter. By 1725, the first purely fictionalized portrayals of her life began to be published, most of which met with great commercial success.[19] Probably influenced by the wider public fascination with the Lady Jane Grey Dudley, Harley carefully preserved her prayer book in his own library.

Robert Harley left his collection to his son, who bequeathed it in turn to his widow Henrietta Cavendish Holles Harley, Countess of Oxford and to their daughter Margaret Cavendish Harley Bentinck, Duchess of Portland. In 1753, Henrietta and Margaret sold the massive Harley collection to the British nation for £10,000, a fraction of the collection's contemporary monetary value. The Harley collection, together with the collections of Sir Robert Cotton and Sir Hans Sloane, became the foundational basis of the British Museum. The prayer book remained with the Library Department of the British Museum until Parliament authorized the creation of a

---

[16] The Roman Catholic James II of England and VII of Scotland had been deposed in 1688 for reasons of religion. He fled to the continent with his infant son James Stuart, and his adult Protestant daughter Mary assumed the throne together with her husband, William of Orange, also a Protestant. Mary died without surviving issue and was succeeded by her Protestant sister Anne in 1707. Anne also died without surviving issue, and the throne passed to George of Hanover as the senior heir of James II and VII's Protestant maternal aunt, Elizabeth Stuart, Queen of Bohemia and Electress of Hanover.

[17] Anon., *The Life, Character, and Death of the most Illustrious Pattern of Female Virtue, the Lady Jane Gray, Who was Beheaded in the Tower at 16 Years of Age, for her Steadfast Adherence to the Protestant Religion* (London: James Roberts, 1714).

[18] The Act of Settlement, passed in 1701 (12 and 13 Will. 3 c.2), barred Roman Catholics from the royal succession. Setting aside all Catholic descendants of the deposed James II and VII, it vested the crown in the Protestant descendants of Elizabeth Stuart, daughter of the James VI of Scotland, who had himself become the first Stuart King of England when he succeeded Elizabeth I in 1603. Elizabeth Stuart was the elder sister of King Charles I and thus a paternal aunt to Charles II and James II. Elizabeth's daughter Sophia became in 1660 the mother of the future King George I of the United Kingdom of Great Britain and Ireland.

[19] James Roberts, *The History and Fall of the Lady Jane Grey* (London: Printed by J. Watts for J. Roberts, 1725).

Figure 1: *Spine of the modern binding of British Library Harley Manuscript 2342, "Lady Jane Grey's Prayerbook." Shown actual size (the ruler at left is in centimeters).*

separate British Library. Since 1997, the prayer book has been held in the British Library's modern facility at St Pancras, London. The Lady Jane's prayer book has on occasion been displayed among the *Treasures of the British Library* exhibition in the Sir John Ritblatt Gallery.

The prayer book was written entirely by hand on parchment pages or 'folios' measuring just 85 by 70 millimeters, or 3.3 by 2.75 inches. The original binding of the book has been lost, and it has been rebound by the British Library in a modern dark blue leather binding with gold lettering (Figure 1). The folios are in a very fragile condition, to be expected of a book that is more than four and a half centuries old. They have suffered significant damage over the years. Curious hands have left their smudges, folios have been crumpled, liquids have soaked some, and the ink has faded away and/or leeched through in many places. As a result, portions of the text can no longer be read in full, especially at the beginning of the volume. The book is on display only periodically, and access to it is otherwise strictly prohibited, even for scholars and historians. Instead, the British

Library many years ago produced a microfilm of the entire volume, but the film is of rather poor quality, due in part to primitive filming techniques at the time the microfilm was created. More recently, the British Library has digitized each of the 142 folios and made the images available via the Internet. This volume represents the first time the book has been photographically reproduced in print in its entirety.

While the provenance for the Lady Jane Grey Dudley's prayer book is well documented in the centuries following her death in 1554, no such documentation survives to indicate how the book came into Jane's possession. The authorial origin of a portion of its content indicates that the volume dates to no earlier than 1540, however. The literary historian Janel Mueller has recently suggested that the book was a deathbed gift from Queen Katherine Parr to Jane in September 1548.[20] Mueller went so far as to claim—without offering any supporting evidence or argument—that the book was written and decorated entirely by Parr's own hand, though that "revolutionary" claim has since been challenged.[21] The lettering is in a style of Gothic blacklettering known as *lettera cursiva formata*, a specialized style of handwriting not commonly utilized beyond the ranks of professional scribes. No examples of writing in that style that can be firmly attributed to Parr are known.[22] All extant examples of Parr's own handwriting are instead in a style known as secretarial script. And while the two styles are markedly different in overall appearance, certain habitual hand motions occurring during writing and that result from muscle memory cause an individual writer to form letters in a similar manner even when writing in different styles.[23] Careful comparison of the formation of individual letters in the prayer book to the formation of the same letters in a document firmly attributed to Parr's hand reveals

---

[20] Janel Mueller, ed., *Katherine Parr: Complete Works and Correspondence* (Chicago: University of Chicago Press, 2011), 18 n.51.

[21] Mueller, *Parr*, 18, 489, and 511 n.1; James Carley, "Italic Ambitions: The Works of Henry VIII's last queen and the problem of identifying exactly what Katherine wrote," *Times Literary Supplement* 5644 (3 June 2011), 3–5.

[22] Though the Kendall Town Hall prayer book has traditionally been associated with Parr and closely resembles the Lady Jane Grey's prayer book, no documentation survives to link definitively the Kendall book with Parr. And the same conclusions drawn from detailed handwriting analysis of the Lady Jane Grey's prayer book apply equally to the Kendall Town Hall prayer book.

[23] Muscle memory occurs when a movement is repeated frequently and over time, creating a long-term automatic response for that task that eventually allows it to be performed without conscious effort.

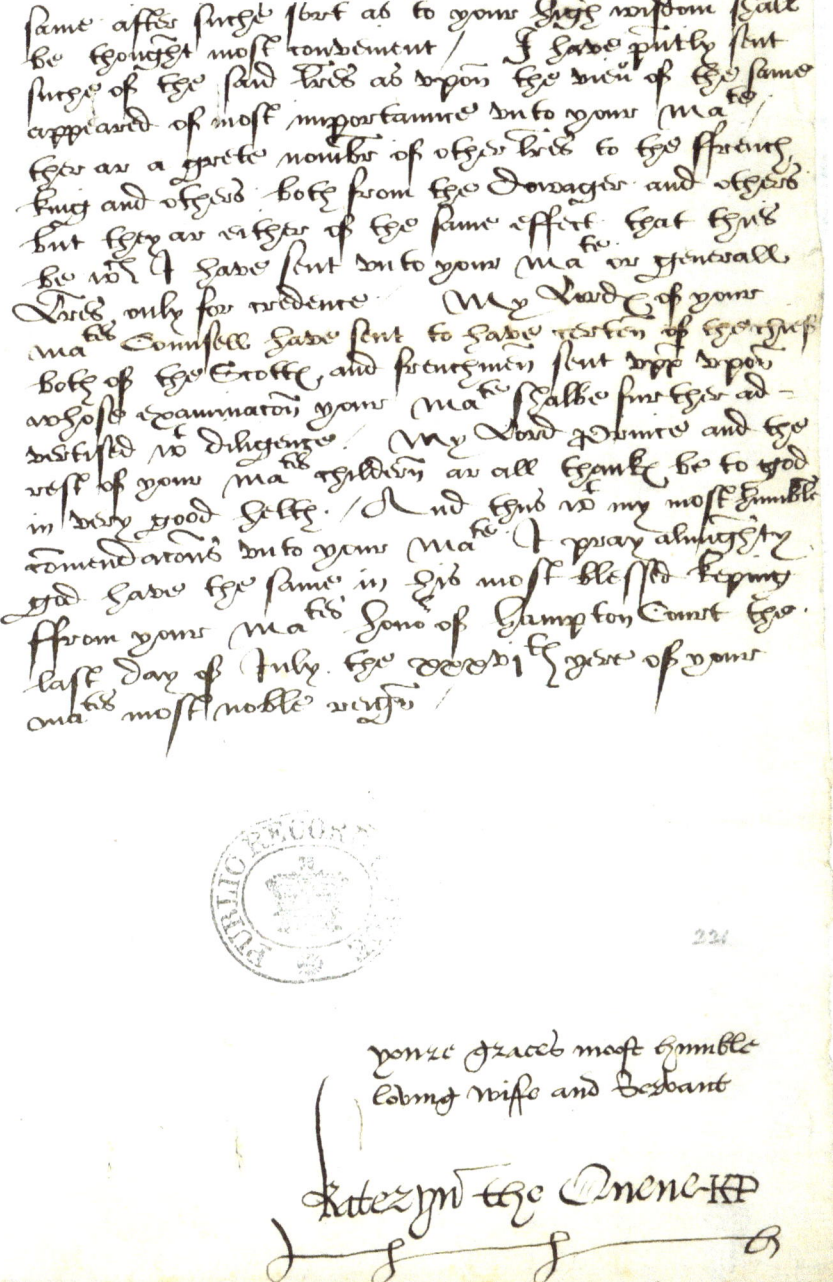

Figure 2: *Detail of a letter written by Katherine Parr to Henry VIII in her own hand, dated at Hampton Court, 31 July 1544*

critical differences (Fig. 2).[24] While the stems of the letter d are straight lines in the prayer book, for example, the stems of Parr's d's are open loops. Similarly, the circular bodies of the letter g in the prayer book all have an open top, while those in Parr's handwriting are closed. And where the tails of y's in the prayer book form a gentle and shallow curve to the right, the tails of Parr's y's form a much sharper and more pronounced curve to the right and continue upward. The handwriting seen in the book unquestionably differs from Parr's own hand, even when we account for the different writing styles used. The prayer book was certainly penned by a professional scribe, not by Katherine Parr.

Like the writing produced by professional scribes, manuscript illumination was also a very highly specialized skill that required equally specialized materials, plus knowledge and mastery of techniques that could be acquired only through years of apprenticeship with a master illuminator or limner. Pigments could not be purchased ready-to-use, for example. They were instead manufactured by the individual limner using raw materials such as bone powder, juice of red nettle, mercury, and even "child's urine." These substances were mixed with turpentine, linseed and other "oils that make smoke," egg yolk, gum arabic, or "water and grease of snails" prior to application to the vellum, parchment, or paper.[25] And only a trained limner might know that certain materials should not be mixed. When lead white is mixed with verdigris, for example, it produces a corrosive chemical that soon destroys any vellum or paper to which it is applied.[26] Additionally, the decorations themselves are exceedingly small in scale, and working in miniature is a challenging skill to acquire.[27] It is difficult to imagine Katherine Parr acting as her own amateur limner, since manuscript illumination was a pursuit largely limited to low-born men. No English aristocratic or royal women are known to have taken up illumination, even as a hobby.[28] But when one considers the detail

---

[24] See, for example, Katherine Parr to Henry VIII, 31 July 1544, National Archives, Public Record Office, SP 1/190, f.220.

[25] *A very proper treatise, wherein is briefly sett forthe the arte of limming....*(London: Richard Tottill, 1571), f.12v.

[26] Christopher de Hamel, *British Library Guide to Manuscript Illumination* (Toronto: University of Toronto Press, 2001), 78.

[27] The incipit W illustrated one the next page is 15 millimeters or 0.6 inches square, while the initials that begin to appear regularly on and after folio 62r of the prayer book are each approximately 5mm or 0.2 inches square.

[28] Only two female limners are reasonably well known from the first half of the sixteenth century in England, though both were Dutch by birth. The first of these chronologically

INTRODUCTION   11

Figure 3: *Decorated incipit W from folio 74 verso. Actual size at left; enlarged at right to reveal detail.*

contained within each of the many five- and fifteen-millimeter initials that appear repeatedly between folios 62 recto and 137 recto, it becomes all but impossible to imagine her having created them herself, even as a hobby (Fig. 3). The skill evidenced by the decoration of the prayer book strongly indicates that the decorations were produced by a specially-trained professional illuminator or limner.

No connection between the book and Katherine Parr can today be verified. The book may as easily have been given to Jane by any of a number of family members, friends, or admirers. Jane is known to have received gifts of books from others, including a volume in Greek of the works of St. Basil presented to her by Mildred Cecil, wife of the up-and-coming

---

was Susanna Horenbout (or Horenbolt), who immigrated to England from the Low Countries in about 1522 together with her father Gerard and her brother Lucas, both also limners. Horenbout married into the upper gentry in 1525 and served as an attendant to Henry VIII's fourth wife, Anne of Cleves, briefly in 1540 and to Queen Katherine Parr in 1543. There is nonetheless no evidence whatsoever to indicate that she taught the complex art of illumination to either of her royal mistresses during the short few months she was in attendance on each. See Lorne Campbell and Susan Foister, "Gerard, Lucas, and Susanna Horenbout," *The Burlington Magazine* 128: 1003 (October 1986), 719–727. The other female limner working in England prior to 1550 was Levina Teerlinc, daughter of Simon Bening (or Benninck), himself a leading illuminator from Bruges. Teerlinc came to England in about 1545 and would go on to serve as a limner to Queen Mary Tudor and Queen Elizabeth I. Teerlinc is even less well documented than Horenbout, and no surviving work has yet been definitively confirmed as hers. See *Oxford Dictionary of National Biography*, s.v. 'Teerlinc, Levina.'

William Cecil, future chief minister to Elizabeth I.[29] And while Jane did live with Parr between about 1546 and the latter's death late in 1548, Parr surrounded herself with a coterie of educated and wealthy women who shared both Jane's and Parr's religious interests. The group included Jane's step-grandmother Katherine Willoughby Brandon, Dowager Duchess of Suffolk, Joan Champernowne Denny, and Mary Fitzalan, future Duchess of Norfolk, each of whom was renowned for her learning.[30] A prayer book would have been an entirely appropriate gift from any of these women to Jane. It has also been suggested that Jane may have commissioned the book herself, though that is perhaps doubtful in light of the fact that Jane was entirely financially dependent upon her parents throughout her short life.[31]

Professionally-produced small or miniature books intended for personal religious devotion were relatively popular among the extremely small percentage of English women who could both read and afford such luxurious items.[32] They had been fashionable in England since at least the fourteenth century. The most common such books were psalters, or collections of psalms, and books of hours, or collections of prayers for use in the daily cycle of prayers known as the Divine Office (Fig. 4).[33] Prayer books were usually smaller in size than psalters in order to allow for carrying them on one's person throughout the day, sometimes enclosed in a protective leather pouch.[34] By the sixteenth century, English ladies had developed the practice of suspending their prayer books by means of decorative chains from the jeweled belts or 'girdles' worn at the waist, giving rise to the terms 'girdle book' and 'girdle tablet,' or 'pendant prayer books.'[35] The books were usually bound in leather covers, often

---

[29] National Archives, Public Record Office, State Papers 10/15/79, ff.1787–1789.
[30] Susan E. James, *Catherine Parr: Henry VIII's Last Love* (Strond: Tempus Publishing, 2008), 127–129.
[31] Carley, "Italic Ambition," 5.
[32] Perhaps no more than five percent of the female population of England in the middle of the sixteenth century could read, while even fewer could write. See David Cressy, *Literacy and the Social Order: Reading and Writing in Tudor and Stuart England* (Cambridge: University of Cambridge Press, 1980).
[33] Nigel Morgan, "Books for the liturgy and private prayer," *Cambridge History of the Book in Britain* (Cambridge: Cambridge University Press, 1999–2012), II:307 and 309.
[34] Margit Smith and Jim Bloxam, "The Medieval Girdle Book Project," *The International Journal of the Book* 3:4 (2006), 15–24.
[35] Hugh Tait: "The girdle-prayerbook or 'tablett': An important class of Renaissance jewellery at the court of Henry VIII," *Jewellery Studies* 2 (1985), 54–55, n.8.

INTRODUCTION 13

Figure 4: A Latin pocket Book of Hours, circa 1480, showing rich illlumination.

Figure 5: A book of psalms with cover in calf leather tooled in gold and painted, sixteenth century. *Figure 6:* Book of prayers with embroidered cover showing combined cypher of King Henry VIII and Queen Katherine Parr.

Figure 7: Enameled gold cover of pendant prayer book, shown actual size.

Figure 8: Unknown woman with prayer book suspended by gold chain from unseen girdle at waist, England, 1550s

Figure 9: Unknown woman with small prayer book open in her hands, England, 1550s

with designs stamped in gold leaf, or in textiles such as velvet and satin embroidered with heraldic emblems, monograms, or other designs (Figs. 5 and 6). The wealthiest owners sometimes even had their miniature prayer books custom bound using precious metals, enameling, and jewels (Fig. 7). Both loose and pendant prayer books are depicted in a number of portraits of English women of the period (Figs. 8 and 10). A handful of paintings of women of the sixteenth and seventeenth centuries would even become mis-identified in later centuries as portraits of the Lady Jane Grey Dudley specifically because they depicted the otherwise unidentified woman holding or reading a book. By the end of the seventeenth century, a small book had in effect become an artistic trope associated in female portraiture with the Lady Jane Grey Dudley in particular.[36]

The Lady Jane's prayer book offers a window onto the character of the religious transition that took place over the course of the second quarter of the sixteenth century as the English Church abandoned Roman Catholicism in favor of a reformed faith that would later come to be known as Protestantism.[37] Historians have long observed that the transition was a gradual process occurring over the course of decades rather than a sudden cataclysmic shift confined to a single historical moment or event. And it must be remembered that the "new" faith was not in fact really new. Theological reformers claimed to be seeking a return to what they considered the "true" primitive church based solely on scripture that had been lost owing to an accumulation over more than a millennium of extra-scriptural beliefs and practices. But the "return" was to prove a slow one. Between Henry VIII's assumption of supremacy over the Church in England in 1534 and his death in January 1547, very few real changes occurred in theology, doctrine, or the liturgy. The Convocation of Bishops approved the Ten Articles in 1536, just months before Jane's birth, reaffirming for the English Church the traditional Roman Catholic doctrines of the real presence in the Eucharist, the salvific necessity for good works, the efficacy of holy images, the invocation of saints, and the

---

[36] See J. Stephan Edwards, *A Queen of a New Invention: Portraits of Lady Jane Grey Dudley, England's Nine Days Queen* (Palm Springs: Old John Publishing, 2015).

[37] The modern word Protestant is derived from the Latin *protestantem*, meaning "those who protest." It was first used at the Diet of Speyer in 1529 to describe very narrowly those followers of Martin Luther who protested the ruling of the Diet of 1526 that had severely curtailed church reform within the territories of the Holy Roman Empire. As a descriptor of a wider system of doctrine and belief, the term *Protestant* did not enter common usage in any language until the end of the sixteenth century.

existence of purgatory, as well as the practices of infant baptism, auricular confession, prayers for the dead, and the sprinkling of holy water and anointing with oil, among other rituals. Over the course of the following two years, many reformers sought to introduce some of the reforms then being implemented among the followers of Martin Luther, but they met with resistance from the Crown. In 1539, the Act of Six Articles reaffirmed many of the stipulations of the Bishop's Ten Articles, especially the traditional doctrines of transubstantiation and the real presence plus auricular confession to a priest, by codifying them as statute law.[38] Yet the first authorized English edition of the Bible, translated by Miles Coverdale, was published in the same year and proved to be a seminal event in the history of the English Reformation.

Reformers continued to press for changes of a more radical nature, however, including outright abolition of the Mass, reduction in the number of the sacraments from seven to two, denial of the existence of purgatory, and a prohibition on the invocation of saints. To combat this rising tide of reform, Henry VIII authorized the publication in May of 1543 of a book entitled *A Necessary Doctrine and Erudition for any Christen* [sic] *Man* (commonly known as *The King's Book*), for which Henry himself wrote the preface.[39] The book again reaffirmed the doctrines outlined by the various Articles. But in the following year, Henry allowed the publication of Cranmer's *Exhortation and Litany*, an exposition of an English-language liturgy for worship services. Still, the Latin Mass would not be abolished in England until two years after Henry's death in January 1547. His son and successor, Edward VI, was a supporter of religious reform and was surrounded by pro-reform advisors, enabling the passage in January 1549 of the First Act of Uniformity and the introduction in that same year of the *First Book of Common Prayer*.[40] Nonetheless, while the *First Book* did provide for services in English and communion in two kinds, it drew heavily upon a traditional liturgy known as the Sarum Use that had guided Roman Catholic worship in England for half a millennium.[41] The

---

[38] 31 Hen.8 c.14, titled *An Act abolishing diversity in Opinions*.
[39] *A Necessary Doctrine and Erudition for any Christen Man* (London: Thomas Berthelet, 1543). The Preface can be found on folios 2r–5r.
[40] 2 & 3 Edw. 6, c.1.
[41] Protestant Christian communion is commonly observed using two 'kinds' or 'species': bread and wine. Traditional Roman Catholic practice limits the distribution of communion to the laity to bread alone, while the receiving of the wine is restricted to the clergy.

Second Book of Common Prayer, issued in 1552, incorporated numerous revisions reflective of reformist teachings, including references to "Holy Communion" instead of "the Mass" and a complete expungement of the word "altar," replacing it with "table." But even as late as 1552, the English Church had taken only a few halting steps on the long road from traditional Roman Catholic beliefs and observances to those of the Protestant Church of England that would finally be established during the reign of Elizabeth I. The official English church to which the Lady Jane Grey Dudley adhered in the final year of her life retained far more of the traditional Roman Catholic doctrines and practices than did the reformed churches on the European continent.

Like both editions of the English *Book of Common Prayer*, the Lady Jane's prayer book draws heavily upon traditional Roman Catholic sources. It does so in a more indirect manner, however, utilizing English translations, called primers, of Latin-language Roman Catholic books of hours. Such translations began to appear in middle of the 1530s, one of the earliest being William Marshall's *A primer in English* issued under royal license in 1534.[42] Marshall's primer included many elements found in traditional Roman Catholic books of hours, such as a liturgical calendar noting the feast days of saints, a Passion narrative, and a catechism. But consistent with reformist teachings, Marshall conspicuously edited the Roman Catholic *Credo* (literally, "I believe..."), eliminating the statement of belief in "one Holy, Catholic and Apostolic Church." In its place, Marshall substituted the very carefully worded statement, "I believe the holy church everywhere to be the company or the congregation of holy and faithful men."[43] And while Marshall similarly expunged from his primer the otherwise ubiquitous *Ave Maria*, a traditional prayer to the Virgin Mary, he did nonetheless reaffirm the Roman Catholic doctrines on the communion of saints and the efficacy of good works towards achieving salvation, both of which were denied by many reformers.[44] His translation of *The Song of Austin and Ambrose* was transcribed verbatim into the Lady Jane's prayer book (74v–77r), as were his renderings of the Roman Catholic collects *A prayer to the Father* (106r–107r), *A Prayer to the Holy Ghost* (107r–107v), and *A prayer to the*

---

[42] William Marshall, *A primer in English with certain prayers & godly meditations, very necessary for all people that understand not the Latin tongue* (London: John Byddell, 1534).

[43] Marshall, *A primer*, 80v (see also 29r).

[44] Marshall, *A primer*, 29r–v.

Trinity (107v–108v).⁴⁵ Marshall published a revised version of his primer in 1535, from which the author of the Lady Jane's prayer book transcribed the untitled prayer beginning "Our merciful father, which in teaching us to pray ... ," which was in turn taken from the traditional Roman Catholic prayers for the ninth canonical hour of the Divine Office.⁴⁶

Sources other than primers also provided material for incorporation into the Lady Jane's prayer book. Thomas Godfray's printing from 1534 of *The Fountain or well of life*, a collection of Biblical prayers and psalms, provided the English-language source for a lengthy expansion of the *Pater Noster* or *Lord's Prayer* (f.109v–136v).⁴⁷ Richard Taverner's *An epitome of the Psalmes*, translated from Wolfgang Capito's *Precationes Christianae ad imitationem psalmorum compositae* and published in 1539, provides not only the source for *A prayer in adversity and grievous distress* (f.21r–v), but also allows for dating the Lady Jane's prayer book to no earlier than 1540.⁴⁸ Three short prayers toward the front of the Lady Jane's volume were each authored by Sir Thomas More, executed in 1535 for refusing to swear the oath required of all Englishmen in acceptance of Henry VIII's assumption of royal supremacy over the church in England (f.9r–16r).⁴⁹ More's prayer *O Holy Trinity* (f.9r–15r) in its original form included reference to the Roman Catholic doctrine on the existence of purgatory, but the reference was omitted when transcribing the prayer into the Lady Jane's prayer book. Lastly, the preface of an early printing of Miles Coverdale's translation of the Bible also served as the source for two short prayers originally composed by Nicholas Shaxton, Bishop of Salisbury (f.16r–17v).⁵⁰ Intriguingly, the latter of Shaxton's two prayers, beginning

---

⁴⁵ Marshall, *A primer*, 106r–108v. "Collects" are structured prayers composed of five parts: the invocation, the acknowledgement, the petition, the aspiration, and the pleading. The form would also later be utilized by the Church of England in its *Book of Common Prayer*.

⁴⁶ Mueller, *Parr*, 501.

⁴⁷ Anonymous, *The fountayne or well of life ... translated out of latyn in to Englysshe* (London: Thomas Godfray, 1534), 18r–29v. (STC:11211)

⁴⁸ Mueller, *Parr*, 18; Richard Taverner, *An epitome of the Psalmes, or briefe meditacons upon the same, with diverse other moste Christian prayers, translated by Richard Taverner* (London: Printed by R. Bankes for A. Clerke, 1539), f.138v. Taverner published his work at precisely the time that Anne of Cleves was pausing in Tournai on her journey to England to become Henry VIII's fourth wife. Taverner's dedication to Henry VIII includes his wish for Anne's safe arrival in England. See f.4r–v.

⁴⁹ Thomas More is today revered as a martyr-saint by the Roman Catholic Church.

⁵⁰ Mueller, *Parr*, 495; Miles Coverdale, *Biblia the Byble, that is, the holy Scrypture of the Olde*

"Lead me O Lord...," was apparently inserted in the Lady Jane's prayer book after the book was originally transcribed, as evidenced by both the smaller handwriting used to fit the prayer into the limited space available at the bottom of folio 17v and the different color of ink used.[51]

The handwritten personal messages inserted by the Lady Jane into the book (ff.74v–77r and 78r–80r) offer clear evidence that she was not herself the transcriber of Shaxton's second prayer. Neither did she pen the text appearing on folios 137 through 142, which likewise appears to have been added after the book was first created. The Lady Jane's own handwriting was in a style that her contemporaries referred to as "Italic," a very neat and legible style quite similar to modern 'print' handwriting. The variation between the two handwritings utilized in the main text of the book suggests the likelihood that the book was owned by someone else prior to the Lady Jane. There is no evidence available, however, to indicate who that person may have been. But Katherine Parr can be excluded based on the same evidence derived from handwriting analysis discussed above.

The Lady Jane's own placement of her inscription to Sir John Brydges offers a very rare glimpse into her thought processes, albeit an indirect and tentative one. The inscription begins on the first page of an ancient and traditional prayer here entitled *The Song of Austin and Ambrose* but known more commonly among Roman Catholics by its Latin name, *Te Deum*.[52] The prayer reiterates the longstanding Christian doctrine of the Holy Trinity, or the deity as consisting of three co-equal and consubstantial entities. That doctrine was shared by both Roman Catholics and reformers,

---

and *New Testament, faithfully translated in to Englyshe* (Southwark?: J. Nycolson, 1535), f.1v (STC 2063.3).

[51] Shaxton is himself an example of the personal turmoil experienced by many as the English Reformation proceeded. Having risen to his bishopric on the strength of his reformist credentials, Shaxton was compelled to resign his see in 1539 on account of having married, a direct violation of the Act of Six Articles. By 1546, he was preaching in denunciation of the efficacy of Masses for the dead and refuting the doctrine of transubstantiation. He was arrested and condemned to the stake, but was spared following a full and public recantation of his reformist ideas. After Mary's accession in 1553, Shaxton sat as an examiner in the trials of others accused of reformist heresies. See *Oxford Dictionary of National Biography*, s.v. 'Shaxton, Miles.'

[52] Saint Austin is an alternate name for Saint Augustine of Hippo (d.430 CE), author of such seminal theological texts as *City of God* and *Confessions*. Augustine converted to Christianity at age 31, in 386, and was baptized by Ambrose (d.397), Bishop of Milan. The *Song of Austin and Ambrose* is traditionally said to have been composed extemporaneously on the occasion of Augustine's baptism.

allowing the Lady Jane to situate her subtle appeal to the Roman Catholic Brydges on a ground of common fundamental belief. Her inscription itself, however, encourages Brydges to appeal to God for guidance and "not to take the words of truth utterly out of your mouth," i.e., not to be misguided by false teachings, by which Jane of course meant Roman Catholicism. Jane then writes of her own optimism even in the face of death, secure in her own belief that her death is but a rebirth into an eternal life. Yet despite the Lady Jane's entreaties, Brydges died a Roman Catholic in April of 1557, having preserved the prayer book as a small memento of his brief acquaintance with the Lady Jane Grey Dudley.[53]

---

[53] Why a Roman Catholic official serving Queen Mary would preserve a gift from that queen's religious and political foe is unclear. Perhaps Brydges valued the book solely as a historical curiosity. He likely found its content inoffensive since it was largely derived from traditional Roman Catholic sources.

A Brief History of the Lady Jane Grey Dudley

The Lady Jane Grey was born of royal blood as a great-granddaughter of Henry VII, founder of the Tudor dynasty and father of Henry VIII. Jane's mother Frances Brandon was the daughter of Henry VIII's younger sister Mary Tudor, making Frances a niece of Henry VIII and Jane his grandniece. And Jane's father Henry Grey was a cousin to Henry VIII, Grey's grandfather Thomas Grey having been half-brother to Henry VIII's mother, Elizabeth of York. In other words, Jane, her mother, and her father were all close kinsmen of King Henry VIII.

The Lady Jane was most probably born in late 1536, entering the world at an exceptionally dynamic point in English history.[1] The English Church had ended its allegiance to the Roman Catholic system of church governance just two years previously. English monasteries were beginning to be closed en masse, and new doctrines were challenging the long-established system of religious belief and practice. Those changes were fueled in part by the rapid expansion of education among the wealthy, aided by the newly-invented printing press. For the first time in English history, appreciable (though still very limited) numbers of women began to be academically educated. Politically, Queen Anne Boleyn had been executed just months earlier in May 1536, and a new queen, Jane Seymour, had taken her place. Henry VIII's only children to survive from his two previous marriages, daughters Mary and Elizabeth, had both been declared illegitimate and removed from the royal succession. Despite his near-obsessive pursuit of a male heir, Henry had as yet failed to sire son that could survive infancy.[2] The Second Act of Succession of June 1536 had empowered Henry to set aside traditional inheritance patterns and to name a successor of his choice, and many believed his only acknowledged illegitimate son, Henry Fitzroy, was

---

[1] See note 1, page 1 above.
[2] Henry's first queen, Katherine of Aragon, bore six children, including three sons. The first son, named Henry after his father and grandfather, died after 52 days. A second son was stillborn, while the third died within days of his birth. Only Katherine's fifth child and second daughter, Mary, survived infancy and reached adulthood.

the likely candidate.³ But Fitzroy died unexpectedly in July 1536, leaving only the descendants of Henry's two sisters, Margaret and Mary, within the legitimate Tudor blood line. Yet many sixteenth-century legal and political theorists argued that persons born under a foreign allegiance or continuing to hold such allegiance could not inherit the English crown, which would have eliminated Henry's elder sister Margaret Tudor Stuart Douglas.⁴ In such case, Jane was, at her birth, second in line to the throne after her own mother Frances, as senior lineal descendants of Henry's deceased younger sister Mary Tudor Brandon. Still, it was assumed by all that God would provide Henry with sons by Jane Seymour.

Tradition holds that the Lady Jane Grey was raised almost exclusively at the Grey family seat of Bradgate in Leicestershire, and that she lived a life of "splendid isolation."⁵ Supposedly her only comfort was her studies, guided by her tutor John Aylmer.⁶ Jane was genuinely exceptional in that her education was relatively extensive in scope, especially since the literacy

---

³ Henry Fitzroy (1519–1536), born of Henry VIII's mistress Elizabeth Blount, was acknowledged by his father, made Duke of Richmond and Somerset, and established in a household in semi-royal estate and style. Some historians today argue that, prior to his death in July 1536, Fitzroy was being groomed to succeed his father in the event no legitimate male heir was born. See Beverley A. Murphy, *Bastard Prince: Henry VIII's Lost Son* (Stroud: Sutton, 2001).

⁴ A Parliamentary statute of 1351 (25 Edward III c.1, more commonly referred to as *De Natis Ultra Mare*) limited inheritance of lands within England by persons born outside that realm to only those "whose fathers and mothers at the time of their birth be and shall be of the faith and allegiance of the King of England." Though Henry VIII's next heir-in-blood, his older sister Margaret Tudor (*d.*1541), had been born in England to parents who were clearly English in allegiance, her own allegiance as an adult was contestable, since she was Dowager Queen of Scotland and mother of the reigning Scots king. Indeed, Margaret had sworn fealty to her son James V of Scotland upon his coronation in 1513. And were Margaret to succeed Henry, her own first heir would be her Scottish son. James himself was presumably excluded outright under the law of 1351, especially since England and Scotland were enemies of long standing (James V would later die at the Battle of Solway Moss in 1542 while attempting to invade England).

Margaret's daughter by her second marriage, Margaret Douglas, had been born in England (1515), thanks to her mother's careful planning, making her eligible to inherit under the law of 1351. And Henry VIII had treated her as such until July 1536, when it was discovered that young Margaret had secretly entered into a betrothal with Thomas Howard without the king's permission. The couple were immediately imprisoned, and Margaret remained in prison and out of favor until after the birth of Prince Edward on 12 October 1537.

⁵ Richard Davey, *The Nine Days Queen: Lady Jane Grey and her Times*, ed. and intro. Martin Hume (New York: G.P. Putnam's Sons and London: Metheun, 1909), 173.

⁶ John Aylmer (*c.*1520–1594) studied at Cambridge with the financial support of the Lady Jane's father, Henry Grey, earning an MA in 1545. He then took up a post as tutor to Jane

rate in England in the middle of the sixteenth century was as low as perhaps ten percent of men and five percent of women.[7] Jane's curriculum focused primarily on languages, consistent with the new humanist methodology that advocated the study of texts in their original language rather than in translation.[8] She was well-versed in Latin and Greek, and functional in Hebrew. Jane probably also read and wrote French, a traditional court language in England. She studied Tuscan, a dialect similar to modern Italian, and may have learned some Spanish as well. At least one contemporary stated that Jane also delved into Chaldean, today called Aramaic.[9] She also studied rhetoric, theology, moral and natural philosophy, logic, and history while reading many of the ancient Greek and Roman classical authors, from Plato and Aristotle to Cicero and Livy.[10]

Tradition also holds that the Lady Jane was a life-long committed Protestant. She was, however, born and raised in a church that until 1549 still utilized mostly Roman Catholic doctrine and ritual, as discussed above.[11] Only after about 1545, when John Aylmer was hired as her principal tutor, did she begin to be exposed to the religious reform movement that would in later decades be called Protestantism. Between about 1549 and her death in February 1554, Jane corresponded with some of the leading

---

and her sisters, remaining in the Grey household exclusively until at least 1549 and intermittently thereafter until 1553. Aylmer was a keen supporter of reformist theology and began corresponding regularly with leaders of the movement, both within England and on the continent, as soon as he joined the Grey household. Following a period of exile during the reign of Queen Mary, he would eventually become Bishop of London in 1577, though his tenure there, and indeed his entire ecclesiastical career, was fraught with controversies. Aylmer has been characterized as having "a genius for antagonizing supporters and opponents alike and was in many respects a typical bully." See *ODNB*, s.v. 'Aylmer, John.'

[7] See David Cressy, *Education in Tudor and Stuart England* (London: E. Arnold, 1975).

[8] "Humanism" is a much-misused and misunderstood term, thanks to the co-opting of the term by the modern movement for social justice, so-called "secular humanism." True humanism derives its English name from the Italian *umanista* and the Latin *studia humanitatis*, studies in the humanities (i.e., grammar, rhetoric, history, poetry, and moral philosophy). Those studies were intended to prepare the student for an active civic life.

[9] Thomas Chaloner, *De rep. Anglorum instauranda libri decem...* (London: Vautrollerius, 1579), 296–299.

[10] See J. Stephan Edwards, *'Jane the Quene': A New Consideration of Lady Jane Grey, England's Nine Days Queen*, Unpub. PhD dissertation, University of Colorado – Boulder, 2007, 36–84.

[11] The quasi-Protestant *First Book of Common Prayer* was issued in 1549, though it met with considerable resistance at the local level.

figures of the reformist movement, both in England and on the European continent. These notably included Martin Bucer and Heinrich Bullinger.[12] Her personal theology evolved over time, so that by the end of her life she was indeed committed to the new theology.

The Lady Jane was influenced in her theological development as much by women as by men, and perhaps even more so by women. As noted above, Jane spent most of the period between 1546 and late 1548 in the household of Queen Katherine Parr, where she had daily contact with Katherine's coterie of educated women, all of whom were advocates of the new religion. In addition to the women already named, the group included Elizabeth Brooke Parr, Anne Stanhope Seymour, Elizabeth Stoner Hoby, and others. Precisely during the time that Jane was resident in the Parr household, these women were engaged, both directly and as patronesses, in efforts to translate pro-reform non-English texts into English. They also actively corresponded with and financially supported many of the male reformers, both in England and on the continent.[13] Jane was at least an observer of these activities, and may well have actively participated in the translation efforts.[14]

The Lady Jane's parents seem to have hoped that she would eventually wed her reform-minded cousin King Edward VI, but it became clear by the early spring of 1553 that the king was dying. The king and his advisors therefore initiated a set of plans to alter the royal succession. Anxious to preserve his reformation of the English church, Edward sought to remove as his heirs his half-sisters Mary (a staunch Roman Catholic) and Elizabeth (never fully committed to Edward's version of reformism). Jane was put forward in their place. The Lady Jane was wed to Lord Guildford Dudley, a younger son of John Dudley, Duke of Northumberland, who was himself the

---

[12] Martin Bucer immigrated to England in 1549 from the German Free Imperial City of Schlettstadt, despite being by then almost sixty years old. He served as Regius Professor of Divinity at Cambridge until his death in 1551. Heinrich Bullinger was the elected head of the Reformed Churches of Switzerland from 1532 until his death in 1575. He was a prolific author on reformist theology. His *Second Helvetic Confession* is today incorporated into the *Book of Confessions* used by the Presbyterian Church (USA).

[13] For a detailed discussion of the feminine court of Katherine Parr and its religious activities, see Susan E. James, *Catherine Parr: Henry VIII's Last Love* (Stroud: Tempus Publishing, 2008), 121–134 and 157–226.

[14] The only theological work that the Lady Jane is known to have translated was Heinrich Bullinger's *Decades*, a collection of that reformer's sermons. But that translation was from Latin into Greek, not English. No copy of her translation of Decades is known to have survived.

king's chief minister and a strong supporter of the Edwardian reformation (though he would eventually profess the Roman Catholic faith at his death). The wedding occurred on Thursday, 25 May 1553. At the same time, Jane's sister Katherine was wed to Henry Herbert, the son and heir of another of the King's principal supporters, William Herbert. Jane's sister Mary was betrothed to her cousin Arthur Grey, while John Dudley's daughter Katherine was married to Henry Hastings, son and heir of yet another of the Dudleys' main allies, Francis Hastings. Together these marriages cemented a seemingly reliable alliance of several leading families of the realm that should have been capable of carrying out Edward's long-term plans. In the event, the alliance was a fragile one that failed all too quickly.

Edward died on 6 July 1553. Jane was proclaimed Queen of England, France, and Ireland on 10 July 1553. Mary immediately announced her intention of pursuing her own claim. Within hours, supporters began traveling toward Mary's base at Framlingham Castle in Suffolk. As Mary's forces increased with each passing day, Queen Jane's own supporters began abandoning her. Nine days later, on 19 July 1553, Jane was deposed by the same alliance that had been formed to promote her, and Mary was proclaimed queen in her place. Jane and her new husband Guildford were imprisoned in the Tower of London. John Dudley was tried for treason and executed in late August.[15] Henry Grey and most of the others were pardoned and released. Jane and Guildford, however, remained imprisoned and were tried and convicted of treason in November 1553.

Meanwhile, Mary returned the English church to Roman Catholic allegiance and practice. She also announced her decision to wed Philip of Spain, an action that would make him King of England. Queen Mary's decision to wed Philip produced considerable anxiety among Englishmen, who feared the imposition of foreign rule.[16] Men such as Sir Thomas Wyatt, Sir Peter Carew, and Jane's own father soon acted to prevent the marriage of Mary and Philip. Known as Wyatt's Rebellion, it erupted in late January 1554, sooner than planned and before it could be fully coordinated. The rebels reached the gates of London but were suppressed by Mary's forces.

---

[15] Despite having personally championed Edward's reformation of the English Church, Dudley famously publicly professed the Roman Catholic faith in the days before his execution.

[16] Fear of Philip assuming direct personal rule of England was so great that Parliament passed an act that limited his powers and influence and that also limited the ability of his children by other marriages to inherit in England should Mary die before him. See The Act for the Marriage of Queen Mary to Philip of Spain (1 Mary 3.c.2).

The rebellion had forced Mary's hand, however, so that she was compelled to allow the death warrants against the Lady Jane and Lord Guildford to be carried out.

The execution was initially set for Friday, 9 February 1554, but was delayed until the following Monday.[17] Queen Mary consented to the brief delay after one of her personal chaplains, John Howman de Feckenham, convinced the Queen through unknown arguments to allow him to engage in a theological debate with the Lady Jane. It has often been said that Feckenham's goal was to convert Jane to Roman Catholicism, and that Mary offered to spare Jane's life if she would in fact convert. This is untrue, however. Even in the very unlikely event that she converted, Jane might still be put forward in future by malcontents and rebels as a candidate to replace Mary on the throne. But more importantly, Philip and the Spanish made Jane's death a pre-condition of Philip's coming to England to wed Mary, and Mary was unwilling to place her own marriage at risk. Further, theological debates were common in the era, though it was very uncommon for a woman to be one of the debaters. Yet Jane was well-known for her erudition, and Feckenham no doubt viewed the possibility of a debate with her with some personal relish. Such debates or disputations were often held in public, as a form of entertainment, but the circumstances of Jane's imprisonment meant that only a handful of witnesses were allowed. The anonymous author of the *Chronicle of Queen Jane* was unaware of the debate, for example, even though he certainly lived and worked within the Tower. But the debate was witnessed, and that witness transcribed what the participants said. The transcription was later published, most famously in John Foxe's *Actes and Monuments* (more commonly called *The Book of Martyrs*).[18] Jane remained politely intransigent throughout the debate, conceding nothing, so that Feckenham eventually withdrew.

The Lady Jane wrote a number of farewell messages during her last days, in addition to the brief note to her father on folios 78r–80r of her prayer book. A letter to her younger sister Katherine was published soon after Jane's death, together with her speech from the scaffold and other writings attributed to her.[19] It has been asserted that Jane's mother, Frances Brandon Grey, facilitated the publication of that pamphlet, though

---

[17] *Chronicle of Queen Jane*, 55.
[18] John Foxe, *Actes and Monuments of these latter and perillous dayes...* (London: John Day, 1563), Book 5, pp. 985-986.
[19] See note 13, page 4 above.

it is noteworthy that no farewell letter from Jane to her mother is known.[20]

The Lady Jane Grey Dudley was beheaded in the Tower of London on 12 February 1554. Her remains are traditionally said to have been buried in an unmarked grave beneath the floor of the Chapel of St. Peter-ad-Vincula within the Tower. Almost immediately, religious reformers appropriated her name for use in anti-Catholic propaganda, and successive generations of authors repeatedly reshaped her narrative to suit changing agendas. And across those generations, one owner of the Lady Jane's prayer book after another has carefully preserved the miniature volume, very much—and quite ironically, in light of her reformist beliefs—like a holy relic.

---

[20] Leanda de Lisle, *The Sisters Who Would Be Queen: the Tragedy of Mary, Katherine and Lady Jane Grey* (Hammersmith: Harper Press, 2008), 159.

Notes on the Transcriptions

The transcriptions presented here repeat the spelling used in the original, including the scribe's use of the Roman v for u, J and ʄ for upper-case I, i for lower-case j, the long s (ſ) at the beginning and within words and the abbreviation symbol ℓ to replace some terminal -s's or -es's. Other abbreviations and contraction symbols commonly used in sixteenth-century script are also retained in the transcription, as are the punctuation, word spacing, lineation, and line breaks of the original manuscript text. This is all intended to allow readers to correlate more easily a given line of the printed transcription with the handwritten text depicted in each photographic image.

The text as presented in modern English usage similarly seeks to maintain the word choice, syntax, and line breaks of the original, to the extent that doing so is grammatically possible. Spelling and punctuation are modernized, and words that are contracted or abbreviated in the original are extended here. Words or letters not present in the original but necessary in the modern text for purposes of proper meaning are marked by square brackets: [ ]. Letters or words that are entirely illegible in the original are indicated in the transcription by the use of an ellipsis (...). Words no longer in common English usage or for which the meanings have changed are defined in footnotes where necessary.

The pages of the volume were not originally numbered. At some point in the modern era, page numbers were inserted in pencil in the upper right-hand corner of the front (recto) side of each folio or page. The reverse (verso) side of each folio remains un-numbered. The penciled numbering already present in the book is utilized for the transcription below, though two consecutive folios were originally inadvertently numbered 4 and are here numbered 4A and 4B instead.

All images from the original manuscript are reproduced as near as possible to actual size. Each original photographic image has been cropped at the outer edges of the manuscript page to remove extraneous elements such as page clamps, rulers, and color calibration targets. Each has also been straightened and corrected for perspective. The original photographic images can be accessed via the British Library's website at:

http://www.bl.uk/catalogues/illuminatedmanuscripts/
record.asp?MSID=7220

The site allows for enlargement and detailed viewing of individual pages, revealing numerous features not readily visible in the photographic images.

The Lady Jane Grey's Prayer Book

British Library
Harley Manuscript
2342

Folio 1 recto

...	...
...	...
...	...
all ...	all ...
...	...
...	...
the labores ...	the labors ...
or lorde and sauyor ...	or Lord and Savior ...
le far... and to re...	le far ... and to re ...
selffes and ...	selves and ...
fholde be ...	should be ...

** This first page of the manuscript bears a later inscription in ink in the upper left corner by Humfrey Wanley, Librarian to the Harley Earls of Oxford, marking the date on which the 1st Earl of Oxford acquired the book, 17 May 1715, and the Oxford Collection cataloguing number.

Folio 1 verso

... chaunces of this present
aduerſitie ſeinge my lorde god
... he was in erth de
...este but in
........deſiered any pleſure
... but tribulations
...
... of wicked folkₑ
and the moſte bitter & ſpitfull
deth on the croſſe he albeit that
he was god toke vpon hym the
nature of man to ſaue me w^ch
was loſte and after he was

... chances of this present
... adversity seeing my Lord God
... He was in Earth de-
...est but in
... desired any pleasure
... but tribulations
...
... of wicked folks
and the most bitter and spiteful
death on the Cross, He, albeit that
He was God, took upon Him the
nature of man to save me which
was lost. And after He was

Folio 2r

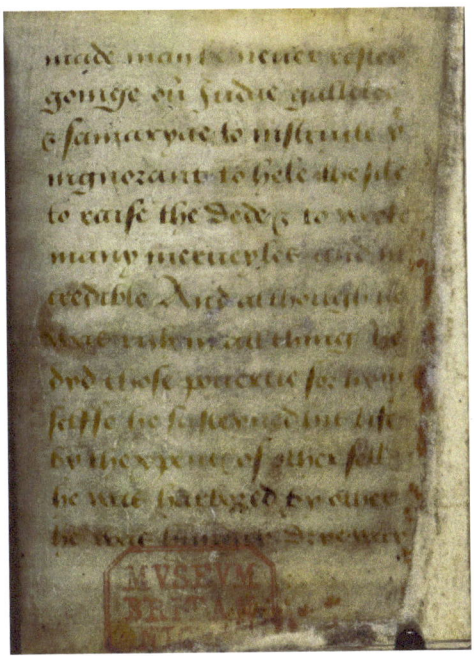

made man he neuer cefted
goinge ou͞r Judae gallelee
& famaryae to inftructe yᵉ
ingnorant to hele the fike
to raife the dede & to worke
many merucyles and in
credible And although he
was in him all thing he
dyd thofe pouertie for hym
felffe he fufteyned his life
by thexpenc℮ of other self℮
he was harbored by other
he was hungry dryeway

made man, He never ceased
going over [into] Judah, Galilee,
and Samaria to instruct the
ignorant, to heal the sick,
to raise the dead, and to work
many miracles and in-
credible [things]. And although He
was in Him all thing[s], He
did those povertie[s] for Himself. He sustained His life
by the expenses of other selves.
He was harbored by other[s].
He was hungry, dry-way.*

* From the early-modern pseudo-science of alchemy, meaning devoid of water; i.e., thirsty

we haue often redde of his
wepinge but neuer of his
laughing when he was x
but achilde he was fought
to haue hym dyſtroyed x
afterwarde whan he grew
to more adge he alweis x
fuffered the hates of wicked
folkₑ he was folde and be
trayed of his owne diſſiple:
taken and poniſſhed of the
Jues and he which dyd no
fin is bounde accuſed com//

Folio 3r

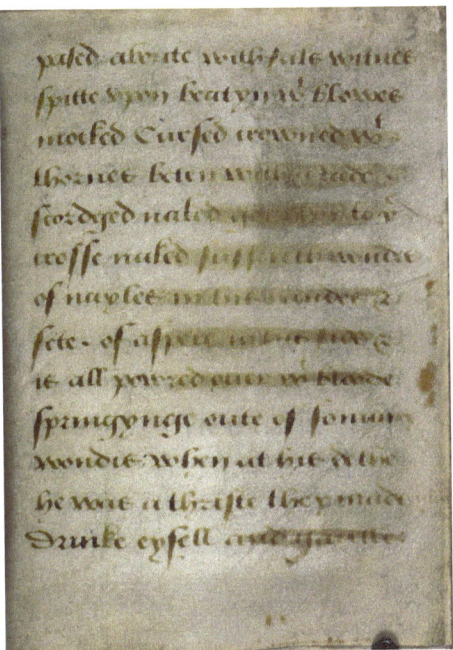

paſed aboute with fals witnes
fpitte vpon, beatyn w^t blowes
mocked Curſed crowned w^t
thornes beten with a Reede
ſcordged naked geuen vp to y^e
croſſe naked ſuffereth wondes
of nayles in his handes &
fete. of aſpere in his ſide &
is all powred over w^t bloode
ſpringynge oute of ſomany
wondis: when at his dethe
he was athriſte they made
drinke eyſell and gaulle:

passed about with false witness,
spit upon, beaten with blows,
mocked, cursed, crowned with
thorns, beaten with a reed,
scourged naked, given up to the
cross naked, suffered wounds
of nails in His hands and
feet, of a spear in His side, and
is all poured over with blood
springing from out of so many
wounds. When at His death
He was thirsty, they made Him
drink eisel* and gall.

* vinegar

Folio 3v

and beinge ſo cruelli confound
he offered hymſelfe a ſacrifice
to god his father for vs all x
who am I then that I ſhulde
diſpayre and ſuffer with x
an vnpatient mynde yf xx
any trouble do chaunce xx
vnto me: yf I ſuffer any incô//
moditie: yf any perſecution
of enuyous perſones comber
me ſpecially ſeinge non evyll
can be don vnto me which x

And being so cruelly confounded,
He offered Himself [as] a sacrifice
to God His Father for us all.
Who am I, then, that I should
despair and suffer with
an impatient mind if
any trouble does chance
unto me? If I suffer any incom-
modity, if any persecution
of envious persons encumber
me, especially seeing no evil
can be done unto me which

my fynnes hath not deserued
Therfor J will not suffer greuo
usly that thinge which ys
bestowed rightuously. but J
shal pray my lorde (gode) to graunt
me pasience in all thinges. &
in that patience pourgynge
and forgeuenes of myne vn
graciousnes that he which
vouchesaued to make me par
taker of his paynes may also
make me ptaker of his glorie
accordinge to thaposteles

my sins have not deserved?
Therefore I will not suffer grevio-
usly that thing which is
bestowed righteously. But I
shall pray my Lord God to grant
me patience in all things, and
in that patience, purging
and forgiveness of my
ungraciousness, that He which
vouchesafed to make me partaker of His pains may also
make me partakter of His glory
according to the Apostles,

Folio 4Av

sayinge/ as ye be felowes of his passions so shal ye be of his comforte. And ageyne and we die w^t hym saith he: we shal all lyve w^t hym: And yf we suffer with hym: we shal also raigne w^t hym/ therfore whether we be prouoked w^t priuate envy: or ell ani vyolente power take away our ryches or haue cruell sikenes/ or oftyn deth of oure dere frend/ or any other: ad

saying, "As you be fellows of His Passions, so shall you be of His comfort."* And again, "And we die with him," sayeth He, "we shall all live with Him. And if we suffer with Him, we shall also reign with Him."† Therefore whether we be provoked with private envy, or else any violent power take away our riches, or have cruel sickness, or often death of our dear friends, or any other ad-

---

* Romans 8:17

† 2 Timothy 2:12

uerfitie chaunce vnto vs/ we mufte gyve thank₍ₑ₎ for all thing₍ₑ₎: confeff and fay: lord: thow x art Jufte and thie Judgment ys true: Reproue not the rebu// kinge of our lorde. ffor he x wondeth and gyueth medy fynes/ he fmyteth & his hand₍ₑ₎ fhall hele / Paul and Sci las beinge betyn with rodd₍ₑ₎ in macidone put in prefon and laide in feteres sange prayfes to oʳ lorde. and our	versity chance unto us, we must give thanks for all things, confess and say, "Lord, Thou are just and Thy judgment is true." Reprove not the rebu- king of our Lord, for He wounds and gives medi- cines. He smites and His hands shall heal. Paul and Si- las being beaten with rods in Macedonia, put in prison, and laid in fetters sang praises to our Lord.* And our

* Acts 16:16-40

Folio 4Bv

lord hymſelf whan he
toke the challis: gaue thankₑ
to tech vs: to gyve thankₑ to
god as oftyn as we be greved
and poniſſhed wᵗʰ any adver//
ſitie: for by the Challys ys
vnderſtoude the tribulatiôs
of this worlde/ accordinge
to that ſayeinge lette this ₓ
Challes paſſe from me: ther
fore lette thankₑ be gyven ₓ
vnto hym for all thingₑ: by
whoſe prouidence all thingₑ

Lord Himself, when He
took the chalice, gave thanks
to teach us to give thanks to
God as often as we be greived
and punished with any adversity. For by the chalice is
understood the tribulations
of this world, according
to that saying, "Let this
chalice pass from me."* Therefore, let thanks be given
unto Him for all things, by
whose providence all things

* Matthew 26:39, Luke 22:42

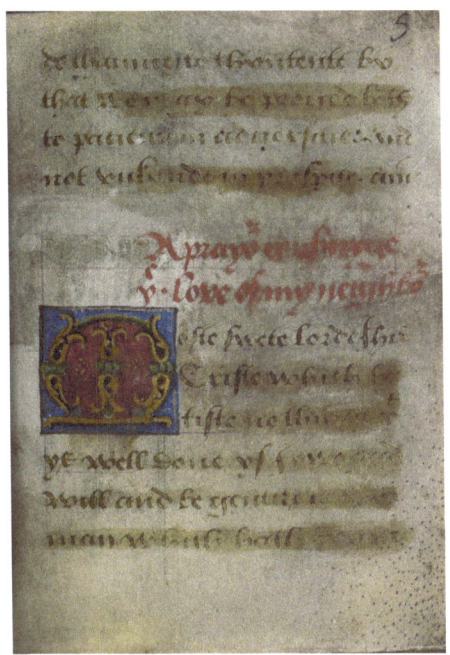

do chaunce to thyintent by that we may be proued both to patience in aduerſitie: And not vnkynde in proſpitie. amê

A prayeʳ ...yge
yᵉ love of my neighboʳ

Moste swete lord Jhũ Criste which ha taſte no thinge yᵗ ys well done yf J owe good will and be gentile to ... man which hath ...

do chance to the intent by that we may be proved* both to patience in adversity and not unkind in prosperity. Amen.

A prayer ...yge
the love of my neighbor

Most sweet Lord Jesus Christ which hates nothing that is well done. If I owe good will and be gentle to ... man which has ...

* to be shown able

Folio 5v

no hurte. But lord it ys
amoch gretter thinge and
liker to thie moste highe.
benignite yf I love myn
enymy/ and alweis will
good & do it yf I can to hym
which hath done me hurte
this procedeth of thie grace
and goodnes/ no thinge is
liker to the in nature then
that man which is gentill
& peaseble to his yll wil//
lers and enymyes that

no hurt. But Lord, it is
a much better thing and
liker* to Thy most high
benignity if I love my
enemy, and always will†
good and do it if I can to him
who has done me hurt.
This proceeds from Thy grace
and goodness. Nothing is
liker to Thee in nature than
that man which is gentle
and peaceable to his ill-wil-
lers and enemies that

---

* more pleasing

† used here as a verb: to desire

Folio 6r

hurte hym: ffor he that loueth
his enemyſe folowᵗ the: wᶜʰ
dideſte love vs/ and not on
ly didest love vs/ but alſo
woldeſte then die for vs: the
moste ſhamfull deth: and
dideſt pray for thie cruſifiers
Alſo thow haſte commaūded
vs to love oʳ enymyſe/ as it
ys wrettyn/ love yoʳ enymys/
and do good to them which
hate you/ and the rewarde
that thow pmiſeſte folowᵗ.

hurt him. For he that loves
his enemies follows Thee, which
did love us. And not on-
ly did love us, but also
would then die for us the
most shameful death, and
did pray for Thy crucifiers.
Also, Thou hast commanded
us to love our enemies, as it
is written, "Love your enemies,
and do good to them which
hate you,"* and the reward
that Thou promised follows

* Matthew 5:44, Luke 6:27

Folio 6v

to thintent ye may be ^the^ chil//
dren of your fader wch ys
yn hevyn: for o^r lorde Jhū x
Criſte/ whoſe propertie ys
to haue mercy and to for
gyve. The only and hole
profe of love ys: yf we love.
hym which is ageynſte
vs and letteth o^r welth xx
Also love ys wonte to be p̄
ued by the only contrietie
of hate/ Wherfore as man
ys ouer com with wordely

to the intent you may be children of your Father which is
in heaven, for our Lord Jesus
Christ, whose property is
to have mercy and to for-
give. The only and whole
proof of love is if we love
him which is against
us and lets* our wealth.
Also, love is wont to be proved by the only contrary
of hate, wherefore† as man
is overcome with worldly

---

* hinders, prevents

† for which reason, as a result of which

Folio 7r

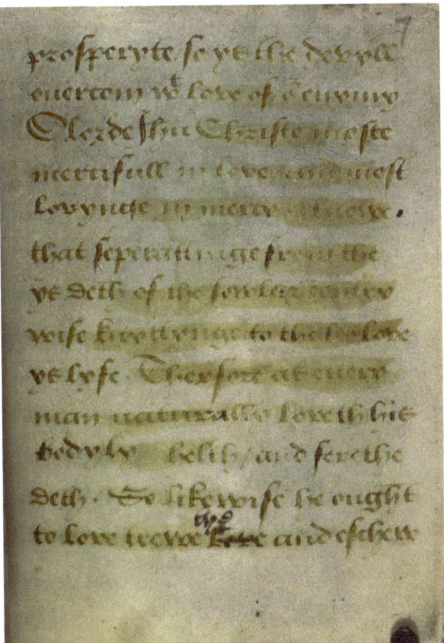

prosperyte/ so ys the devyll
ouercom wth love of o^r enymy
O lord Jhũ Chrifte mofte
mercifull in love/ and moft
lovynge in mercy. I knowe.
that feperattinge from the
ys deth of the fowle: & contry
wise knyttynge to the by love
ys lyfe. Therfor as euery
man naturally loveth his
bodyly helth/ and ferethe
deth. So likewise he ought
to love trewe^{lye} ~~love~~ and efchew

prosperity, so is the Devil
overcome with love of our enemy.
Oh Lord Jesus Christ, most
merciful in love and most
loving in mercy, I know
that separating from Thee
is death of the soul. And contrary-
wise, knitting to Thee by love
is life. Therefore, as every
man naturally loves his
bodily health and fears
death, so likewise he ought
to love truly and eschew

Folio 7v

hate. ffor he that hathe not
that love remayneth in deth
of fynne and detto^r of etñal
deth. O mofte merciful lord
Jhũ Chrifte. from whom love
cannot be banefhed: although
thofe thyngₑ be not hyd from
the which J moste wicked
fynner haue commytted &
if J confesse with my harte
and mouth that J haue xx
lyved vngracioufly. and by /
the reafon of my malles and

hate. For he that has not
that love remains in death
of sin and debtor of eternal
death. O most merciful Lord
Jesus Christ, from whom love
cannot be banished, although
those things be not hidden from
Thee which I, most wicked
sinner, have committed, and
if I confess with my heart
and mouth that I have
lived ungraciously, and by
the reason of my malice and

Folio 8r

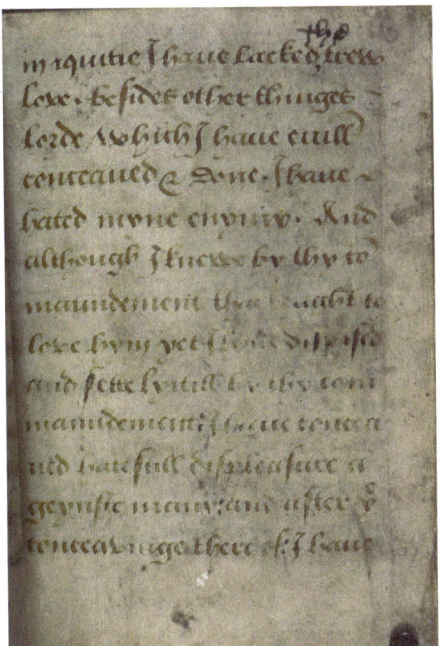

iniquitie ſ haue lacked ^(the) trew
love. beſides other thinges x
lorde which ſ haue euill
conceaued & done. ſ haue x
hated myne enymy. And
although ſ knewe by thy cō
maundement that ſ ought to
love hym yet ſ hym diſpiſed
and ſette lyitill by thy com
maundement: ſ haue concea
ued hatefull diſpleaſure a
geynſte many: and after y^e
conceavinge thereof: ſ haue

iniquity I have lacked the true
love. Besides other things,
Lord, which I have evil
conceived and done, I have
hated my enemy. And
although I knew by Thy com-
mandment that I ought to
love him, yet I him despised
and set little by Thy com-
mandment. I have concei-
ved hateful displeasure a-
gainst many. And after the
conceiving thereof, I have

Folio 8v

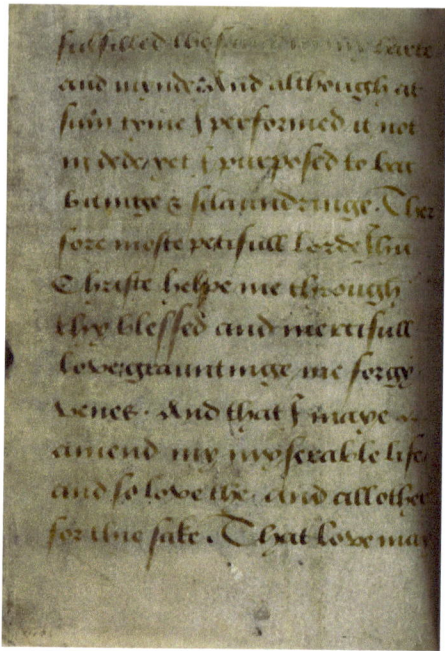

fulfilled the fame in my harte
and mynde: And although at
ſum tyme Ȉ performed it not
in dede/ yet Ȉ purpoſed to bac//
bitinge & felaunderinge. Ther
fore moſte petifull lorde Jhū
Chriſte helpe me through
thy bleſſed and mercifull
love: grauntinge me forgy
venes. And that Ȉ maye x
amend my myſerable life/
and ſo love the and all other
for thie ſake. That love may

fulfilled the same in my heart
and mind. And although at
some time I performed it not
in deed, yet I purposed* to backbiting and slandering. Therefore, most pitiful Lord Jesus
Christ, help me through
Thy blessed and merciful
love, granting me forgi-
veness. And [grant] that I may
amend my miserable life
and so love Thee and all other[s]
for Thy sake. That love may

* inclined, tended or leaned toward

Folio 9r

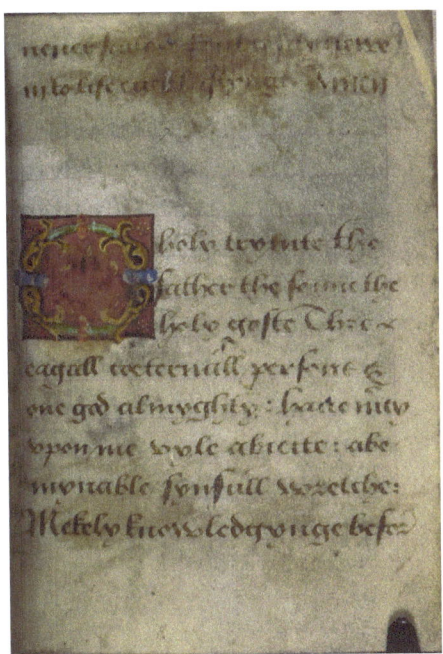

neuer faile ... ynewe
into life euerlaftinge. Amen.

O holy trynite the father the fonne the holy gofte Thre x eagall coeternall perfons & one god almyghty: haue m{r}cy vpon me vyle abiecte: abo// mynable/ fynfull wretche: Mekely knowledgynge befor

never fail ..ynew
into life everlasting. Amen.

O Holy Trinity: the Father, the Son, the Holy Ghost, three equal co-eternal persons and one God Almighty. Have mercy upon me, vile, abject, abominable, sinful wretch, meekly acknowledging before

Folio 9v

thy hye maiefte my longe
contynued fynfull life/ euen
fro my childhed hetherto/
thow good gratious lorde as
thow gyuefte me thy grace
to knowledge them/ fo gyve
me thie grace not in only xx
woorde but in harte alfo. w^t
forowful contrition to repente
them and vtterly to forfake
them/ fforgyf me thofe fyñes
also in whiche myne owne
defaulte throwe euyl affecti

Thy high majesty, my long
continued sinful life, even
from my childhood hitherto.
Thou good gracious Lord, as
Thou gives me Thy grace
to acknowledge them, so give
me Thy grace not only
in word but in heart also, with
sorrowful contrition to repent
them and utterly to forsake
them. Forgive me those sins
also in which my own
default, through evil affecti-

Folio 10r

ons and euel ſuſtume my
reſon is wᵗ ſenſualitie ſo blyn
ded that Ī cannot deſſerne x
them for ſyn: And illumin ~
good lord myn ĥte & gyue me
grace to knowelege them. And x
for gyve me my syñes xx
necligently for getten/ And
bringe them to my mynde
wᵗ grace to be prierly conſeſ
ſed of them: Gloryous god x
gyve me from hens forthe
thie grace wᵗ litell reſpecte

ons and evil custom, my
reason is with sensuality so blin-
ded that I cannot discern
them from sin. And illumine,
good Lord, my heart and give me
grace to acknowledge them. And
forgive me my sins
negligently forgotten, and
bring them to my mind
with grace to be properly confes-
sed of them. Glorious God,
give me from henceforth
Thy grace with little respect

unto the world, so to set and fix
firmly my heart upon Thee
that I may say with the Blessed
Apostle Saint Paul, "The
world is crucified to me and I
to the world.* Christ is to me
life, and to die is my gain and
advantage.† I desire to be loosed
and to be with Christ."** Lord,
give me Thy grace to amend
my life and to have an eye
to my end without any
grudge or fear of death, which

* Galatians 6:15　　† Philippians 1:21　　** Philippians 1:23

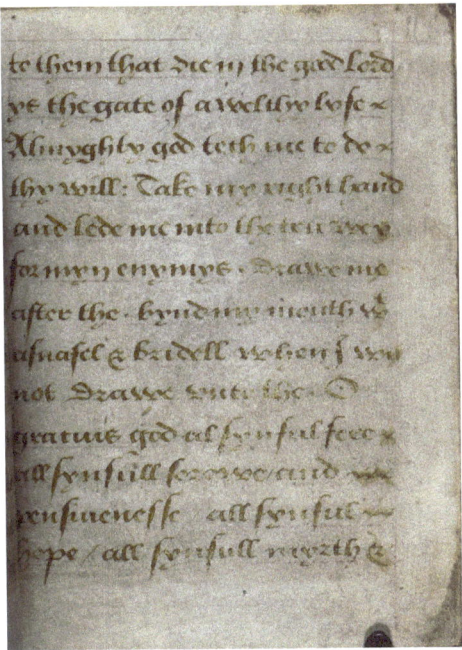

to them that die in the good lord
ys the gate of a welthyy lyfe x
Almyghty god tech me to do x
thy will: Take my right hand
and lede me into the tru wey
for myn enymys. drawe me
after the. bynd my mouth wt
a snafel & bridell when I wil
not drawe vnto the. O
gracius god al fynful fere x
all fynfull forowe/ and xxx
penfiueneffe / all fynful xx
hope / all fynfull myrth &

to them that die in Thee, good Lord,
is the gate of a wealthy life.
Almyghty God, teach me to do
Thy will. Take my right hand
and lead me into the true way
from my enemies. Draw me
after Thee. Bind my mouth with
a snaffle* and bridle when I will
not draw unto Thee. O
gracious God, all sinful fear,
all sinful sorrow, and
pensiveness, all sinful
hope, all sinful mirth and

* The bit of a horse's bridle.

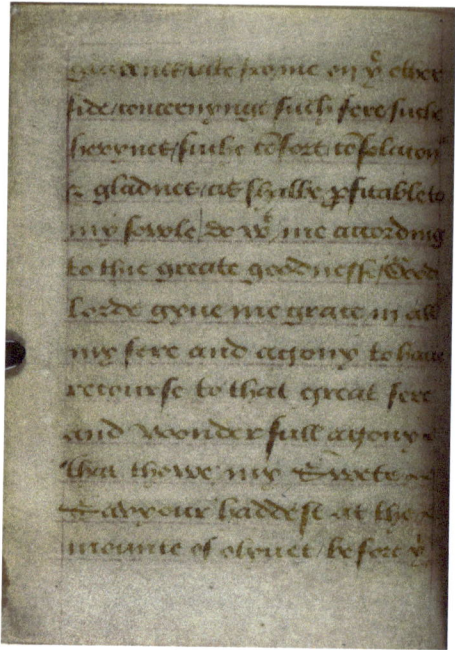

gladnes/ take fro on yᵉ other
fide/ concernynge fuch fere/ fuche
hevynes/ fuche côfort/ côfolacon
& gladness/ as fhalbe pfitable to
my fowle/ do wᵗ me according
to thie greate goodneffe/ Good
lorde gyue me grace in all
my fere and agony to haue
recourfe to that great fere
and wonderfull agony ₓ
that thowe my Swete ₓₓ
Savyour haddefte at the ₓ
mounte of olyuet/ before yʳ

gladness. Take from the other
side, concerning such fear, such
heaviness, such comfort, consolation
and gladness, as shall be profitable to
my soul. Do with me according
to Thy great goodness, good
Lord. Give me grace in all
my fear, and again to have
recourse to that great fear
and wonderful agony
that Thou, my sweet
Savior, had at the
Mount of Olives before Your

Folio 12r

moſte bitter paſſion and in yᵉ	most bitter Passion, and in the
meditacon thereof to cõceave	meditation thereof to conceive
goſtely cõfort & conſolacon x	ghostly* comfort and consolation
p̱fitable for my ſoule: Almyghty	profitable to my soul. Almighty
god take fro me al veyneglori℮	God, take from me all vainglorious
myndes: all apetit℮ of myne x	thoughts, all appetites of my
owne prayſe: al enuy: couetuſnes,	own praise, all envy, covetousness,
ſlewth: & lechery: all wrathful [glotony]	gluttony, sloth, and lechery, all wrathful
affections: all apetite of reven	affections, all appetite of reven-
gynge: all deſire or delite of x	ging, all desire or delight in
other fok℮ harme: all pleaſure	other folks' harm, all pleasure
in provokynge any parſen to	in provoking any person to
wrath and anger: all delite of	wrath and anger, all delight in

* spiritual

Folio 12v

tauntynge or mockynge any
parſon: in their affliction or trou
ble: And gyue me good lord an
humble lowly yet pefable pa
tient/ cheritable/ kynd/ tender &
petyfull mynde: in all my war
kes/ all my wordes/ and all
my thoughtₑ/ to have a taſte
of thye holye bleſſed ſprite/
Gyve me good Lord afull
faithe/ aferme hope/ afervent
Cheryty/ A Love to xxx
the Good Lorde/ incomperable

taunting or mocking any
person in their affliction or trouble. And give me, good Lord, an
humble, lowly, yet peaceable, patient, charitable, kind, tender, and
pitiful mind. In all my works, all my words, and all
my thoughts to have a taste of
Thy Holy Blessed Spirit.
Give me, good Lord, a full
faith, a firm hope, a fervent
charity, a love to
Thee, good Lord, incomparable

Folio 13r

aboue the love of my ſelfe/ and that I loue no thing to thie difpleaſure/ but every thinge in adwe order to the: Gyue me good lorde alongynge to be wᵗ the/ not for the advoydîge of the calymities of this wretched worlde/ nor ſo much for the aduoidynge of the paŷes of helle/ nother ſo muche for the atteynynge of the Ioyes of hevyn in the reſpect of myne owne cômoditie/ as

above the love of myself, and that I love nothing to Thy displeasure, but everything in a due order to Thee. Give me, good Lord, a longing to be with Thee, not for the avoiding of the calamities of this wretched world, nor so much for the avoiding of the pains of Hell, nor so much for the attaining of the joys of Heaven in respect of my own commodity,* as

* "In respect of my own commodity" = "by virtue of my own merits"

Folio 13v

evyn for avery love to the:
And bere me thie love & faur
which thinge my love to the//
warde ware it neuer fo grete/
coulde not but of thie greate
goodnes difserve. And pdon
me good lorde that I am fo
bolde to aske the so hye petici
ons beinge fo vyle a fynfull
wretche and fo vnwerthy to
atteyne the lowefte. but yet
fuche they be as I am bounden
to defire & wiffhe & fhulde be

(interlinear: goo'ls lorde; goode lorde; x)

even* for a very love to Thee.
And bear me, good Lord, Thy love and
    favor,
which thing to my love to Thee-
ward, were it never so great,
could not but of Thy great
goodness deserve. And pardon
me, good Lord, that I am so
bold to ask Thee so high petitions, being so vile a sinful
wretch and so unworthy to
attain the lowest. But yet,
good Lord, such they be as I am
    bounden
to desire and wish and should be

* "As even" = "but rather" or "but instead"

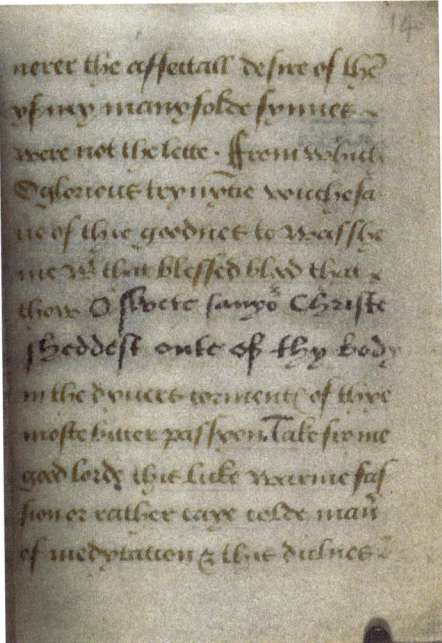

never the affectal defire of the
yf my manyfolde fynnes x
were not the lette. ffrom which,
O glorious trynytie wuche sa
ue of thie goodnes to waffhe
me w^t that bleffed blud that x
thow O fwete fauyo^r Chrifte
sheddeft oute of thy body
in the dyvers torment℮ of thye
mofte bitter paffyon. Take fro me
good lorde this luke warme faf//
fion or rather caye colde man^r
of medytations & this dulnes x

never the effectual desire of Thee
if my manifold sins
were not the less. From which,
oh glorious Trinity, which save of Thy goodness, to wash
me with that blessed blood that
Thou, oh sweet Savior Christ,
shed out of Thy body
in the diverse torments of Thy
most bitter Passion. Take from me,
good Lord, this lukewarm passion, or rather cold manner
of meditations and this dullness

Folio 14v

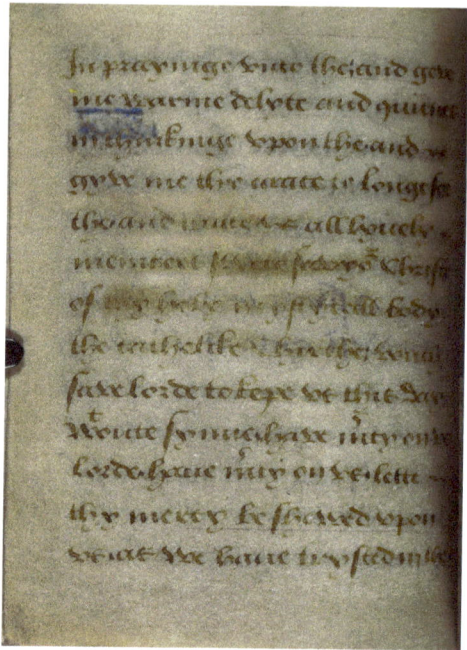

ʃn prayinge vnto the: and geve
me warme delite and quitnes
in thinkinge vpon the and xx
gyve me thy grace to longe for
the and make vs all lyuely x
members ʃwete ʃavyo^r Chriʃte
of thy holy myʃtycall body
the catholike Churche: which
ʃave lord to kepe vs this day
w^toute ʃynne. have m^rcy on vs
lorde haue m^rcy on us. lette ~
thy mercy be ʃhowed vpon
vs. as we haue tryʃted in the.

in praying unto Thee. And give
me warm delight and quietness
in thinking upon Thee, and
give me Thy grace to long for
Thee, and make us all lively
members, sweet Savior Christ,
of Thy holy mystical body,
the catholic* Church, which
save Lord to keep us this day
without sin. Have mercy on us,
Lord, have mercy on us. Let
Thy mercy be shown upon
us, as we have trusted in Thee.

* "Catholic" as used here refers to the universal church of Christian believers generally, not to the Roman Catholic Church specifically.

Folio 15r

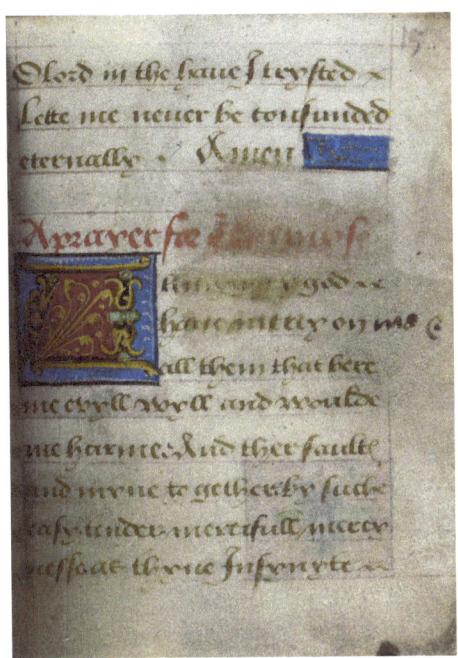

Olord in the haue J tryſted x
lette me neuer be confunded
eternally ~   Amen.

Aprayer for o^r enemyse

llmyghty god xx
haue mercy on me &
all them that bere
me harme: And ther faultₑ
and myne to gether: by ſuche
eaſy tender mercifull mercy
nesse as thyne Jnfynyte xx

Oh Lord, in Thee have I trusted.
Let me never be confounded
eternally.   Amen.

A prayer for our enemies

lmighty God,
have mercy on me and
all them that bear
me harm. And their faults
and mine together, by such
easy, tender, merciful merci-
ness as Thine infinite

Folio 15v

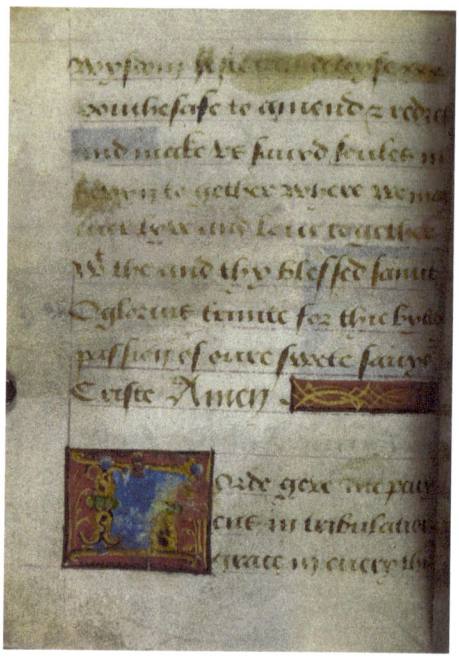

wyſdem & ſtead... eyſe xxx
vouchſafe to amend & redres
and make vs ſauyd ſoules in
hevyn to gether where we may
euer lyve and loue to gether
wᵗ the and thy bleſſed sainctₑ
Oglorius trinite for thie bytter
paſſion of oure swete sauyoʳ
Criſte   Amen

ord geve me paty
ens in tribulation
grace in euerythîg

wisdom and stead... eys.
Vouchsafe to amend and redress
and make us saved souls in
Heaven together, where we may
ever live and love together
with Thee and Thy blessed saints,
Oh glorious Trinity, for Thy bitter
Passion of our sweet Savior
Christ. Amen.

ord give me pati-
ence in tribulation,
grace in everything

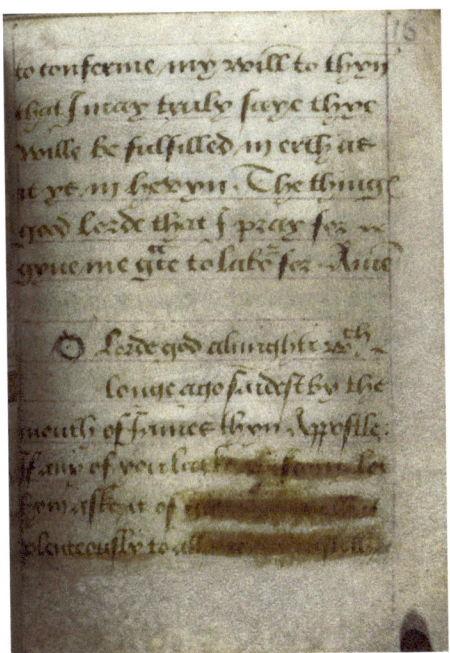

to conferme my will to thyn
that J may truly faye thye
wille be fulfilled in erth as
it ys in hevyn. The thing*e*
good lorde that J pray for xx
gyue me g^ace to labo^r for. Amê

O lorde god almighte wch x
   longe ago been faideft by the
   mouth of James thyn Appoftle:
Jf any of you lacke wifdem let
hym afke it of god ... eth it
plenteoufly to all men ... afketh

to conform my will to Thine
that I may truly say, "Thy
will be fulfilled in Earth as
it is in Heaven." The things,
good Lord, that I pray for,
give me grace to labor for. Amen.

O* Lord God Almighty, which
   long ago [have] been said by the
   mouth of James Thine Apostle,
"If any of you lack wisdom, let
him ask it of God ... eth it
plenteously to all men ... asketh

* Space was left by the scribe for the insertion of a decorated initial O, but the decorator failed to provide the decoration.

Folio 16v

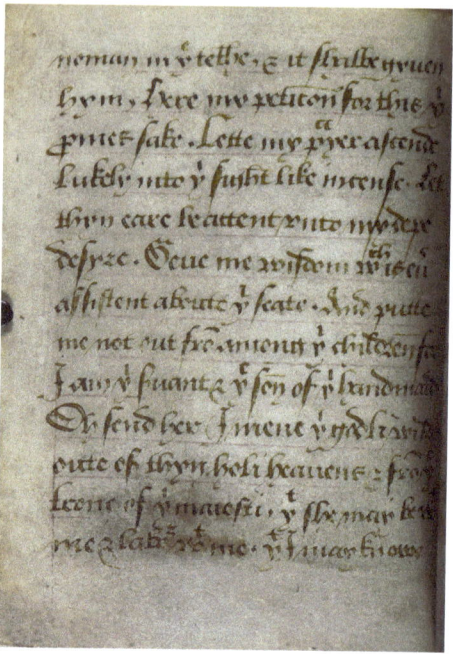

noman in ye tethe, & it fhalbe gyuen hym, here my peticon for thys yi pmes fake. Lette my payer afcende lukely into yi fight like incenfe. Let thyn eare be attent vnto my depe defyre. Geue me wisdom wch ys eur affiftent aboute yi feat. And putte me not out frô among yi children for J am yi fuant & ye son of yi handmaid Oh fend her (J mene yi godliwifdô) oute of thyn holi heauens & frô ye trone of yi maiefti, yt fhe may be wt me & labor wt me. yt J may knowe

no man in the teeth, and it shall be given him."* Hear this petition for this Thy promise's sake. Let my prayer ascend warmly† into Thy sight like incense. Let Thine ear be attentive unto my deep desire. Give me wisdom, which is ever assitant about Thy seat. And put me not out from among Thy children for I am Thy servant and the son of Thy handmaiden.
Oh send her (I mean Thy godly wisdom) out of Thine Holy Heavens and from the throne of Thy majesty, that she may be with
me and labor with me, that I may know

*James 1:5   † "lukely" is an obsolete word meaning "warmly"

Folio 17r

what is acceptable in yᶦ fight. Oh lern
me goodnes, nurtʳ & knowlege, for Ɉ
beleve yᶦ cõmañdmentℓ. Thow art
good & gᵃcious, inftruct me in thyn
ordinancℓ. Let myn herti befichŷng
afcend into yᶦ prfens. Geve me vn//
derftonding according to yᶦ worde.
Oh geve me vnderftonding & I fhall
kepe yᶦ lawe, yee Ɉ fhall keep it wᵗ
all myn ĥte. Shewe me thie
weis o lorde, & teche me thy
patthes. Led me into yᶦ trueth

what is acceptable in Thy sight. Oh learn
me goodness, nurture, and knowledge, for I
believe Thy commandments. Thou are
good and gracious, instruct me in Thine
ordinances. Let my heart beseeching
ascend into Thy presence. Give me understanding according to Thy Word.
Oh give me understanding and I shall
keep Thy Law. Yea, I shall keep it with
all my heart. Show me Thy
ways, O Lord, and teach me Thy
paths. Lead me into Thy truth

Folio 17v

& lerne me, for thow art ye god of my helth & on the do J depêd alwei. Here now my hert O lord w^t wch J haue cryed vnto … haue m^{r}ci vpon me & g^{a}ci oufly here me for Jefus xx Crift℮ fake o^r lord whiche lyueth and reigneth with the hys father and the holi goefte worlde withoute ende. Amen. Lede me O lord in thy way & lette me walke in y^i trewth Oh lette my ḣte delyte in fearing y^i na….. Ordre my going℮ after y^i worde y^t no wi kednes raigne in me/ kepe my ftepes … y^i pathes leste my fete turne into … contrayrye waye/

and learn me, for Thou are the God of my health and on Thee do I depend always. Hear now my heart Oh Lord, with which I have cried unto …. Have mercy upon me and graci- ously hear me for Jesus Christ's sake, our Lord which lives and reigns with Thee, His Father, and the Holy Ghost, world without end. Amen. Lead me, oh Lord in Thy ways and let me walk in Thy truth. Oh let my heart delight in fearing Thy na[me]. Order my goings after Thy Word that no wi- ckedness [may] reign in me. Keep my steps [on] Thy paths lest my feet turn into … contrary ways.

| myſerable ſynner, am not wor//
thie to name or caule vpon nor
thynke on in my harte/ Jhumbly
beſyche the (good lorde) mercyfulli
to looke on me thyne vnkynde xx
ſervaunte and haue petie on me,
lyke as thow haddeſte petye and
dydeſte forgeue the woman of
Chanane, Mary magdaleyne, ye
Publican, and the thefe hanging
on the croſſe. | confeſſe vnto the
moſte m{r}cyfull father, all my
synnes whiche yf | wolde I …

I, miserable sinner, am not worthy to name or call upon nor
think on. In my heart I humbly
beseech Thee, good Lord, mercifully
to look on me, Thine unkind
servant, and have pity on me,
like as Thou had pity and
did forgive the woman of
Canaan*, Mary Magdalen†, the
publican**, and the thief hanging
on the cross.†† I confess unto Thee,
most merciful Father, all my
sins which if I would I …

* Matthew 15: 21-28 † John 3: 7-8 ** Luke 18: 10-14 †† Luke 23: 39-43

Folio 18v

not hide frome the/ fforgeue me my lorde jhu chryſte, where as J wretched ſynner haue offended the, in pride, in covetouſnes, in flouthe, in wrathe, in enuye, in glotenye, in lechery, in vayn glo//rye, in adulterie, in thefte, in lying, in blaſphemynge, in wanton geſtes and ſportes, in heringe in seinge, in taſtinge, in felyng, in ſpekynge, in thinkinge, in workinge, and in all manner waies wherein J (an vnſtable

not hide from Thee. Forgive me, my Lord Jesus Christ, whereas I, wretched sinner, have offended Thee in pride, in covetousness, in sloth, in wrath, in envy, in gluttony, in lechery, in vainglory, in adultery, in theft, in lying, in blaspheming, in wanton jests and sports, in hearing, in seeing, in tasting, in feeling, in speaking, in thinking, in working, and in all manner [and] ways wherein I, an unstable

Folio 19r

and frayle creature) myghte
offende my maker by anny fa
ate or trespas. Therefore J be
syche thie mercye and goodneſſe
whiche cãm downe frome he
uen to erthe for my soul helth
(whyche also reysed vp kynge
Dauyd frome the faule of syñ)
to forgeuc me/ fforgeue me
good lorde whiche forgaueste
Peter that denyed & forsoke y^e
Thow arte my maker, my hel
per my redemer my gou^r no^r

and frail creature, might
offend my Maker by any fact or trespass. Therefore I beseech Thy mercy and goodness,
which came down from He-
aven to Earth for my soul's health
(which also raised up King
David from the fall of sin)
to forgive me. Forgive me,
good Lord, which forgave
Peter that denied and forsook Thee.
Thou are my Maker, my Helper, my Redeemer, my Governor,

Folio 19v

my father my lorde my king
my god/ thow arte my hope/
my trufte my gouernaunce/
my helpe/ my comforte/ my
ftrength/ my defence my de//
lyueraunce/ my lyfe/ my x
helth/ my refurrection
T how arte my ftaye & my
Refuge my lighte my defire &
my focoure good lord Ɉ befich
the helpe me & Ɉ fhalbe faffe,
gouerne me and defende me
Comforte me and confirme

my Father, my Lord, my King,
my God. Thou are my hope,
my trust, my governance,
my help, my comfort, my
strength, my defense, my deliverance, my life, my
health, my resurrection.
T hou are my stay and my
refuge, my light, my desire, and
my succor. Good Lord, I beseech
Thee [to] help me, and I shall be safe.
Govern me and defend me.
Comfort me and confirm

me in gladnes Geue me light
& viſet me/ Reuyue me yt am
dede in ſynne Deſpiſe me nat
good lorde for Ɉ am the worke of
yi handes yi ſeruaunt Ɉ am thou
gh Ɉ be euell/ though Ɉ be a syner
& vnworthie, yet howſover Ɉ be
good lorde Ɉ am thyne. To whom
than ſhoulde Ɉ fle good lorde, but
onelie to ye. Ɉf thow caſte me oute,
who will receyve me, Ɉf thow x
deſpiſe me, who will regarde me
Therefore good lorde though Ɉ be

me in gladness. Give me light
and visit me. Receive me that am
dead in sin. Despise me not,
good Lord, for I am the work of
Thy hands. Thy servant, I am. Though I be evil, though I be a sinner
and unworthy, yet howsoever I be,
good Lord, I am Thine. To whom
then should I flee, good Lord, but
only to Thee? If Thou caste me out,
who will receive me? If Thou
despise me, who will regard me?
Therefore, good Lord, though I be

Folio 20v

vnworthie, vyle and vncleane,	unworthy, vile, unclean,
yet knowlege me returnyng xx	yet acknowledge my returning
agayne vnto ye ffor yf J be vyle &	again unto Thee. For if I be vile and
filthie, thow mayfte make me	filthy, Thou may make me
cleane/ Jf I be blynde thow maift	clean. If I be blind, Thou may
make me fe agayne/ Jf J be seke	make me see again. If I be sick,
thow mayfte make me hole/ Jf J	Thou may make me whole. If I
be dede & buried in fynne thow	be dead and buried in sin, Thou
mayfte reuyue me/ ffor y^i m^{r}cye	may revive me. For Thy mercy
is gretter than myne Jnyquyte,	is greater than my iniquity.
y^u maifte forgeue more than J cã	Thou may forgive more than I can
offende/ Therefore good lorde con	offend. Therefore, good Lord, con-
fydre not y^e nomber of my faut$_e$	sider not the number of my faults

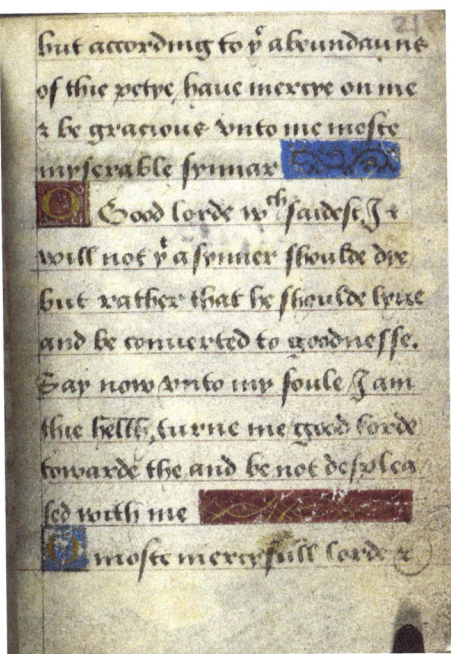

but according to yᵉ aboundauns
of thie petye/ haue mercye on me
& be gracious vnto me moste
myferable fynnar

🅞 Good lorde wᶜʰ faideft, J
will not yᵗ a fynner fhoulde dye/
but rather that he fhoulde lyue
and be conuerted to goodneffe.
Say now vnto my foule/ J am
thie helth, turne me (good lorde)
towarde the and be not defplea
fed with me.

🅞 mofte mercyfull lord &

but according to the abundance
of Thy pity. Have mercy on me
and be gracious unto me, most
miserable sinner.

🅞 good Lord, which said, "I
will not that a sinner should die,
but rather that he should live
and be converted to goodness."
Say now unto my soul, "I am
thy health." Turn me, good Lord,
toward Thee and be not displea-
sed with me.

🅞 most merciful Lord and

Folio 21v

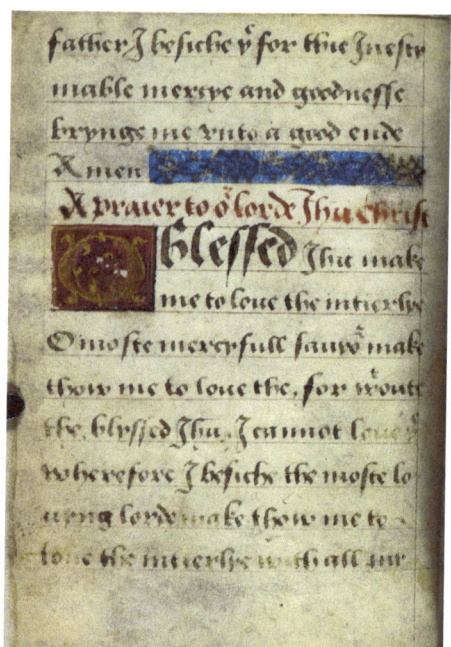

father, J besiche yͤ for thie Jnesty mable mercye and goodneſſe brynge me vnto a good ende Amen

A praier to oʳ lorde J̄hu Chriſt

O bleſſed J̄hu make me to loue the intierlye O moſte mercyfull ſauyoʳ make thow me to loue the, for wᵗoute the, blyſſed J̄hu, J cannot loue yͤ wherefore J beſiche the moſte lo// uyng lorde make thow me to ₓ loue the intierlye with all my

Father, I beseech Thee for Thy inestimable mercy and goodness, bring me unto a good end. Amen

A prayer to our Lord Jesus Christ

O blessed Jesus, make me to love Thee entirely. O most merciful Savior, make Thou me to love Thee, for without Thee, Blessed Jesus, I cannot love Thee. Therefore I beseech Thee, most loving Lord, make Thou me to love Thee entirely with all my

Folio 22r

harte w^t all my mynde & withe
all my power and ſtrength.
O moſte bliſſed Jh̄u, J wolde
fayne loue y^e, but J cannot w^t//
oute thie helpe. O moſte ſwete
Jh̄u my comforte and ſolace fa
yne woulde J loue the but w^tout
thie helpe J can do nothinge. my
great enemyes, the worlde, the
fleſſhe, and the feende, be right
fearce and cruell & euermore
Redye to lette me frome yⁱ loue.
helpe me therefore good lorde

heart, with all my mind, and with all my power and strength. Oh most Blessed Jesus, I would fain* love Thee, but I cannot without Thy help. Oh most sweet Jesus, my comfort and solace, fain would I love Thee, but without Thy help I can do nothing. My great enemies, the world, the flesh, and the fiend, be right fierce and cruel and evermore ready to let[†] me from Thy love. Help me therefore, good Lord,

* readily

† remove

and ftrength me wt thie grace
fo that J may euer loue the as
thie will is. O blyssed Jhu lett
me depelye confidre the contentℓ
of thie loue towardes me O my
lorde god almyghtie thow arte
my maker, thow arte my rede
mer, thow arte my favyoʳ, thow
good lorde hafte made me not
a ftone wtout life, nor of a tre
wtoute sensyble parceyuyng,
nor a beefte withoute refonne,
but thow hafte made me a ꝑfite

and strengthen me with Thy grace
so that I may ever love Thee as
Thy will is. Oh Blessed Jesus, let
me deeply consider the contents
of Thy love towards me. Oh my
Lord God Almighty, Thou are
my Maker, Thou are my Redeemer, Thou are my Savior. Thou,
good Lord, have made me not
a stone without life, not of a tree
without sensible preceiving,
nor a beast without reason,
but Thou have made me a perfect

Folio 23r

creature hauyng lyfe sencyble parceyuyng and reaſonable vndreſtanding. Alſo thow haſte Redemed me not wᵗ corruptible golde and filuer. but wᵗ thie moſte precyous bloode. wherby thow haſte made me partaker of thie grete glorie & Joye in heuen. Moreouer thow haſte preſerued me frome myche yll & yet daylie thow doeſte preſerue me & noryſſhe ᵐᵉ both bodely and goſtely. Graunte me myne

creature having life, sensible perceiving, and reasonable understanding. Also Thou have redeemed me not with corruptible gold and silver, but with Thy most precious blood, whereby Thou have made me a partaker of Thy great glory and joy in Heaven. Moreover, Thou have preserved me from much ill, and yet* daily Thou do preserve me and nourish me both bodily and ghostly. Grant me, my

* still

Folio 23v

owne good lorde depely to plante wᵗin my breſte, the remembrau nce of this thie greate loue towa rdes me. O blyſſed Jh̄u geue me grace, hartely to thanke the for yⁱ benefites. O moſte gracious lorde J am full of frayltie & feble as thow knoweſt beſte & vtterly Jnsufficyent of my selffe to ren dre thank℮ vnto thie goodneſſe for my creacõn. for my redemp cõn and conſeruacõn. Thow therefore blyſſed lorde Jh̄u xx

own good Lord, deeply to plant within my breast the remembra- nce of this, Thy great love towa- rds me. Oh Blessed Jesus, give me grace, heartily to thank Thee for Thy benefits. Oh most gracious Lord, I am full of frailty and feeble, as Thou knows best, and utterly insufficient of myself to ren- der thanks unto Thy goodness for my creation, for my redemp- tion and conservation. Thou therefore, Blessed Lord Jesus,

Folio 24r

Receyue me after thy wyll and
geue me grace hartely to thank
the for this and other of thye ma
nyfold benefett*e*. O blyffed x
Jhu geue me good will to ferue
the & fuffer for y^e. O mofte good
and lyberall lorde thow arte y^e
very gyuer of all good thynges.
geue me good lorde a good will
to loue y^e, to dreade the, and to fuf
fre my dewtye good lorde is gret
and my power ys but fmalle
J oughte to loue ye above all cre

receive me after Thy will and
give me grace heartily to thank
Thee for this and other of Thy manifold benefits. Oh Blessed
Jesus, give me good will to serve
Thee and [to] suffer for Thee. Oh most good
and liberal Lord, Thou art the
very giver of all good things.
Give me, good Lord, a good will
to love Thee, to dread Thee, and to suffer my duty, good Lord, is great
and my power is but small.
I ought to love Thee above all cre-

Folio 24v

creatures and my neyghbour
as my ſelffe J aught to fle ſynne
for thye ſake & onely to folow yᵉ
J aught to be content wᵗ all my
trybulacõn, and gladlye to ſuf
fre theym for the loue of the, but
in nowyſe J canne do this by ˣ
myne owne power & ſtrength/
Helpe me therefore blyſſed Jh̃u
wᵗ thy ſpecyall grace and geue
me good wille thus to ſerue yᵉ
obediently, and pacyently to ſuf
fre. Oſwete Jh̃u geue me con/

creatures and my neighbor
as my self. I ought to flee sin
for Thy sake and only to follow Thee.
I ought to be content with all my
tribulation, and gladly to suffer them for the love of Thee. But
in no way can I do this by
my own power and strength.
Help me therefore, Blessed Jesus,
with Thy special grace, and give
me good will thus to serve Thee
obediently, and patiently to suffer. Oh sweet Jesus, give me con-

tynuall remembraunce of thy passyon. O moſte benyng Jhu myne hole helthe & welthe J conﬃeſſe and lowly ſubmitte my ſelffe vnto y{i} greate mercy and goodneſſe for J haue lytle remêbred the, and leſſe J haue thanked ye for y{i} great kyndnes ſhewed vnto me and almankynde. Where as thow werte ryche, for o{r} ſakes thow becameſt full poore, thow tokeſt great labo{r} to eaſe vs, thou ſuffreſte many paynes to Releue

tinual remembrance of Thy Passion. Oh most benign Jesus, my whole health and wealth, I confess and lowly submit myself unto Thy great mercy and goodness, for I have little remembered Thee, and less I have thanked Thee for Thy great kindness showed unto me and all mankind. Whereas Thou were rich, for our sakes Thou became full poor. Thou took great labor to ease us. Thou suffered many pains to relieve

Folio 25v

vs. Where we were bounde y__u__ madeſt vs fre, we were condem ned by Juſtice of the paynefull pryſon of hell/ And thow by y__i__ m__r__cye madeſt vs inheritours to y__e__ Joyful kingdome of heuyn x
Thow werte vnkyndely betraied. Thow werte traiterouſely taken and cruelly bounde w__t__ harde ropes Thow werte mocked & ſcorned and ſpitted vpon. Thow werte beaten and bobbed, and crow// ned w__t__ ſharpe thornes. Thow

us. Where we were bound, Thou made us free. We were condem- ned by justice of the painful prison of Hell, and Thou, by Thy mercy, made us inheritors to the joyful Kingdom of Heaven. Thou were unkindly betrayed. Thou were traitorously taken and cruelly bound with hard ropes. Thou were mocked and scorned and spat upon. Thou were beaten and bobbed, and crow- ned with sharp thorns. Thou

werte drawen and ſtretched and
through perced into thy harte/ yⁱ
ſenewes and vaynes were bro
ken and thy skynne and fleſſh
was torne, thie handes and
feete nayled to yᵉ croſſe. Thowe
ſhedeſte all yⁱ bloode and yelded
vp yⁱ goſte All this and mych
more thow dideſte and ſuffreſt
for ſynfull mannes ſake x
Moyste my drye harte, blyſſed
Jhu wᵗ thie swete droppes of yⁱ
grace and geue me contynuall

were drawn and stretched and
through-pierced into Thy heart. Thy
sinews and veins were broken, and Thy skin and flesh
were torn, Thy hands and
feet nailed to the Cross. Thou
shed all Thy blood and yielded
up Thy ghost. All this and much
more Thou did and suffered
for sinful man's sake.
Moisten my dry heart, Blessed
Jesus, with the sweet drops of Thy
grace and give me continual

Folio 26v

remembraunce of this thie
paynefull paffyon O swete
Jhu poffeff my harte and kepe
it onely to yᵉ. O mofte noble &
myghtye prynce lorde of all
lordes and kynge of all kingₑ
thow madefte heuen and erth
& all yᵉ creatures in theym .
Now than like as J am thyn
by creacõn/ fo make thow me
euer thyne by poffeffion xx
make thow me mekely to con
feffe myne owne dedes, wordes,

remembrance of this Thy
painful Passion. Oh sweet
Jesus, possess my heart and keep
it only to Thee. Oh most noble and
mighty prince, Lord of all
lords, and King of all kings,
Thou made Heaven and Earth
and all the creatures in them.
Now, then, just as I am Thine
by creation, so make Thou me
ever Thine by possession.
Make Thou me meekly to confess my own deeds, words,

Folio 27r

and thoughtes, and to put my
hole truste and confidence in y^i
grace/ Make me vtterly to des
pyse this wretched worlde &
all ye vnlawfull pleasures &
desyres of the same, make thow
me meke pacyent and petyfull
and geue me parfecte faythe
hope and charyte Make thow
my harte also O moste swete
Jhu a pleasaunte Palles for
thie high magestye and posseffe
it holde it and kepe it onelye to

and thoughts, and to put my
whole trust and confidence in Thy
grace. Make me utterly to despise this wretched world and
all the unlawful pleasures and
desires of the same. Make Thou
me patient and pitiful
and give me perfect faith,
hope, and charity. Make Thou
my heart also, oh most sweet
Jesus, a pleasant palace for
Thy high majesty, and possess
it, hold it, and keep it only to

Folio 27v

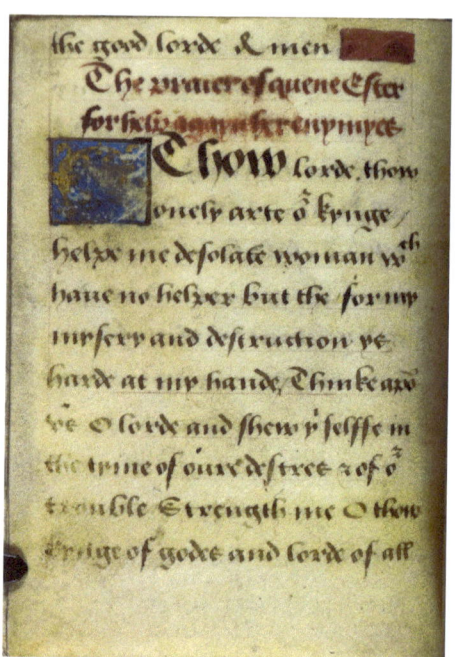

the good lorde Amen

The praier of quene Efter for help agayn her enymyes
O Thow lord, thow onely arte o^r kynge/ helpe me defolate woman wch haue no helper but the/ for my myfery and deftruction ys harde at my hande/ Thinke apõ vs O lorde and fhew y^i felffe in the tyme of oure deftres & of o^r trouble Strength me O thow kynge of godes lorde of all

Thee, good Lord. Amen.

The prayer of Queen Esther for help against her enemies
O Thou, Lord, Thou only are our King. Help me, desolate woman which has no helper but Thee, for my misery and destruction is hard at my hand. Think upon us, oh Lord, and show Thyself in the time of our distress and of our trouble. Strengthen me, oh Thou King of gods, Lord of all

Folio 28r

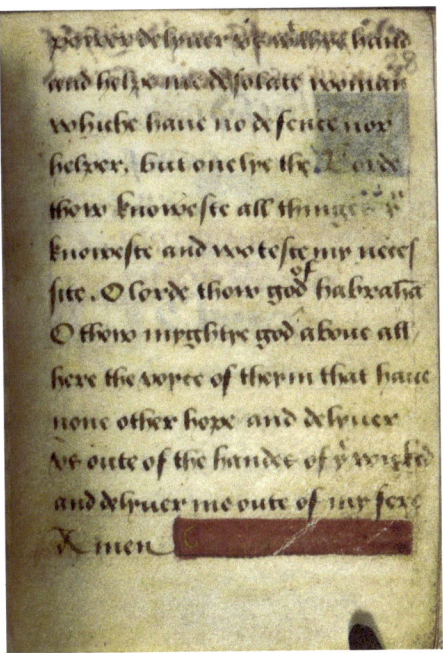

power delyuer vs w^t thye hand
and helpe me deſolate woman
whiche have no defence nor
helper, but onelye the lorde
thow knoweſte all thinges y^u
knoweſte and woteſte my neceſ
fite. O lorde thow god of habrahã
O thow myghtye god aboue all/
here the voyce of theym that haue
none other hope and delyuer
vs oute of the handes of ye wicked
and delyver me oute of my fere
Amen

power, deliver us with Thy hand
and help me, desolate woman
which has no defense nor
helper, but only Thee, Lord.
Thou know all things. Thou
know and wot* my neces-
sity. Oh Lord, Thou God of Abraham,
oh Thou mighty God above all,
hear the voice of them that have
no other hope and deliver
us out of the hands of the wicked
and deliver me out of my fear.
Amen.

* wot: obsolete word meaning "to understand"

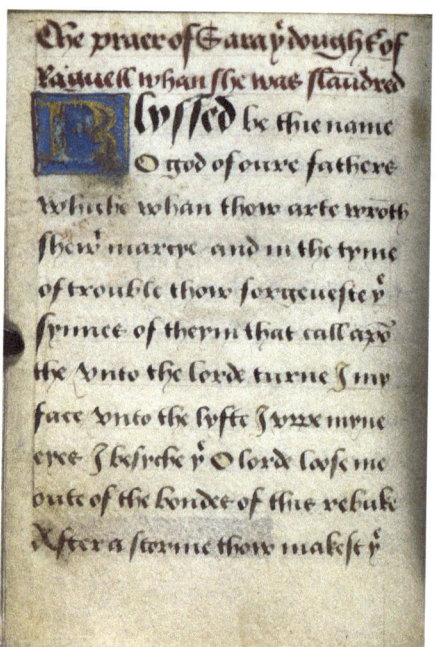

The praer of Sara yͤ dughtʳ of Raguel whan ſhe was flaũdred

Blyſſed be thie name
O god of oure fathers
whiche whan thow arte wroth
ſhewᵗ marcye and in the tyme
of trouble thow forgeueſte yͤ
ſynnes of theym that call apõ
the vnto the lorde turn J my
face vnto the lyfte J vp myne
eyes J beſyche yͤ O lorde looſe me
oute of the bondes of this rebuke
After a storme thow makeſt yͤ

The prayer of Sara, the daughter of Rachel, when she was slandered.

Blessed be Thy name,
oh God of our fathers,
which when Thou are wrathful
shows mercy, and in the time
of trouble Thou forgives the
sins of them that call upon
Thee. Unto Thee, Lord, I turn my
face unto Thee. Lift I up my
eyes. I beseech Thee, oh Lord, loose* me
out of the bonds of this rebuke.
After a storm, Thou makes the

* release

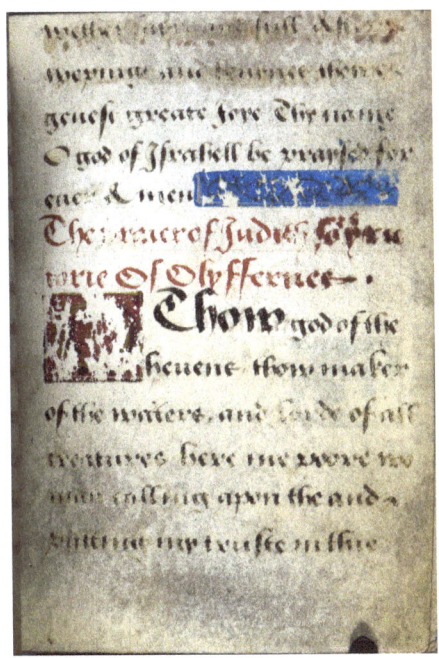

wether fayre and full After
weping and heuynes thowe
geueſt greate ʄoye Thy name
O god of Jſrahell be praysed for
euer Amen
The praier of Judith fo^r **y**^e **vic
torie Of Olyffernes**.
O Thow god of the
hevens, thow maker
of the waters, and lorde of all
creatures here me poore wo
man calling apon the and x
putting my truſte in thie

weather fair and full. After
weeping and heaviness Thou
gives great joy. Thy name,
oh God of Israel, be praised forever. Amen.
**The prayer of Judith for the vic-
tory of** [i.e., over] **Holofernes.**
O Thou, God of the
Heavens, Thou maker
of the waters, and Lord of all
creatures, hear me, poor woman, calling upon Thee and
putting my trust in Thy

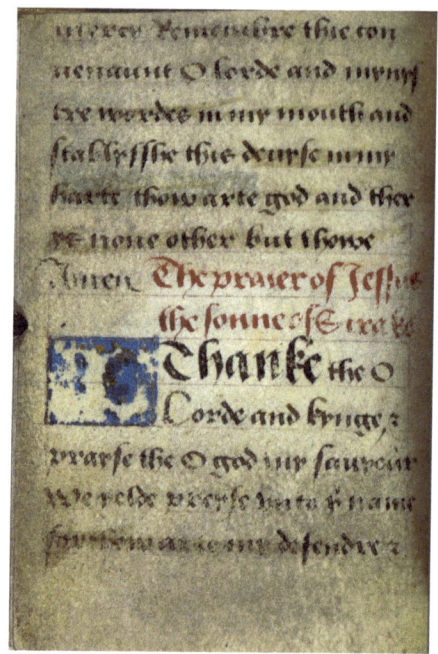

mercy Remembre thie con
uenaunt O lord and mynyſ
tre wordes in my mouth and
ſtablyſſhe this deuyſe in my
harte thow arte god and ther
is none other but thowe
Amen **The praier of Jeſſus
the sonne of Sirake**
I Thanke the O
Lorde and kynge &
prayſe the O god my ſauyour
We yelde preyſe vnto y^i name
for thow arte my defendre &

mercy. Remember Thy co-
venant, oh Lord, and minister words in my mouth and
establish they device in my
heart. Thou are God and there
is none other but Thou.
Amen. **The prayer of Jesus,
the son of Sirach.**
I Thank Thee, oh
Lord and King, and
praise Thee, oh God my Savior.
We yield praise unto Thy name,
for Thou are my defender and

Folio 30r

helper and haſte preſerued
my bodye frome deſtruction x
frome the ſnare of traitorous
tonges and from the lippes yᵗ
are occupied wᵗ lyes/ Thow haſte
bene my helper frome suche x
as ſtood vppe agaynſte me and
haſte delyuered ^me after the mul
tytude of thie mercy and for yⁱ
holy name is ſake/ Thow haſte
delyuered me frome the roring
of theym that prepared them
ſelffes to deuoure me/ ~~After~~
out of the handes of

helper and have preserved
my body from destruction,
from the snare of traitorous
tongues, and from the lips that
are occupied with lies. Thou have
been my helper from such
as stood up against me and
have delivered me after the mul-
titude of Thy mercy and for Thy
holy name's sake. Thou have
delivered me from the roaring
of them that prepared them-
selves to devour me,
out of the hands of

Folio 30v

fuche as foughte after my lyfe
ffrome ye multytude of theym
that troubled me and went
aboute to sette fier apon me
on euery fide fo that J am not
burned in the myddes of the
fyer/ ffrom the depe of helle
ffrome an vncleane tonge
ffrom lying wordes/ ffrom
an vnryghtuous tonge xx
my foule fhall prayfe the x
lorde vnto deth. for my lyfe
drew nye vnto hell/ They

such as sought after my life,
from the multitude of them
that troubled me and went
about to set fire upon me
on every side, so that I am not
burned in the midst of the
fire, from the deep of Hell,
from an unclean tongue,
from lying words, from
an unrighteous tongue.
My soul shall praise Thee,
Lord, unto death, for my life
drew nigh unto Hell. They

Folio 31r

compaſſed me rounde aboute on euery ſyde and there was no man to helpe me J loked aboute me yf there were any man that woulde focoure me but there was none Then thought J apon thye mercye O lorde, and apon thye actes, that thow haſte done euer of olde/ namely thou delyuereſte ſuche as put ~~as~~ theire truſte in the and reddeſste them oute of the handes of their enemyes	compassed* me roundabout on every side, and there was no man to help me. I looked about me [to see] if there was any man that would succor me but there was none. Then thought I upon Thy mercy, oh Lord, and upon Thy acts that Thou have done ever of old. Namely, Thou delivered such as put their trust in Thee and rid them out of the hands of their enemies.

* archaic, meaning to encircle or surround

Folio 31v

Thus lyfted J vp my prayer
frome the erth, and prayed
for delyueraunce frome mỹ
enemyes. J cauled apon the x
lorde my father that he wolde
not leue me w^toute helpe in
the day of my trouble and in
the tyme of the proude J pray
fed thye name contynuallye
yelding hono^r and thankes x
vnto yt And fo my prayer x
was harde/ thow fauefte me
frome deftruction and dely//

Thus lifted I up my prayer
from the Earth and prayed
for deliverance from my
enemies. I called upon Thee,
Lord my Father, that He would
not leave me without help in
the day of my trouble and in
the time of the proud. I praised Thy name continually,
yielding honor and thanks
unto it. And so my prayer
was heard. Thou saved me
from destruction and deli-

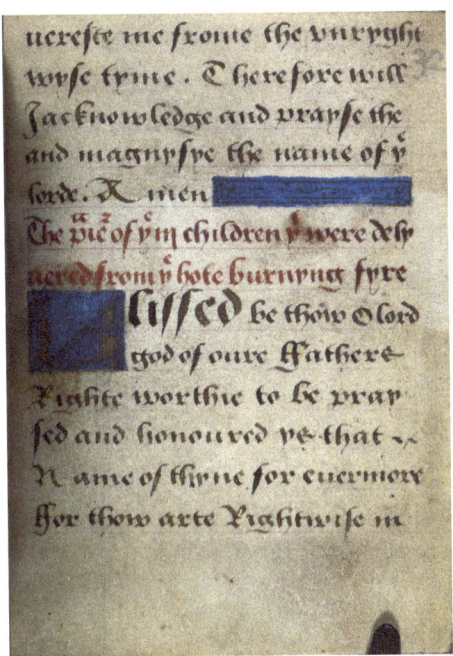

uerefte me frome the unright-
wise* time. Therefore will
I acknowledge and praise Thee
and magnify the name of the
Lord. Amen

**The prayer of the 3 children that were deli-
vered from the hot burning fire**

Blessed be Thou, oh Lord
God of our Father,
right worthy to be prai-
sed and honored is that
name of Thine for evermore.
For Thou are righteous in

* unrighteous

Folio 32v

all thoſe things that thow x
haſte doone to vs/ yea fayth
full are all thye woorkes/ thye
wayes are righte and thye
Judgmentes trew/ yea ac/
cordinge to righte and equy
te haſte thow broughte theſe
thinges apon vs bycauſe
of oure ſynnes/ for whye
we haue offended and doone
wickedlye/ departinge from
the/ in all thinges haue we x
treſpaſſed and not obeied thye

all those things that Thou
have done to us. Yea, faithful are all Thy works. Thy
ways are right and Thy
judgments true. Yea, ac-
cording to right and equity have Thou brought these
things upon us because
of our sins. For while
we have offended and done
wickedly, departing from
Thee, in all things have we
trespassed and not obeyed Thy

Folio 33r

commaundementes/ nor x
kepte theym/ neyther done as
thow hafte beden vs. that we
myghte profpere wherefore
all that y{u} hafte broughte apõ
vs and euery thinge yt thow
hafte done to vs, thow hafte
done theym in trew Judgemet
as in delyuerynge vs into ye
handes of oure enemyes. Yet
for thy names fake we befych
ye geue vs not uppe foreuer
breke not thy conuenaunte

commandments, nor
kept them, neither done as
Thou have bidden us that we
might propser. Wherefore*
all that Thou have brought upon
us and everything that Thou
have done to us, Thou have
done them in true judgment,
as in delivering us into the
hands of our enemies. Yet
for Thy name's sake we beseech
Thee, give us not up forever.
Break not Thy covenant

* thus

Folio 33v

and take not away yⁱ mercye
frome vs/ for thy beloued xx
Abrahames ſake/ for yⁱ ſeru
ante Jſaac is ſake/ and for yⁱ
holy Jſrael is ſake/ to whom
thow haſte ſpoken and pro//
myſed that thow woldeſt mul//
typlye theire ſede as the ſtar//
res of heuen and as the ſande
that lyeth apon the ſe ſide/ for
we O lorde are become leſſe/
then any people and be kept
vndre this day in all yᵉ world

and take not away Thy mercy from us, for Thy beloved Abraham's sake, for Thy servant Isaac's sake, and for Thy Holy Israel's sake, to whom Thou have spoken and promised that Thou would multiply their seed as the stars of Heaven and as the sand that lies upon the seaside. For we, oh Lord, are become less than any people and be kept under this day in all the world

Folio 34r

bycaufe of oure fynnes/ neur
theleffe in a contryte harte &
an humble fpyrytte/ let vs
be receyued yt we may optaȳ
yi mercy/ for yr is no confufion
vnto yem that put theyre truft
in the/ and now we folowe ye
wt all or harte/ we fere ye and
feke thy face/ Put vs not to
fhame but deale wt vs after
thy louyng kyndnes & accor
ding to ye multytude of thy
mercyes delyuer vs by thy

because of our sins. Never-
theless, in a contrite heart and
an humble spirit let us
be received, that we may obtain
Thy mercy, for there is no confusion
unto them that put their trust
in Thee. And now we follow Thee
with all our heart. We fear Thee and
seek Thy face. Put us not to
shame, but deal with us after
Thy loving kindness and according to the multitude of Thy
mercies. Deliver us by Thy

Folio 34v

myracles O lorde and gette
thy name an honoʳ/ that all
they whiche do thy feruauntₑ
euyll may be confounded.
Let them be affhamed thro//
ugh thy almyghty power/
& let yʳ ftrength be broken yᵗ
they may know how that thou
onely arte the lorde god/ and
honoʳ worthy through oute
all the worlde/ Blyffed be yᵉ
holy name of thy glory for it
is worthy to be prayfed and

miracles, oh Lord, and get
Thy name an honor, that all
they which do Thy servants
evil may be confounded.
Let them be ashamed thro-
ugh Thy almighty power,
and let their strength be broken, that
they may know how that Thou
only are the Lord God, and
honor-worthy throughout
all the world. Blessed be the
Holy Name of Thy glory, for it
is worthy to be praised and

Folio 35r

magnyfied in all worldes.
Blyſſed be thow in the holye
temple of yⁱ glory/ for aboue
all thinges, thow arte to be pra//
ſed, yea and more worthye x
to be magnyfied for euer.
Blyſſed be thow in the trone
of yⁱ kyngedome/ for aboue all
thow arte worthye to be well
ſpoken of and to be more then
magnyfied foreuer/ Blyſſed
be thow that lokeſte through yᵉ
depe & ſitteſte apon the Cherubym

magnified in all worlds.
Blessed be Thou in the Holy
Temple of Thy glory, for above
all things, Thou are to be praised, yea, and more worthy
to be magnified forever.
Blessed be Thou in the throne
of Thy Kingdom, for above all
Thou are worthy to be well
spoken of and to be more than
magnified forever. Blessed
be Thou that looks through the
deep and sits upon the cherubim,

for thow arte worthy to be
prayſed and aboue all to be
magnyfied foreuer/ Blyſſed
be thow in the firmament of
heuen for thow arte prayſe
& honor worthye foreuer Amen

The praier of Maneſ eth kinge of Juda.

O lorde almyghty, god of oʳ fathers, Abrahᵃm, Jſaac and Jacob, and of the ryg htwys ſede of them which xx haſte made heuen and earth wᵗ

for Thou are worthy to be
praised and above all to be
magnified forever. Blessed
be Thou in the firmament of
Heaven, for Thou are praise
and honor-worthy forever. Amen.

The prayer of Manas- seh, King of Judah.

O Lord Almighty, God of our Fathers, Abraham, Isaac, and Jacob, and of the rig- hteous seed of them, which have made Heaven and Earth with

Folio 36r

all the ornamentₑ thereof/ wᶜʰ
haſte ordened the ſee by the word
of the cõmaundement: which
haſte ſhute vp yᵉ depe/ and haſte
ſealed it for thy fearefull and
laudable name/ whiche all
men fear and tremble be-
fore the face of thy .../ &
for the angre of thy thretnỹg
the whiche is importable to ₓ
ſynners. But the mercy of
thy promes ys great & vnfear
cheable: for thow arte the lorde

all the ornaments thereof, which
have ordained the sea by the word
of the commandments, which
have shut up the deep, and have
sealed it for Thy fearful and
laudable name, which all
men fear and tremble be-
for the face of Thy ..., and
for the anger of Thy threatening,
the which is importable* to
sinners. But the mercy of
Thy promise is great and unsearchable, for Thou are the Lord

* not able to be borne, unbearable

Folio 36v

god moſte high/ aboue all therth
longe ſuffring/ and exceding
mercyfull/ and repentaunt for
yᵉ malice of men/ Thow lorde
after thy goodnes haſte promy
ſed repentance of the remyſſyon
of ſynnes: and thow that arte
the god of the ryghtwes haſt not
put repentaunce to yᵉ ryghtwes
Abraham/ Jſaac/ and Jacob
vnto them that haue not ſyn//
ned agaynſte the But bicauſe
J haue ſynned aboue the nomber

God most high above all the Earth,
long suffering and exceedingly
merciful, and repentant for
the malice of men. Thou, Lord,
after Thy goodness, have promised repentance of the remission
of sins. And Thou that are
the God of the righteous have not
put repentance to the righteous
Abraham, Isaac, and Jacob, [neither]
unto them that have not sinned against Thee. But because
I have sinned above the number

Folio 37r

of the sandes of the see/ and that
myne Jnyquytees are multy/
plyed. J am humbled wt many
bandes of Iron, and there ys
in me no breathinge. J haue
prouoked thyne angre and
haue done euyll before the in
cõmyttyng abhomynacons
& multyplying offences/ and
now J bow the knees of my xx
harte requyring goodnes of
the O lorde J haue synned lord
J haue synned and know mỹ

of the sands of the sea, and that
my iniquities are multi-
plied, I am humbled with many
bands of iron and there is
in me no breathing. I have
provoked Thine anger and
have done evil before Thee in
committing abominations
and multiplying offenses. And
now I bow the knees of my
heart, requiring goodness of
Thee, oh Lord. I have sinned, Lord
I have sinned and know my

Folio 37v

Jnyquyte. J defyre the by prayer
O lorde forgeue me, forgeue
me and deftroy me not wᵗ myn
Inyquytees, neyther do thow al
wayes remembre myne euylls
to punyffhe them/ but faue me
(whiche am vnworthy) after yⁱ
great mercye/ and J will preyſ
the euerlaftyngly all the dayes
of my lyfe for all ᵗʰᵉvertu of heuen
prayfeth the/ and vnto the be
longeth Glory worlde with/
oute ende A men

iniquity. I desire Thee by prayer,
oh Lord, forgive me. Forgive
me and destroy me not with my
iniquities. Neither do Thou always remember my evils
to punish them, but save me
(which am unworthy) after Thy
great mercy, and I will praise
Thee everlastingly all the days
of my life, for all the virtue of Heaven
praise Thee, and unto Thee belongs glory, world with-
out end. Amen.

Ovre mercyfull x
father whiche in tea
chinge vs to pray by
thie fon Chryfte hafte cõma
unded vs to caull the father and
to beleue that we are thye wel//
belouyd children whiche fter
refte vppe none of thyne to pray
but to thentente thow woldeft
heare them/ geuyng vs alfo all
thinges more effectuouflye
& plentyoufly than we can xx
eyther afke or thinke/ we befich

Our merciful
father, which in tea-
ching us to pray by
Thy Son Christ, have commanded us to call Thee Father and
to believe that we are Thy wel-
beloved children, which stir
up none of Thine to pray
but to the intent Thou would
hear them, giving us also all
things more effectively
and plenteously than we can
either ask or think, we beseech

Folio 38v

the for thy fonnes fake geue vs grace to beleue and to knowe ftedfaftely that y{i} fonne oure fauyo{r} Chryfte ys geuen of the vnto vs to be vnto vs o{r} fauyo{r} oure ryghtwyfnes/ o{r} wyfdom o{r} holynes o{r} redempcon, and o{r} fatiffaction / And fuffre xx not vs to trufte in any other faluacõn but in y{i} fonne/ and by y{i} fonne onely o{r} fauyoure Amen	Thee for Thy Son's sake, give us grace to believe and to know steadfastly that Thy Son, our Savior Christ, is given of Thee unto us to be unto us our Savior, our righteous, our wisdom, our holiness, our redemption, and our satisfaction. And suffer not us to trust in any other salvation but in Thy Son, and by Thy Son only, our Savior. Amen.

Folio 39r

O Lorde god geue,
that my harte maye
defyre the/ Jn defiringe, feke yᵉ
Jn fekinge. to fynde the/ Jn fyne
ding to loue yᵉ/ in louyng the. to
fynde remedye of my euylls/ &
remedye had, that J may abide
ftille in the Graunte me O
lorde my god in my harte, re
pentaunce in my Spiritte con
trition/ in my eyes, a fountayn
of teares/ oute of my handes,
lyberalite of almes/ my kyng

Oh Lord God give,
that my heart may
desire Thee; in desiring, seek Thee;
in seeking, to find Thee; in fin-
ding, to love Thee; in loving Thee, to
find remedy of my evils; and
remedy had, that I may abide
still in Thee. Grant me, oh
Lord my God, in my heart, repentance; in my spirit, contrition; in my eyes, a fountain
of tears; out of my hands,
liberality of alms. My King,

Folio 39v

quenche in me the defires and
luftes of the fleffhe/ and kyndle
in me, the fier of thye Love
My redemer put oute of me
the fpiritte of Pride and grau
nte me Of thye mercy the trea
fure of thye mekenes and humy
ite My fauyour expell from
me fumyffhnes and wrathe
and geue me for thye Petye
fake, the buckeler of pacience.
My creature pull oute of me
the rancoure Of mynde and

quench in me the desires and
lusts of the flesh, and kindle
in me the fire of Thy love.
My Redeemer, put out of me
the spirit of pride and grant me of Thy mercy the treasure of Thy meekness and humility. My Savior, expel from
me fumishness* and wrath
and give me, for Thy pity's
sake, the buckler† of patience.
My Creator, pull out of me
the rancor of mind and

* irritability

† a type of shield worn on the forearm

Folio 40r

graunte thow me that arte fo
mercyfull a louyng harte xx
Geue me O mofte tendre and
pytefull father, fure faythe /
lyke hope/ and charyte cõtynuall
My governoʳ put frome me
all vanyte, inconftancye of x
mynde, wavering of the harte
Jeftyng, or rayfyng of my xx
mouthe, proude lokyng/ Glo
teny of the bellye, vncharytable
rebukyng of myne neyghbors/
the loue or defyre of worldely

grant Thou me, that are so
merciful, a loving heart.
Give me, oh most tender and
pitiful Father, sure faith,
like[wise] hope, and charity continual.
My Governor, put from me
all vanity, inconstancy of
mind, wavering of heart,
jesting, or raising of my
mouth, proud looking, glu-
ttony of the belly, uncharitable
rebuking of my neighbors,
the love or desire of worldly

Ryches, the defyre of vayne glory
the myfchefe of hypocryfye, the
poyfon of flattery, the dyfdayne
of the nedye, the oppreffyon of yᵉ
poore and feable, the rufte of
enuye, the death of blafphemy.
Cut away from me (O my
maker) vnryghtfull raffh//
nes, Sturdynes, vnquyetnes
Jdlenes, Slothfulnes, Dul//
nes of the wytte, Blyndenes
of the harte, Obftynacye of yᵉ
mynde, Crewelnes of behauoʳ

riches, the desire of vainglory,
the mischief of hypocrisy,
the poison of flattery, the disdain
of the needy, the oppression of the
poor and feeble, the rust of
envy, the death of blasphemy.
Cut away from me, oh my
Maker, unrightful rash-
ness, sturdiness,* unquietness,
idleness, slothfulness, dullness of the wit, blindness
of the heart, obstinacy of the
mind, cruelness of behaviour,

* harshness, violence

Folio 41r

Dyſobedyence of that ys good xx
Reſyſtence agaynſte good coun/
cell, vnrulynes of my tonge
Pollinge of poore people, vyo
lence dealynge wᵗ the Impotent,
Slaundring of Jnnocentes,
Crabbednes agaynſte thoſe yᵗ
be with me in howſeholde, vn
kyndnes towardes my freendes
and famylyar acquayntaũces,
Rygoure or extreme dealynge
wᵗ my neyghboures. O my
god, my mercy, J pray the for

disobedience of [all] that is good,
resistance against good counsel, unruliness of my tongue,
polling* of poor people, violence dealing with the impotent,
slandering of innocents,
crabbishness against those that
be with me in household, un-
kindness towards my friends
and familiar acquaintances,
rigor or extreme dealing
with my neighbors. Oh my
God, my Mercy, I pray Thee for

* robbing

the loue of thy fonne make me
to do deades of marcy, to exer//
cyfe petye, to haue compaffy//
on on thofe y^t be in afflyctyon,
or trouble. To geue concell
to thofe that be oute of ye ryght
way, To focoure thofe that be
in myfery. To releve the op
preffed, To comforte theym
that be in heuynes, To refrefh
the poore. To chere theym y^t
wepe. To forgeue theym that
trefpas agaynfte me. To loue

the love of Thy Son, make me
to do deeds of mercy, to exer-
cise pity, to have compassion on those that be in affliction
or trouble, to give counsel
to those that be out of the right
way, to succor those that be
in misery, to relieve the op-
pressed, to comfort them
that be in heaviness, to refresh
the poor, to cheer them that
weep, to forgive them that
trespass against me, to love

Folio 42r

thoſe that hate me. To recompen
ce good for euyll. To deſpyſe none
but to honor all men, To folow
the good, To eſchew the euyll. To
embrace vertewes. and to re-
fuſe vyces. Jn aduerſyte, pacy
ence. Jn proſperyte, modera
tyon and kepyng of my tong
and to holde cloſe my lipes warely
To deſpyſe thinges earthly
and to thirſte after thinges
heuenly Amen

those that hate me, to recompen-
se good for evil, to despise none,
but to honor all men, to follow
the good, to eschew the evil, to
embrace virtues and to re-
fuse vices, in adversity patience, in prosperity modera-
tion, and keeping of my tongue
and to hold closed my lips warily,
to despise things Earthly
and to thirst after things
Heavenly. Amen.

Folio 42v

M<!-- -->**oſte** foueraygn & holye Trenyte, the father, the Sonne and the holy goſte thre parſons and one god haue mercy on me. O blyſſed and gloryous Trenyte haue mercy on me O the moſte holy mercyfull & euer laſtynge Trenyte hauee m^{r}cy on me. O the trew and vn// feyned Trenyte ye greate and incomperable goodnes, the euerlaſtyng and ſwete clen//

M<!-- -->**ost** sovereign and Holy Trinity, the Father, the Son, and the Holy Ghost, three persons and one God, have mercy on me. Oh blessed and glorious Trinity, have mercy on me. Oh the most holy, merciful, and everlasting Trinity, have mercy on me. Oh the true and unfained Trinity, the great and incomparable goodness, the everlasting and sweet clean-

Folio 43r

nes, and the inseparate majesty of the Father, the Son,
and the Holy Ghost, have mercy
on me. Oh good Father and
meek Son, oh Holy Ghost,
oh light that cannot be put
out, oh Thee, only Father of Heaven, have mercy on me. Thee,
good Lord, do I call upon. To
Thee do I make my intercessi-
on and prayer. Thee do I laud
and praise now and is ever
in mind so to continue, which

arte the onely begynner of all
vertew and goodnes, and the
fynall ender of all good work₍ₑ₎
O holy god. O ftronge god, O
euerlafting god, haue m︎ʳcy
on me, and remember me
wᵗ thye manyfefte goodnes
that J vnworthye feruaunt
and handeworke/ for my
greate Jnyquyte and fynne
be not wᵗoute thy mʳcy lofte
and dampned, for thow arte
my maker and redemʳ my

are the only beginner of all
virtue and goodness, and the
final ender of all good works.
Oh Holy God, oh strong God, oh
everlasting God, have mercy
on me and remember me
with Thy manifest goodness,
that I, unworthy servant
and handiwork, for my
great iniquity and sin,
be not without Thy mercy lost
and damned. For Thou are
my Maker and Redeemer, my

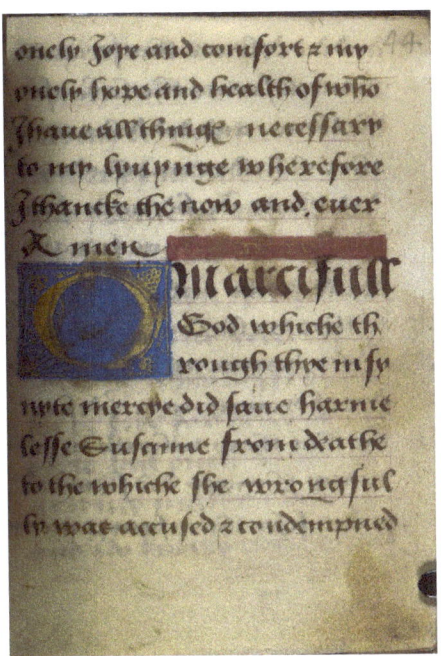

onely joy and comfort and my
only hope and health, of whom
I have all things necessary
to my living, therefore
I thank Thee now and ever.
Amen.

merciful
God, which th-
rough Thy infi-
nite mercy did save from harm-
less Susanna from death,
to the which she wrongful-
ly was accused and condemned,*

* Daniel 13: 7-63

Folio 44v

and did delyuer thye feruaũte
Danyell frome the lake of
the lyons, and did delyuer the
thre Childrenne Sydrack
Myſaac Abdenago, from
the hote burnynge fier and
didde retche oute thy hande
to thy welbelouyd diffiple
Peter beynge in great Jeobar
dye of drownynge. J defire
the that thow whyche in fo
many thinges did fhew and
manyfefte thy infynyte mercy,

and did deliver Thy servant
Daniel from the lake of
the lions,* and did deliver the
three children, Shadrach,
Meshach, and Abednego, from
the hot burning fire,† and
did reach out Thy hand
to Thy well-beloved disciple
Peter, being in great jeopar-
dy of drowning.** I desire
Thee that Thou, which in so
many things did show and
manifest Thy infinite mercy,

* Daniel 6: 1-28   † Daniel 3: 1-30   ** Matthew 14: 28-31

Folio 45r

wolde faue and delyuer me	would save and deliver me
frome all trybulacõn and	from all tribulation and
enymyes/ and from all y̕	enemies, and from all the
power of all myne enemyes	power of all my enemies,
and frome all theym that	and from all them that
confent to my deftructyon	consent to my destruction
and pardicõn, for I am x	and perdition, for I am
Jngnoraunt (mercyfull	ignorant, merciful
lorde) to whom J fholde	Lord, to whom I should
fle or feke for helpe or com	flee or seek for help or com-
forte// but onely to you wᶜʰ	fort. But only to You, which
arte my maker & redemer	are my Maker and Redeemer,
and J do knowe none other	and I do know none other

Folio 45v

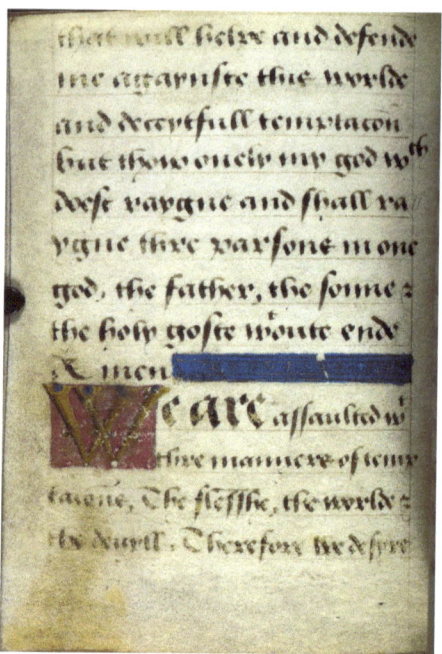

that will helpe and defende
me agaynſte this worlde
and deceytfull temptacõn,
but thow onely my god w^{ch}
doeſt raygne and ſhall ra//
ygne thre parſons in one
god, the father, the ſonne &
the holy goſte w^toute ende
Amen

We are aſſaulted w^t thre manners of temp tacõns, The fleſſhe, the worlde & the deuyll. Therefore we deſyre

that will help and defend
me against this world
and deceitful temptation,
but Thou only, my God, which
does reign and shall re-
ign, three persons in one
God, the Father, the Son, and
the Holy Ghost, without end.
Amen.

We are assaulted with three manners of temp- tations: the flesh, the world, and the Devil. Therefore we desire

Folio 46r

the moſte dere father, endow vs
ſo wyth thy grace, that we may
wᵗſtand the deſyre of the fleſſh
Make that we reſyſte and fyght
agaynſte thys ſuperfluyte of
meate, drynke, ſlepe, ſlouthe
and Jdlenes. Make that we x
may bryng the fleſſhe into
bondage and ſubiecyon wyth
faſtyng, temperate dyete, con
uenrent clothynge, ſlepe, reſt
watch, and laboure, ſo that yt
may be mete and apte to goode

Thee, most dear Father, endow us
so with Thy grace, that we may
withstand the desire of the flesh.
Make that we resist and fight
against this superfluity of
meat, drink, sleep, slouth,
and idleness. Make that we
may bring the flesh into
bondage and subjection with
fasting, temperate diet, con-
venient clothing, sleep, rest,
watch, and labor, so that it
may be mete* and apt to good

* appropriate

woorkes. kepe vs frõ the grete
fynnes of couetoufnes, and defire
of worldly Ryches. Geue vs
grace that we feke not the rule
and honoʳ of thys worlde or con//
fent to fuche defyres. Kepe vs
that the falce fubtlyte of thys
worlde, the conterfet bryght//
nes & entyefemementₑ of the
fame parfwade vs not to folow
yt. Kepe vs that we be not drawen
by the euylles and aduerfytees
of thys worlde, to Jmpacyens

works. Keep us from the great
sins of covetousness and desire
of worldly riches. Give us
grace that we seek not the rule
and honor of this world of consent to such desires. Keep us
that the false subtlety of this
world, the counterfeit bright-
ness and enticements of the
same persuade us not to follow
it. Keep us that we be not drawn
by the evils and adversities
of this world to impatience,

Folio 47r

auendgement, wrathe, or fuch
other vyces. Geue vs grace yt
we may defpyfe ye lyes of the world,
coloures, deceytes, promyfes &
falfehoode. And to be fhorte, yt
we may efteme of lytle reputa
tyon all yt belongeth to hym x
good and euyll, as we haue pro
myfed in baptyfme, and that x
we may contynew in thys pur
pofe, going forwarde daylye x
more and more, kepe vs frõ
the entyefment{e} of the deuyll yt

avengement, wrath, or such
other vices. Give us grace that
we may despise the lies of the world,
colors, deceits, promises, and
falsehood. And, to be short, that
we may esteem of little reputa-
tion all that belongs to him,
good and evil, as we have promised in baptism, and that
we may continue in this pur-
pose, going forward daily
more and more. Keep us from
the enticements of the Devil, that

Folio 47v

we confente not to pryde, w^ch
wolde caufe vs to fette myche
by oure felffes. and defpyfe oy^r
for ryches, kyn, power, fcyence
learnyng, beautye, or anny
other gyftes, or goodes. Kepe
vs that we falle not into the
fynne of hate, and enuye xx
what occafyon foeuer be geuen
to vs. Kepe vs that we doubte
not in the faithe. neyther xx
falle in defperacõ, now no^r
in the poynte of death. Put

we consent not to pride, which
would cause us to set much
by ourselves, and despise other[s]
for riches, kin, power, science,
learning, beauty, or any
other gifts or goods. Keep
us that we fall not into the
sins of hate and envy,
what occasion soever be given
to us. Keep us that we doubt
not in the faith, neither
fall into desperation, now nor
at the point of death. Put

Folio 48r

thy helping hande, oure beſt
heuenly father to theym that
fighte and labour agaynſte
thys harde and manyfolde x
temptacõ. Comforte them
that now do ſtande, and lyfte
theym vp that are fallen &
be ouercom. ffynally, ful
fyll vs all wᵗ thy grace, that
in thys myſerable, and per//
lous lyffe (whyche ys com
paſſed wᵗ ſo many contynu
all enemyes, that neuer ceſe

Thy helping hand, our best
Heavenly Father, to them that
fight and labor against
this hard and manifold
temptation. Comfort them
that now do stand, and lift
them up that are fallen and
be overcome. Finally, full
fill us all with Thy grace, that
in this miserable and peri-
lous life (which is com-
passed* with so many continual enemies, that never cease)

* See note, Folio 31r.

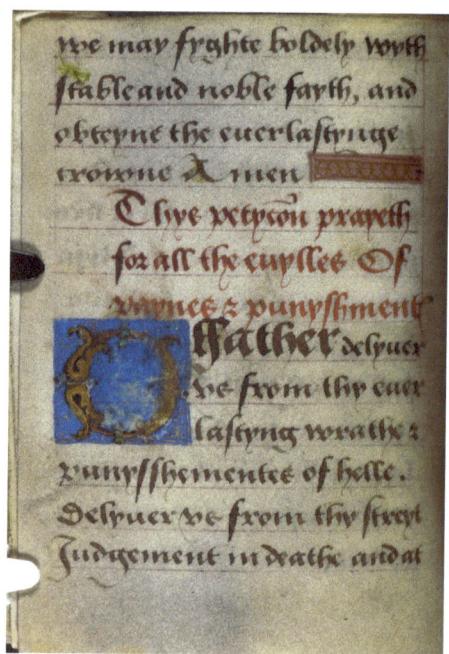

we may fyghte boldely wyth ſtable and noble fayth, and obteyne the euerlaſtynge crowne Amen

    Thys petycõn prayeth for all the euylles Of paynes & punyſhment⁀

O **ffather** delyuer vs from thy euer laſtyng wrathe & punyſſhementes of helle. Delyuer vs from thy ſtreyt Judgement in deathe and at

we may fight boldly with stable and noble faith, and obtain the everlasting crown. Amen.

    This petition prays for all the evils of pains and punishments

O **Father**, deliver us from Thy everlasting wrath and punishments of Hell. Deliver us from Thy straight* judgment in death and at

---

* strict, unbending

Folio 49r

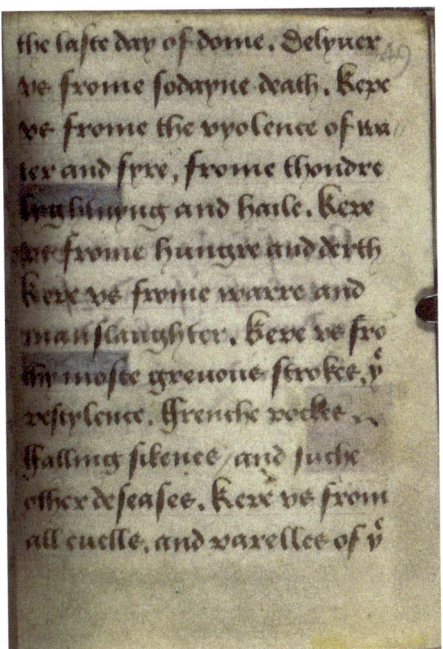

the laſte day of dome. Delyuer
vs frome ſodayne death. Kepe
vs frome the vyolence of wa//
ter and fyre, frome thondre
lyghtnyng and haile. Kepe
vs frome hungre and derth
kepe vs from warre and
manſlaughter. Kepe vs frõ
thy moſte greuous ſtrokes, ye
peſtylence, ffrenche pockes xx
ffalling ſikenes/ and ſuche
other deſeaſes. Kepe vs from
all euells, and parelles of ye

the last day of doom. Deliver
us from sudden death. Keep
us from the violence of water and fire, from thunder,
lightning, and hail. Keep
us from hunger and dearth.
Keep us from war and
manslaughter. Keep us from
Thy most grevious strokes, the
pestilence,* French pox,†
falling sickness,** and such
other diseases. Keep us from
all evils and perils of the

---

* the Black Plague   † syphilis   ** seizures and epilepsy

Folio 49v

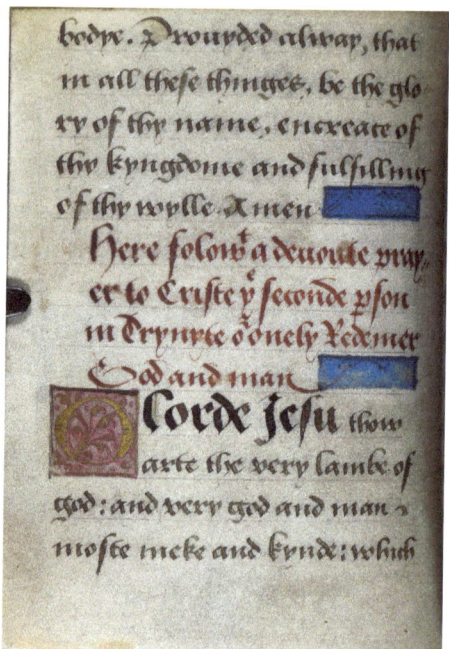

bodye. Prouyded alway, that
in all thefe thinges, be the glo//
ry of thy name, encreace of
thy kyngdome and fulfilling
of thy wylle Amen

Here folow^t a deuoute pray//
er to Crifte y^e feconde pſon
in Trynyte o^r onely Redeemer
God and man

O lorde Jefu thow
arte the very lambe of
god: and very god and man x
mofte meek and kynde: which

body. Provided always that
in all these things be the glory of Thy name, increase of
Thy kingdom, and fulfilling
of Thy will. Amen.

Here follows a devout prayer to Christ the second person
in Trinity, our only Redeemer,
God and man

Oh Lord Jesus, Thou
are the very Lamb of
God, and very God and man,
most meek and kind, which

Folio 50r

waſte offred in the aulter of yᵉ
croſſe and there ſuffredeſt paỹ//
full death. J worſhyppe and
honoʳ the and magnyfye the,
beſychyng thee that my ſoule
may eſcape the daunger of euʳ//
laſtyng paynes of death: ſithen
thow lorde haſte boought me
wᵗ thye precyous bloode Lorde
kynge of glorye, and of mʳcye
and petye. J do beleue and xx
knowledge that thow ſuffreſt
thy moſte holy handes to be

was offered on the altar of the
Cross, and there suffered painful death. I worship and
honor Thee and magnify Thee,
beseeching Thee that my soul
may escape the danger of everlasting pains of death, since
Thou, Lord, have bought me
with Thy precious blood, Lord,
king of glory, and of mercy
and pity. I do believe and
acknowledge that Thou suffered
Thy most holy hands to be

Folio 50v

drawen abrode and nayled
paynefully on the croffe. The...
fore J befyche the mercyfull
lorde, for thy infynyte petye
and goodnes: and for that x
petyfull woundes and paynes
that thow fuffreft in thy blyf//
fed armes, geue thow me gᵃce
lorde that all the dayes of my
lyfe I do not ftretche furth my
armes or handes to do anye
wickednes or harme to my
Cryften brother or neyghbor

drawn abroad* and nailed
painfully on the Cross. Therefore I beseech Thee, merciful
Lord, for Thy infinite pity
and goodness, and for that [i.e., those]
pitiful wounds and pains
that Thou suffered in Thy blessed arms, give Thou me grace,
Lord, that all the days of my
life I do not stretch forth my
arms or hands to do any
wickedness or harm to my
Christian brother or neighbor

* apart

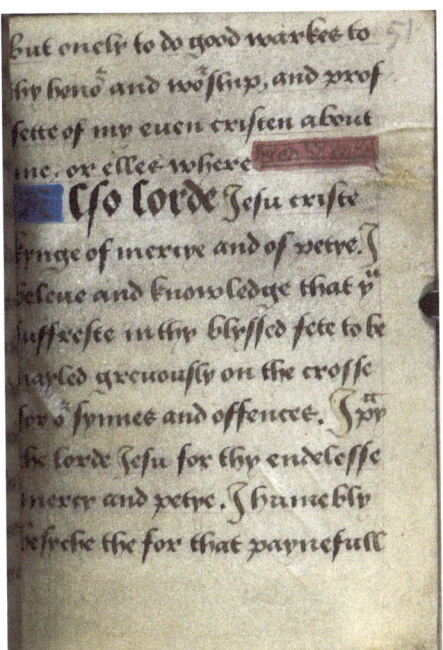

but onely to do good warkes to
thy honor and worſhip, and prof//
fette of my euen criſten about
me, or elles where
Alſo lorde Jeſu criſte
kynge of mercye and of petye. J
beleue and knowledge that yu
ſuffreſte in thy blyſſed fete to be
nayled greuouſly on the croſſe
for or ſynnes and offences. I pay
the lorde Jeſu for thy endeleſſe
mercye and petye. I humebly
beſyche the for that paynefull

but only to do good works to
Thy honor and worship and prof‑
it of my even* Christian about
me, or elsewhere.
Also, Lord Jesus Christ,
King of Mercy and of Pity, I
believe and acknowledge that Thou
suffered in Thy blessed feet to be
nailed grievously on the Cross
for our sins and offenses. I pray
Thee, Lord Jesus, for Thy endless
mercy and pity; I humbly
beseech Thee for that painful

---

* Probably a scribal error. The original was perhaps intended to read, "and profit of every Christian about me...."

Folio 51v

woundes that thow lorde fuf// freſte there in thy fete, that yᵘ lorde forgeue me cleane all my fynne yᵗ J haue doone in going, in working, Jdlenes and vanytees, and geue me grace that all the dayes of my lyffe J go not aboute foly and Jdle vanytees, but to con uerte my fteppes to good worke pleaſante in thy fyghte, that it may be pleaſante to the & proffitable to all aboute me	wounds that Thou, Lord, suf- ferred there in Thy feet, that Thou, Lord, forgive me clean all my sin that I have done in going, in working, idleness, and vanities, and give me grace that all the days of my life I go not about folly and idle vanities, but to con- vert my steps to good work, pleasant in Thy sight, that it may be pleasant to Thee and profitable to all about me

Folio 52r

Alfo lorde Jefu kynge
of Glorye J beleue and I know
ledge that whan thow fawefte
..he Cetye of Jierufalem geuen
to horryble fynnes, for which
it fhoulde be deftroied: thowe
wepefte full tenderly for oy^r
..tnennes fynnes. J praye the
Jefu Crifte and kynge of m^{r}cye
for thyne endeles mercy & pety
which fhedde fo pyteous teares
for o^r fynfulnes oute of thy glo//
rious eyes, that thow lorde for

Also, Lord Jesus, King
of Glory, I believe and I acknowledge that when Thou saw
the city of Jerusalem given
to horrible sins, for which
it should have been destroyed, Thou
wept full tenderly for other
..tnennes sins. I pray Thee,
Jesus Christ and King of Mercy,
for Thy endless mercy and pity, which
shed so piteous tears
for our sinfulness out of Thy glorious eyes, that Thou, Lord, for-

geue me all my fynnes whiche
J haue doone in my fpendinge,
in the fyghte of myne eyes and
geue me grace that all the dayes
of my lyfe I may nomore offend
thy goodnes in vayne and fyn
full fightes, but onelye lorde to
looke on thy creatures, and ftirre
me to thy loue and dreade, and y^t
J may perceyue to do good work$_\ell$
profitable to my foule to thye
pleafure and wille

Alfo lorde Jefu J beleue &

give me all my sins which
I have done in my spending,
in the sight of my eyes, and
give me grace that all the days
of my life I may no more offend
Thy goodness in vain and sinful sights, but only, Lord, to
look on Thy Creation, and stir
me to Thy love and dread, and that
I may perceive to do good works
profitable to my soul, to Thy
pleasure and will.

Also, **Lord** Jesus, I believe and

Folio 53r

knowledge that whan thowe x	acknowledge that when Thou
hongeſte nailed on the croſſe x	hung nailed on the Cross,
thow hardeſte thy enemyes re	Thou heard Thy enemies re-
porte and ſpeke of the myche	port and speak of Thee much
falceneſſe and ſelandre agay	falseness and slander agai-
nſte thy moſte endeles mercye	nst Thy most endless mercy
and pacyence. for all the paynes	and patience. For all the pains
that thow ſuffreſt in thy hering.	that Thou suffered in Thy hearing,
that thow lorde pleaſe to forgeue	that Thou, Lord, please to forgive
me all my ſynnes that I haue	me all my sins that I have
offended, in heringe of euell	offended in hearing of evil
tailes and reaporte agaynſte	tales and report against
my criſten brother. Geue x	my Christian brother. Give

Folio 53v

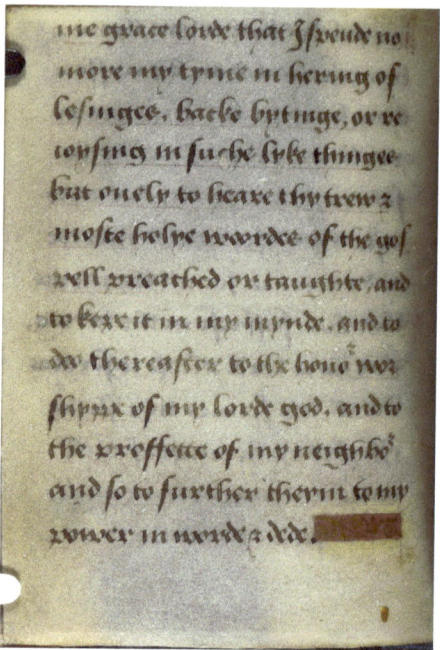

me grace, Lord, that I spend no
more time in hearing of
lessings,* backbiting, or re-
joicing in such-like things,
but only to hear Thy true and
most Holy Words of the Gospel preached or taught, and
to keep in my mind, and to
do thereafter to the honor [and] worship of my Lord God, and to
the profit of my neighbor,
and so to further them to my
power in word and deed.

* criticism of someone or something

Also, Lord Jesus, King of Glory, I believe and acknowledge that when Thou were yet hanging on the Cross Thou, Lord, opened Thy most holy mouth and prayed for Thine enemies, and exorting the unlearned, and comforted them that were comfortless. I pray Thee, Lord Jesus, for Thine endless mercy and goodness, and for the merciful words that proceeded out of Thy holy

Folio 54v

mouthe, fforgeue me vtterly
all the fyunnes the which J
haue doone in my vile fpeking
and geue me grace that all
the dayes of my lyfe, J speke no
lefinges, Backe bytinges
nor harme of any parson
and alfo that J fow no dys//
corde amonge criften people
but only lorde that J speke y^e
treuth, and flattre not for
fauo^r nor lucre and that J
may speke nothing but

mouth, forgive me utterly
all the sins, the which I
have done in my vile speaking,
and give me grace that all
the days of my life I speak no
lessenings, backbitings,
nor harm of any person,
and also that I sow no dis-
cord among Christian people,
but only, Lord, that I speak the
truth and flatter not for
favor or lucre, and that I
may speak nothing but

Folio 55r

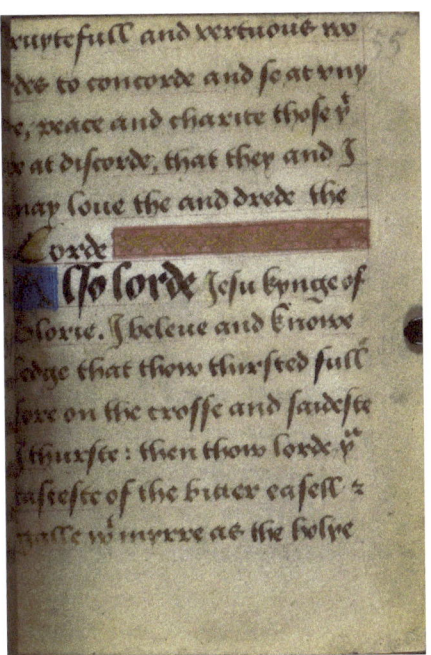

...ruytefull and vertuous wo
...des to concorde and ſo at vny
...e, peace and charite thoſe yᵗ
be at diſcorde, that they and J
may loue the and drede the
Lorde
Alſo lorde Jeſu kynge of
Glorie. J beleue and knowe
ledge that thow thirtſted full
ſore on the croſſe and ſaideſte
J thurſte: then thow lorde yᵘ
taſteſte of the bitter eaſell &
gall wᵗ myrre as the holye

[f]ruitful and virtuous wo-
[r]ds to concord and sow at uni-
[ty], peace and charity those that
be at discord, that they and I
may love Thee and dread Thee,
Lord.
Also, Lord Jesus, King of
Glory, I believe and acknowledge that Thou thirsted full
sore* on the Cross and said,
"I thurst." Then Thou, Lord, Thou
tasted of the bitter eisel and
gall with myrrh, as the Holy

* to an extreme degree

Folio 55v

Gospell witnesseth. J pray the lorde Jesu for thyne endelesse petye and mercye, and for the bitternesse of that drynke y^t thow tastetefte of, that thow lorde please to forgue me all my synnes doone agaynste ye whiche J haue offended in tast tynge and in relysinge of xx meates and drinckes and in superfluous tastetyng there of. Geue me grace Lorde y^t all the dayes of my lyfe, J no

Gospel witnesses.* I pray Thee, Lord Jesus, for Thine endless pity and mercy, and for the bitterness of that drink that Thou tasted of, that Thou, Lord, please to forgive me all my sins done against Thee, which I have offended in tasting and in relishing of meats and drinks, and in superfluous tasting thereof. Give me grace, Lord, that all the days of my life, I no

* The crucifixion of Jesus is detailed in Matthew 27:11-50, Mark 15:1-37, Luke 23:1-46, and John 19:1-37.

Folio 56r

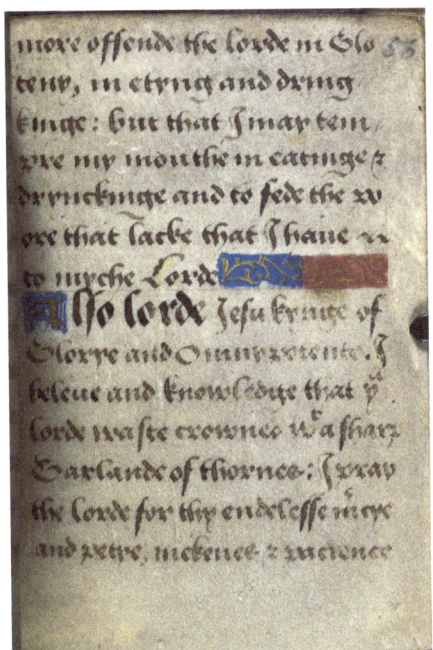

more offende the lorde in Glo
teny, in etyng and dring//
kinge: but that J may tem//
pre my mouthe in eating &
drynckinge and to fede the po//
ore that lacke that J have xx
to myche Lorde
Alſo lorde Jeſu kynge of
Glorye and Omnypotente. J
beleue and knowlsdge that yᵘ
lorde waſte crowned wᵗ a ſharp
Garlande of thornes: J pray
the lorde for thy endeleſſe mʳcye
and petye, mekenes, & pacience

more offend Thee, Lord, in gluttony, in eating, in drinking, but that I may tem-
per my mouth in eating and
drinking and to feed the po-
or that lack what I have
too much [of], Lord.
Also, Lord Jesus, King of
Glory and Omnipotent, I
believe and acknowledge that Thou,
Lord, was crowned with a sharp
garland of thorns. I pray
Thee, Lord, for Thy endless mercy
and pity, meekness, and patience

Folio 56v

that thow lorde clerely for//
geue me all the ſynnes that
J haue doone in Pride, Boſte
and in vayne glorie: and xx
Geue me grace while J dooe
lyue, that J doe vſe no Pride x
but to vſe mekeneſſe and geue
enſample thereof to all men
where J vſe companye with.

Also lorde Jeſu kynge
of mercy and petye J ſtedfaſte
ly beleue and knowledge that
thow lorde suffereſte thy bliſſed
bodie to be beten, rente & torne

that Thou, Lord, clearly forgive me all the sins that
I have done in pride, boast[ing],
and in vainglory. And
give me grace while I do
live that I do use no pride,
but to use meekness and give
example thereof to all men
where I use company with.*

Also Lord Jesus, King
of Mercy and Pity, I steadfast-
ly believe and acknowledge that
Thou, Lord, suffered Thy blessed
body to be beaten, rent, and torn

* all men with whom I keep company.

w{superscript t} fcourges, and thie tendre bodie ftrayned, info myche all the Joyntes of thie precious bodie myghte haue been nom/ bred and tolde, as the prophet David saieth Dinumeraue // runt omnia offa mea. J hum// bly pray the my Lorde god of thie endeleffe fauoure and pety for all the pytefull woundes that thow fufferefte in thy mofte tendre and pitefull bodie to forgeue me all the filthie xx

with scrouges, and Thy tender body strained insomuch [that] all the joints of Thy precious body might have been numbered and told, as the prophet David said, "Dinumeraverunt omnia ossa mea."* I humbly pray Thee, my Lord God, of Thy endless favor and pity, for all the pitiful wounds that Thou suffered in Thy most tender and pififul body, to forgive me all the filthy

* "They have numbered all my bones." Psalm 21:18.

Folio 57v

ſynfulnes of my bodie as in
Lecherie and in all other ſyn
full operacõns that J haue x
wroughte in ſynne of anye
parte of my bodie. Geue me
grace lorde foreuer to deſpice
all woorkₑ of ſynfull lecheri
whiche violeth the temple of
god: whiche is my ſoule wh//
an it is oute of dedely ſynne
ffrome the whiche filthie x
ſynne Geue me grace vtter/
ly to expell frome all partes

sinfulness of my body, as in
lechery, and in all other sinful operations that I have
wrought in sin of any
part of my body. Give me
grace, Lord, forever to despise
all works of sinful lechery,
which violate the temple of
God, which is my soul wh-
en it is out of deadly sin.
From the which filthy
sin, give me grace utter-
ly to expel from all parts

Folio 58r

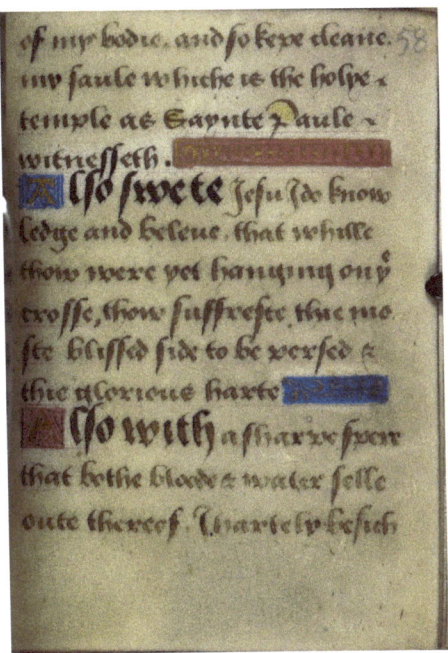

of my bodie, and ſo kepe cleane.
my ſaule whiche is the holye x
temple as Saynte Paule x
witneſſeth.

A lso ſwete Jeſu J do know
ledge and beleue , that whille
thow were yet hanging on yᵉ
croſſe, thow ſuffereſte thie mo
ſte bliſſed ſide to be perced &
thie glorious harte

A lso with a ſharpe ſpere
that bothe bloode & water felle
oute thereof. J hartely beſich

of my body, and so keep clean
my soul, which is the holy
temple, as Saint Paul
witnesses.*

A lso, sweet Jesus, I do acknow-
ledge and believe that while
Thou were yet hanging on the
Cross, Thou suffered Thy mo-
st blessed side to be pierced, and
Thy glorious heart

A lso, with a sharp spear,
that blood and water fell
out thereof. I heartily beseech

* 1 Corinthians 6:19

Folio 58v

the lorde to forgeue me clene
all my crewell fynnes w*ch*
hathe proceded from my vn//
clene harte, by thoughte or
dede in vayne glorie, or in ded//
lye fynne, in ꝺmagynynge
or delytinge that J henfefurth
whiles J lyve fpende no more
my tyme in fuche daunger of
fynne and vanyte of this x
worlde, nor in Jdle thought*e*,
but to vfe deuoute exortacõns
and to haue cõmunycacõns

Thee, Lord, to forgive me clean
all my cruel sins which
have proceeded from my unclean heart, by thought or
deed, in vainglory, or in deadly sin, in imagining
or delighting, that I henceforth
while I live spend no more [of]
my time in such danger of
sin and vanity of this
world, nor in idle thoughts,
but to use devout exhortations
and to have communications,

Folio 59r

feruente praiers and holye
defires, that may be vnto thie
pleafure and wille, and that
all my hartes defire may al
waye joye in the my father xx
eternall: fo that J may thr
ough thy precious bloode &
paynes efcape the Immor
tall daunger of helle and
paynes Jntollerable and fo
furely come to yᵉ eternall
fruycon and heritage, wᶜʰ
thow lorde hafte prepared

fervent prayers, and holy
desires that may be unto Thy
pleasure and will, and that
all my heart's desire may always joy in Thee, my Father
eternal, so that I may through Thy precious blood and
pains escape the immor-
tal danger of Hell and
pains intolerable and so
surely come to the eternal
fruition and heritage, which
Thou, Lord, have prepared

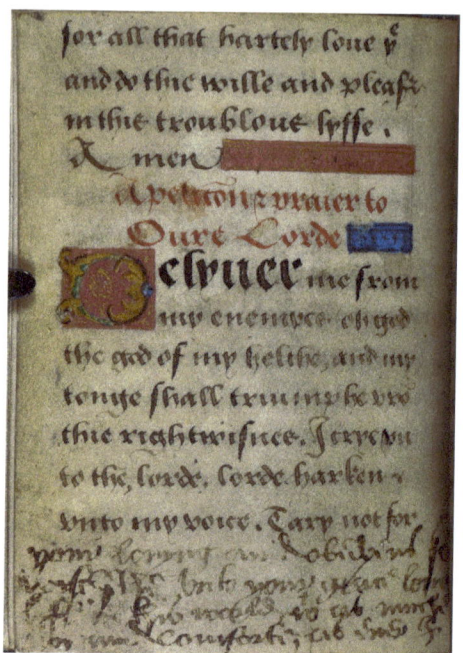

for all that hartely loue yᵉ
and do thie wille and pleaſʳ
in this troublous lyffe.
Amen

A peticõn & praier to Oure Lorde

Delyuer me from
my enemyes (oh god)
the god of my helthe, and my
tonge ſhall triumphe vpõ
thie rightwiſnes. J crye vn
to the, lorde, lorde harken ˣ
vnto my voice. Tary not for

your louing and obiᵉdiᵉnt ſo..
wyſchᵉthᵉ vnto your gracᵉ long
lyffᵉ in this world, wᵗ as muchᵉ
...oy and comforte, as ᵉuᵉr J

for all that heartily love Thee
and to Thy will and pleasure
in this troublous life.
Amen.

A petition and prayer to Our Lord

Deliver me from
my enemies, Oh God,
the God of my health, and my
tongue shall triumph upon
Thy righteousness. I cry unto Thee, Lord. Lord, harken
unto my voice. Tarry not, for

Your loving and obedient son
wishes unto your Grace long
life in this world, with as much
[j]oy and comfort as ever I

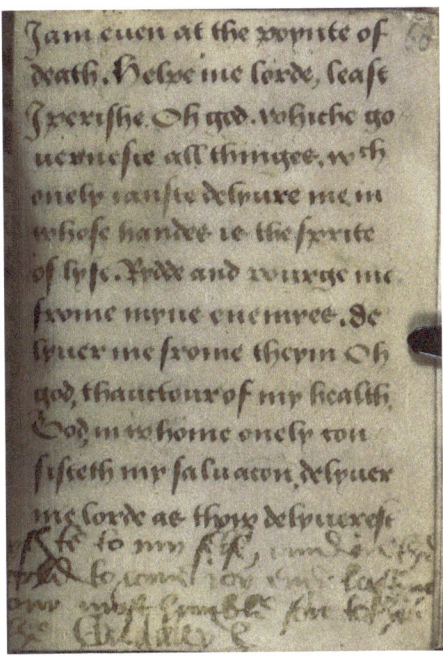

J am euen at the poynte of
death. Helpe me lorde, leaſt
J periſhe. Oh god. whiche go//
uerneſte all thinges, wᶜʰ
onely canſte delyure me in
whoſe handes is the ſprite
of lyfe. Rydde and pourge me
frome myne enemyes. de
lyuer me frome theym oh
god, thauctour of my health
God, in whome onely con/
ſiſteth my ſaluacõn, delyuer
me lorde as thow delyuereſt

..iſh for to my ſelfᵉ, and in this
...orld to comᵉ ioy euerlaſting
..our most humblᵉ ſon to his
..hᵉ GDuddeley

I am even at the point of
death. Help me, Lord, lest
I perish. Oh God, which go-
verns all things, which
only can deliver me, in
whose hands is the spirit
of life, rid and purge me
from my enemies. De-
liver me from them, oh
God, the author of my health.
God, in whom only con-
sists my salvation, deliver
me, Lord, as Thou delivered

[w]ish for myself, and in this
[w]orld for come, joy everlasting.
[Y]our most humble son to his
[deat]h. G[uildford] Dudley

Folio 60v

Noe from the waters of the ffloode. Delyuer me as thow delyuerefte Rothe from the fier of Sodome. Delyuer me as thow delyuerefte the Children of Jfraell from the deapthe of the Reede See Delyuer me as thow delyuerefte Jonas from the bellye of the whall. Delyuer me as thow delyuerefte the thre Children from the ffurnace of brennynge fire

Noah from the waters of the Flood.* Deliver me as Thou delivered Ruth from the fire of Sodom.† Deliver me as Thou delivered the Children of Israel from the depth of the Red Sea.** Deliver me as Thou delivered Jonah from the belly of the whale.†† Deliver me as Thou delivered the three children from the furnace of burning fire.***

* Genesis 6 and 7
** Exodus 14:21
† Ruth is not named in Genesis 19, the story of Sodom
†† Jonah 1 and 2
*** Daniel 3:8-30

Folio 61r

Delyuer me as thow delyue//
refte Peter frome the perell
of the see. Delyuer me as yᵘ
delyuerefte Paule from the
deape of the See. Delyuer
me as thow delyuerefte in//
fynyte fynners from the
power of death and frome
the gates of helle, and than
my tonge fhall tryumphe
apon thie Ryghtwifenes, for
thie rightwifnes as thap//
poftle faieth cõmeth by yᵉ

Deliver me as Thou delivered Peter from the peril
of the sea.* Deliver me as Thou
delivered Paul from the
deep of the sea.† Deliver
me as Thou delivered in-
finite sinners from the
power of death and from
the gates of Hell, and then
my tongue shall triumph
upon Thy righteousness, for
Thy righteousness, as the Apostle says, comes by the

* Matthew 14:28-33

† Acts 27:13-42

Folio 61v

faithe of Jeſus Criſte vnto
all, and apon all theym yt
beleue in hym, than ſhall
my tonge tryumphe in
prayſing this thie right
wiſnes cõmending thie fa
uoure, magnyfiyng thie
petie, knowledging my x
ſynnes that thie mercye x
may be declared in me wch
wolde vouchefaffe to Juſty
fie suche a great ſynnar
and that all men maye xx

faith of Jesus Christ unto
all, and upon all them that
believe in Him.* Then shall
my tongue triumph in
praising this, Thy right-
eousness, commending Thy favor, magnifying Thy
pity, acknowledging my
sins, that Thy mercy
may be declared in me, which
would vouchsafe to justi-
fy such a great sinner,
and that all men may

* Romans 3:22, Philippians 3:9

Folio 62r

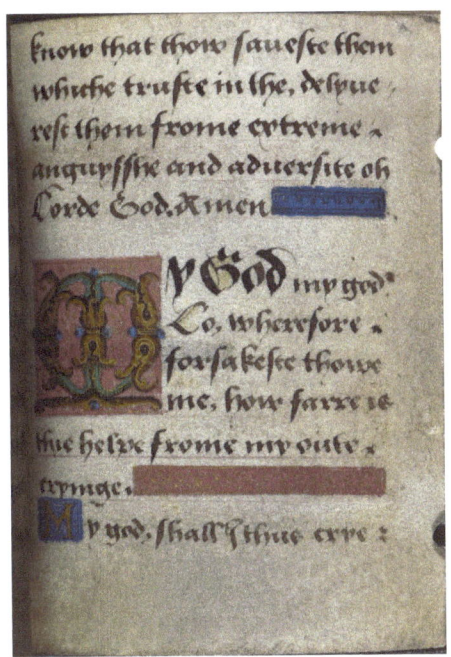

know that thow sauefte them
whiche trufte in the, delyue//
refte them frome extreme x
anguiffhe and aduerfitie oh
Lorde God. Amen

y God my god
Lo, wherefore x
forfakefte thowe
me, how farre is
thie helpe frome my oute x
cryinge.
My god, fhall I thus crye:

know that Thou saves them
which trust in Thee, delivers them from extreme
anguish and adversity, oh
Lord God. Amen.

My God, my God,
Lo, wherefore*
forsake Thou
me? How far is
Thy help from my out-
crying?
My God, shall I thus cry,

* why

Folio 62v

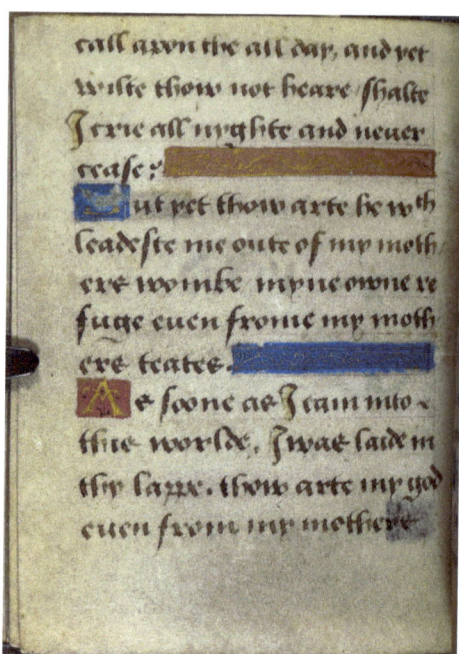

call apon the all day, and yet wilte thow not heare/ ſhalte J crye all nyghte and neuer cease?

But yet thow arte he wch leadeſte me oute of my moth/ers wombe/ myne owne refuge euen frome my moth/ers teates.

As ſoone as J cam into x this worlde, J was laide in thy lappe. thow arte my god euen from my mothers

call upon Thee all day, and yet will Thou not hear? Shall I cry all night and never cease?

But yet Thou are He which led me out of my mother's womb, my own refuge, even from my mother's teats.

As soon as I came into this world, I was laid in Thy lap. Thou are my God even from my mother's

Folio 63r

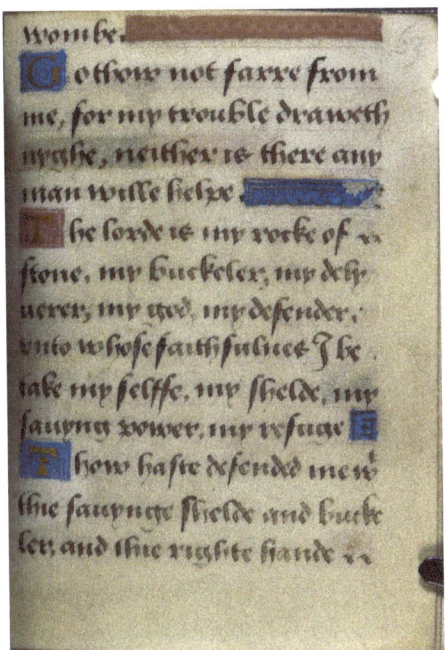

wombe.
Go thow not farre from me, for my trouble draweth nyghe, neither is there any man wille helpe.
The lorde is my rocke of ſtone, my buckeler, my dely// uerer, my god, my defender, vnto whoſe faithfulnes J be// take my felffe, my ſhelde, my ſauyng power, my refuge
Thow haſte defended me wᵗ thie ſauynge ſhelde and buckeler, and thie righte hande

womb.
Go Thou not far from me, for my trouble draws nigh, neither is there any man [that] will help me.
The Lord is my rock of stone, my buckler, my deliverer, my God, my defender, unto whose faithfulness I betake myself, my shield, my saving power, my refuge.
Thou have defended me with Thy saving shield and buckler, and Thy right hand

Folio 63v

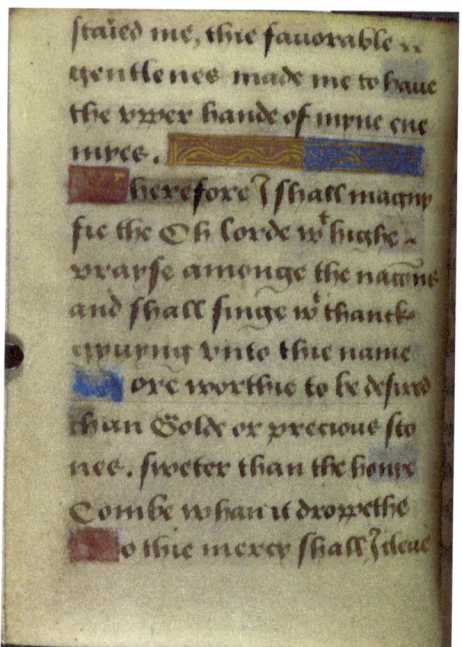

ſtaied me, thie fauorable xx
gentlenes made me to haue
the vpper hande of myne ene//
myes.
Wherefore J ſhall magny//
fie the Oh lorde wt highe xx
prayſe amonge the nacõns
and ſhall ſinge wt thanckℓ
gyuyng vnto thie name
More worthie to be deſired
than Golde or precious ſto
nes. ſweter than the honye
Combe whan it droppethe
To thie mercy ſhall J cleue

sayed me, Thy favorable
gentleness made me to have
the upper hand of [i.e., over] my ene‑
mies.
Therefore I shall magni‑
fy Thee, Oh Lord, with high
praise among the nations
and shall sing with thanks,
giving unto Thy name
More worthy to be desired
than gold or precious sto‑
nes, sweeter than the honey‑
comb when it drops.
To Thy mercy shall I cleave,

Folio 64r

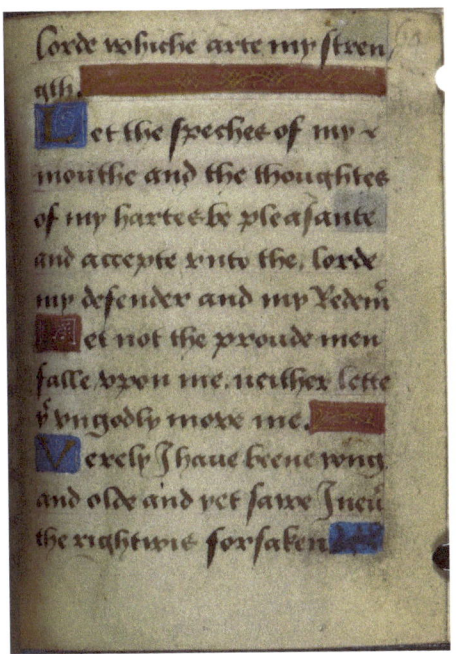

lorde whiche arte my ſtren//
gth.
Let the ſpeches of my x
mouthe and the thoughtes
of my hartes be pleaſante
and accepte vnto the, lorde
my defender and my Redem^r
Let not the proude men
falle vpon me. neither lette
ye vngodly move me.
Verely J haue been yong
and olde and yet ſawe J neu^r
the rightwis forſaken

Lord, which is my stren-
gth.
Let the speeches of my
mouth and the thoughts
of my heart be pleasant
and acceptable unto Thee, Lord,
my defender and my redeemer.
Let not the proud men
fall upon me. Neither let
the ungodly move me.
Verily, I have been young
and old and yet saw I never
the righteous forsaken.

Folio 64v

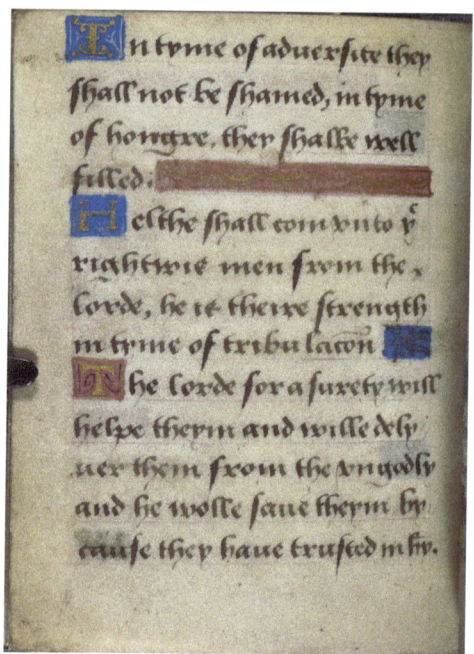

In tyme of aduerſite they
ſhall not be ſhamed, in tyme
of hongre, they ſhalbe well
filled:
Helthe ſhall com vnto yᵉ
rightwis men from the x
lorde, he is theire ſtrength
in tyme of tribulacõn
The lorde for a ſurety will
helpe theym and will dely//
uer them from the vngodly
and he wolle ſaue theym by//
cauſe they haue truſted in hỹ.

In time of adversity they
shall not be shamed; in time of hunger, they shall be well
filled.
Health shall come unto the
rigtheous men from the
Lord. He is their strength
in time of tribulation.
The Lord for a surety* will
help them and will deli-
ver them from the ungodly,
and He will save them be-
cause they have trusted in Him.

* "for a surety" = certainly

Folio 65r

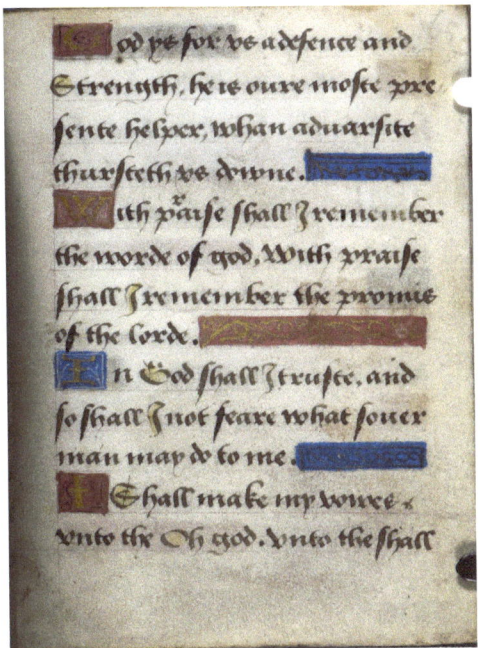

God ys for vs a defence and Strength, he is oure moſte pre// ſente helper, whan aduerſite thurſteth vs downe.
With pʳaiſe ſhall J remember the worde of god, With praiſe ſhall I remember the promiſ of the lorde.
In God ſhall I truſte, and ſo ſhall J not feare what foeuer man may do to me.
I Shall make my vowes x vnto the Oh god. vnto the ſhall

God is for us a defense and strength. He is our most present helper when adversity thrusts us down.
With praise shall I remember the Word of God, with praise shall I remember the promise of the Lord.
In God shall I trust, and so shall I not fear whatsoever man may do to me.
I shall make my vows unto Thee, Oh God. Unto Thee shall

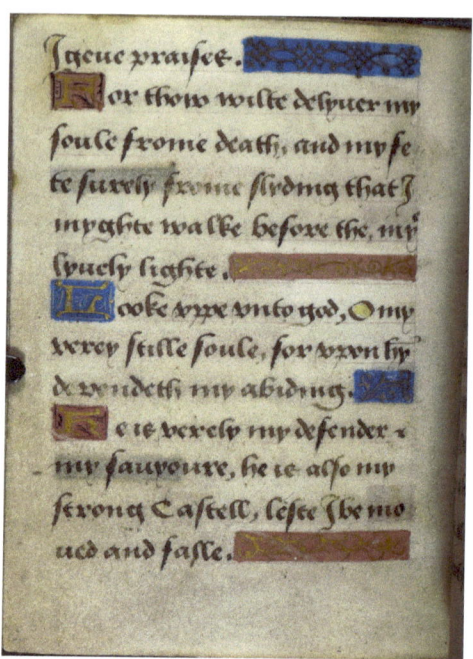

J geue praiſes.
For thow wilte delyuer my ſoule frome death, and my fe//te ſurely frome ſlyding that J myghte walke before the, in yᵉ lyuely lighte.
Looke uppe vnto god, O my verey ſtille ſoule, for vpon hỹ dependeth my abiding.
He is verely my defender x my ſauyoure, he is alſo my ſtrong Caſtell, left J be moued and falle.

I give praises.
For Thou will deliver my soul from death, and my feet from sliding, that I might walk before Thee in the lively light.
Look up unto God, oh my very still soul, for upon Him depends my abiding.
He is verily my defender, my Savior. He is also my strong castle, lest I be moved and fall.

Folio 66r

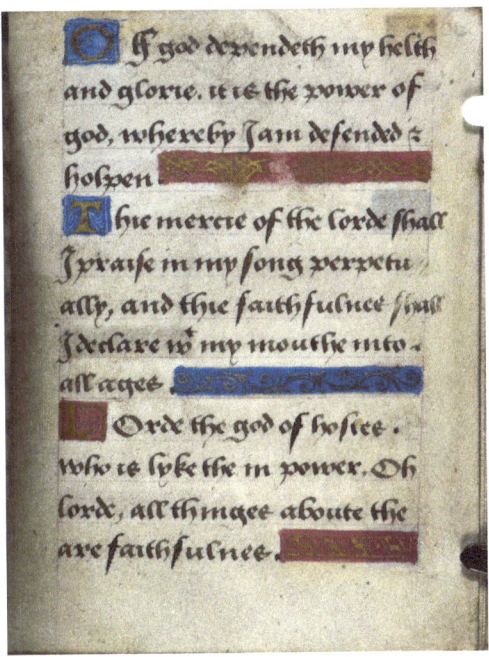

Off god dependeth my helth and glorie. it is the power of god, whereby J am defended & holpen.
Thie mercie of the lorde ſhall J praiſe in my ſong perpetu// ally, and thie faithfulnes ſhall J declare w^t my mouthe into x all ages.
LOrde the god of the hoſtes. who is lyke the in power, Oh lorde, all thinges about the are faithfulnes.

Of God depends my health and glory. It is the power of God whereby I am defended and helped.
The mercy of the Lord shall I praise in my song perpetually, and Thy faithfulness shall I declare with my mouth into all ages.
Lord the God of Hosts, who is like Thee in power? Oh Lord, all things about Thee are faithfulness.

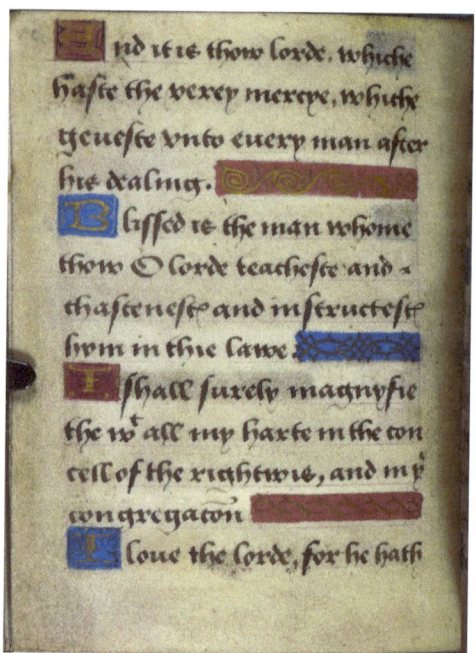

[A]nd it is thow lorde, whiche haſte the verey mercye, whiche geueſte vnto euery man after his dealing.
[B]liſſed is the man whome thow O lorde teacheſte and x chaſteneſtℓ and inſtructeſtℓ hym in thie lawe.
[I] ſhall ſurely magnyfie the w^t all my harte in the con cell of the rightwis, and in ye congregacõn
[I] loue the lorde, for he hath

[A]nd it is Thou, Lord, which have the very mercy, which gives unto every man after his dealing.
[B]lessed is the man whom Thou, Lord, teaches and chastens and instructs him in Thy Law.
[I] shall surely magnify Thee with all my heart in the council of the righteous, and in the congregation.
[I] love the Lord, for He has

Folio 67r

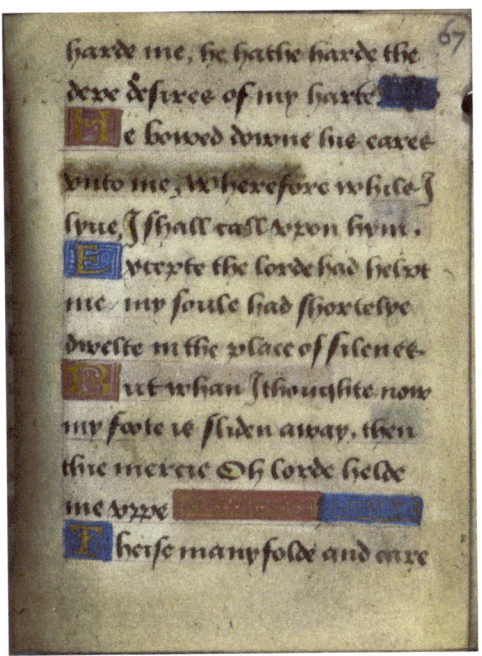

harde me, he hathe harde the
depe deſires of my harte.
He bowed downe his cares
vnto me, wherefore whils J
lyue, J ſhall call vpon hym.
Excepte the lorde had helpt
me/ my ſoule had ſhortelye
dwelte in the place of ſilenes
But whan J thoughte nowe
my foote is ſliden away, then
thie mercie Oh lorde helde
me vppe
Theiſe manyfolde and care

heard me; He has heard the
deep desires of my heart.
He bowed down His cares
unto me, therefore while I
live; I shall call upon Him.
Except the Lord had helped
me, my soul [would have] shortly
dwelled in the place of silence.
But when I thought, "Now
my foot is slidden away," then
Thy mercy, Oh Lord, held
me up.
These manifold and care-

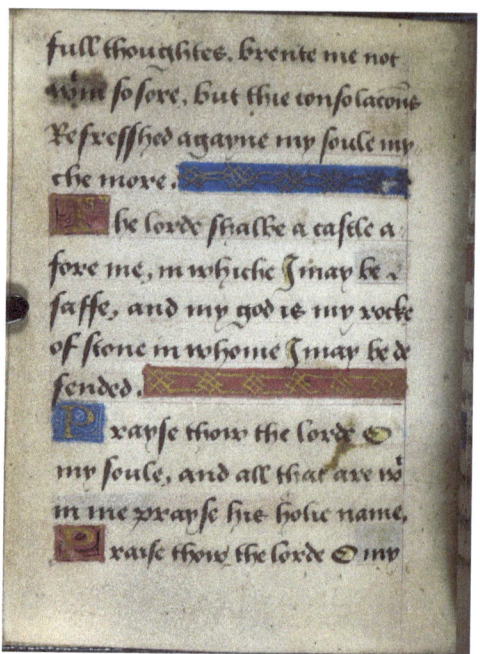

full thoughtes, brente me not
w{t}in fo fore, but thie confolacõns
Refreffhed agayne my foule my//
che more.
The lorde fhalbe a caftle a//
fore me, in whiche J may be x
faffe, and my god is my rocke
of ftone in whome J may be de
fended.
Prayfe thow the lorde O
my foule, and all that are wt
in me prayfe his holie name,
Praife thow the lorde O my

ful thoughts, burnt me not
within so sore, but Thy consolations
refreshed again my soul mu-
ch more.
The Lord shall be a castle a-
fore me, in which I may be
safe, and my God is my rock
of stone in whom I me be e-
fended.
Praise thou the Lord, oh
my soul, and all that are with-
in me praise His holy name.
Praise thou the Lord, oh my

Folio 68r

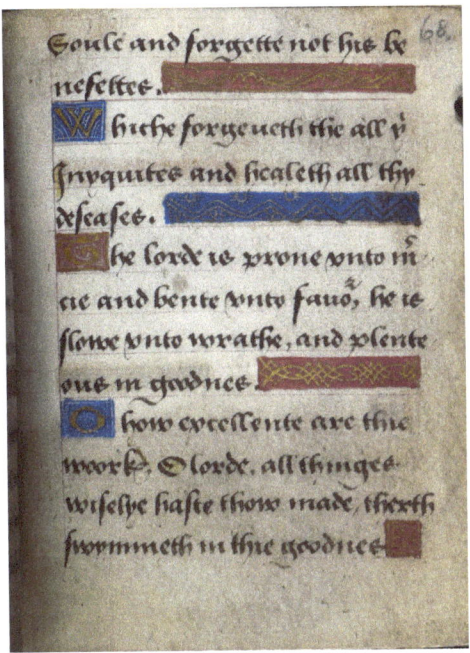

Soule and forgette not his benefettes.
Whiche forgeueth the all y^i Jnyquites and healeth all thy deseases.
The lorde is prone vnto m^r cie and bente vnto fauo^r, he is flowe vnto wrathe, and pleante// ous in goodnes.
O how excellente are thie woork₽, O lorde, all thinges wiselye hafte thow made/ therth fwymmeth in thie goodnes

soul and forget not His benefits,
Which forgives thee all thy iniquities and heals all thy diseases.
The Lord is prone unto mercy and bent unto favor. He is slow unto wrath and plentious in goodness.
O how excellent are Thy works, oh Lord. All things wisely have Thou made. The Earth swims in Thy goodness.

Folio 68v

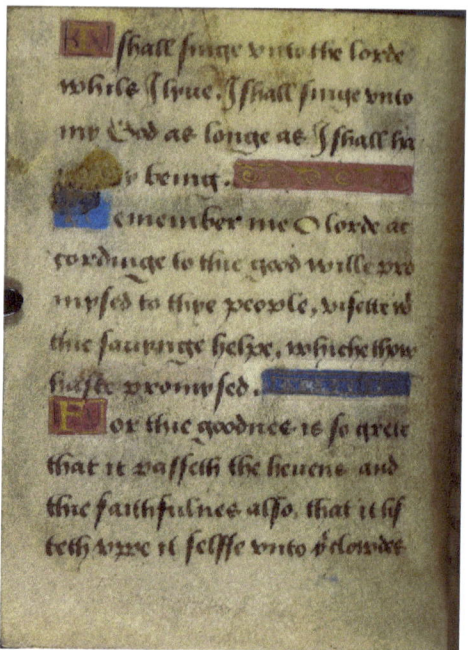

I shall singe vnto the lorde while J lyue. J shall singe vnto my God as longe as J shall ha//
...y being.
Remember me O lorde according to thie good wille promysed to thye people, visette w^t thie sauynge helpe, whiche thow haste promysed.
For thie goodnes is so grete that it passeth the heuens and thei faithfulnes also, that it lifteth vppe it selffe vnto ye clowdes

I shall sing unto the Lord while I live. I shall sing unto my God as long as I shall ha-
...y being.
Remember me, oh Lord, according to Thy goodwill promised to Thy people. Visit with Thy saving help, which Thou have promised,
For Thy goodness is so great that it passes the heavens, and Thy faithfulness also, that it lifts up itself unto the clouds.

Folio 69r

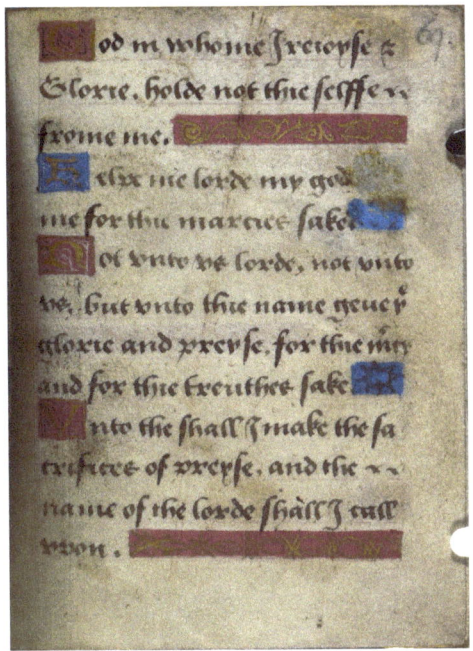

God in whom I rejoice and
glory, hold not Thyself
from me.
Help me, Lord my God …
me for Thy mercy's sake.
Not unto us, Lord, not unto
us, but unto Thy name give the
glory and praise, for Thy mercy
and for Thy truth's sake.
Unto Thee shall I make the sacrifices of praise, and the
name of the Lord shall I call
upon.

Folio 69v

L et my aduerfaries be we//
reid wt fhame, and couered wt
confufion. lyke as wt a cloke
L et theym curffe, but bliffe
thow, Let theym rife agaynfte
me but to theire owne confufi//
on, but lette thie faruantes
reioyce.
I fhall magnyfie the lorde di//
ligently wt my mouthe, J shall
praife hym among manye.
F or he wille ftond at the po//
ore mannes righte hande, to

L et my adversaries be wea-
ried with shame, and covered with
confusion, like as with a cloak.
L et them curse, but bless
Thou. Let them rise against
me, but to their own confusion, but let Thy servants
rejoice.
I shall magnify the Lord diligently with my mouth. I shall
praise Him among many.
F or He will stand at the po-
or man's right hand, to

Folio 70r

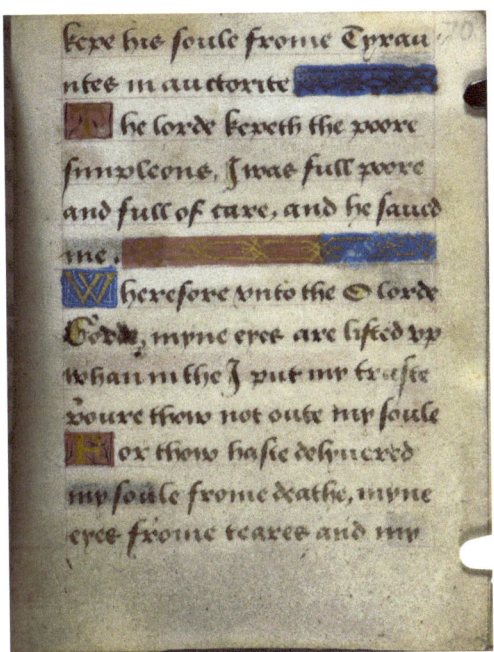

kepe his foule frome Tyrau//
ntes in auctorite
The lorde kepeth the poore
fimpleons. J was full poore
and full of care, and he faued
me.
Wherefore vnto the O lorde
Lorde, myne eyes are lifted vp
whan in the J put my trufte
poure thow not oute my foule
For thow hafte delyuered
my foule frome deathe, myne
eyes frome teares and my

keep his soul from tyra-
nts in authority.
The Lord keep the poor
simpletons. I was poor
and full of care, and He saved
me.
Therefore unto Thee, oh Lord,
Lord, my eyes are lifted up
when in Thee I put my trust.
Pour Thou not out my soul,
For Thou have delivered
my soul from death, my
eyes from tears, and my

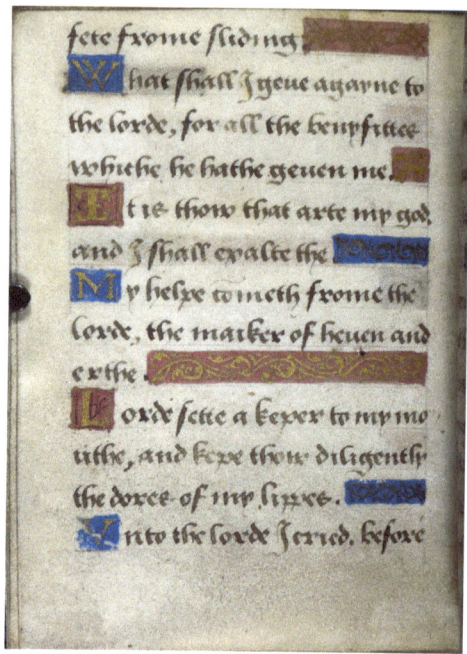

fete frome fliding.
What fhall J geue agayne to the lorde, for all the benyfittes whiche he hathe geuen me.
It is thow that arte my god, and I fhall exalte the
My helpe cõmeth frome the lorde, the macker of heuen and erthe.
Lorde sette a keper to my mo// uthe, and kepe thow diligently the dores of my lippes.
Vnto the lorde J cried, before

feet from sliding.
What shall I give again to the Lord for all the benefits which He has given me?
It is Thou that are my God, and I shall exalt Thee.
My help comes from the Lord, the maker of Heaven and Earth.
Lord, set a keeper to my mo- uth, and keep Thou diligently the doors of my lips.
Unto Thee, Lord, I cried. Before

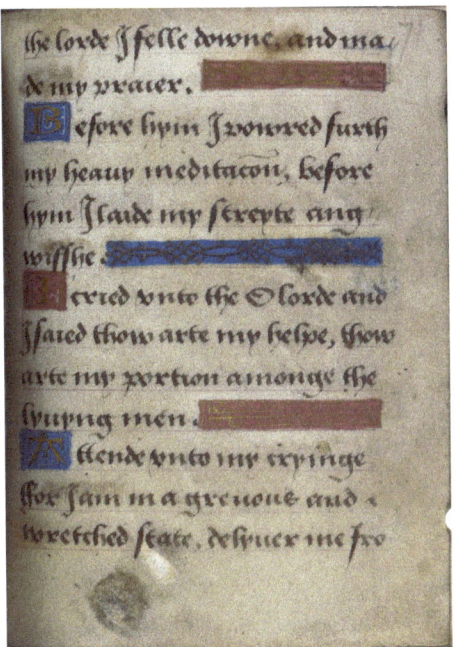

the lorde J felle downe, and ma//
de my praier.
Before hym J powred furth
my heauy meditacõn, before
hym J laide my ftreyte ang//
uiffhe.
I cried vnto the O lorde and
J faied thow arte my helpe, thow
arte my portion among the
lyuyng men.
Attende vnto my crynge
ffor J am in a greuous and x
wretched ftate, delyuer me fro

the Lord I fell down and made my prayer.
Before Him I poured forth
my heavy meditation. Before
Him I laid my straight* anguish.
I cried unto Thee, oh Lord, and
I said, "Thou are my help; Thou
are my portion among the
living men.
Attend unto my crying,
for I am in a grievous and
wretched state. Deliver me from

* heavy

Folio 71v

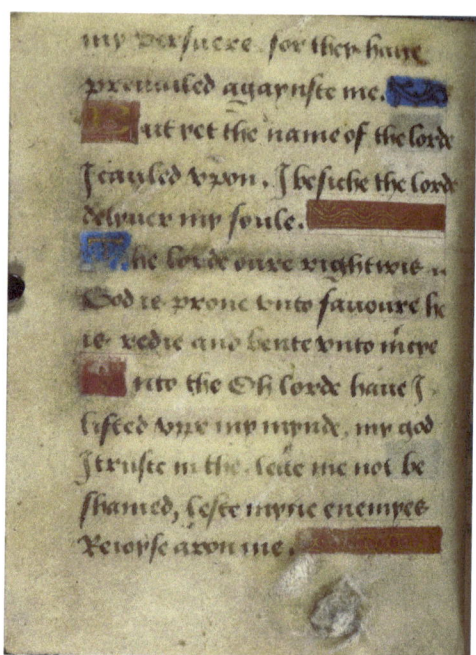

my perſuere, for they haue
preuailed agaynſte me.
But yet the name of the lorde
J cauled vpon. J beſiche the lorde
delyuer my ſoule.
The lorde oure rightwis xx
God is prone vnto fauoure he
is redie and bente vnto m^rcye
Vnto the Oh lorde haue J
lifted vppe my mynde, my god
J truſte in the, lette me not be
ſhamed, leſte myne enemyes
Reioyſe apon me.

my preserve, for they have
prevailed against me."
But yet the name of the Lord
I called upon. I beseech Thee Lord,
deliver my soul.
The Lord, our righteous
God, is prone unto favor. He
is ready and bent unto mercy.
Unto Thee, oh Lord, have I
lifted up my mind. My God,
I trust in Thee. Let me not be
shamed, lest my enemies
rejoice upon me.

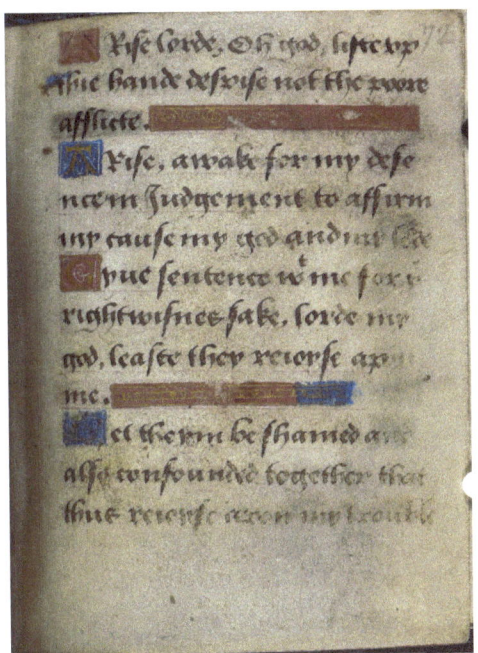

A Rife lorde, oh god, lifte vp thie hande defpife not the poore afflicte.
A rife, awake for my defence in Judgement to affirm my caufe my god and my lo^rde
G yue fentence w^t me for yⁱ rightwifnes fake, lorde my god, leafte they reioyfe apon me.
L et theym be fhamed and alfo confounded together that thus reioyfe apon my trouble

A rise Lord, oh God, lift up Thy hand. Despise not the poor afflicted.
A rise, awake for my defense in judgment to affirm my cause, my God and my Lord.
G ive sentence with me for Thy righteousness sake, Lord my God, lest they rejoice upon me.
L et them be shamed and also confounded together that thus rejoice upon my trouble.

Folio 72v

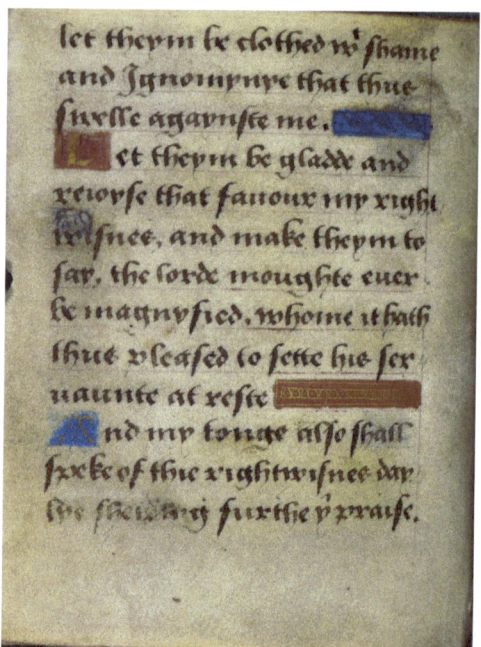

let theym be clothed wt ſhame and Jgnomynye that thus ſwelle agaynſte me.

Let theym be gladde and reioyſe that favour my right/ wiſnes, and make theym to ſay, the lorde moughte euer be magnyfied, whome it hath thus pleaſed to ſette his ſer// uaunte at reſte

And my tonge alſo ſhall ſpeke of thie rightwiſnes day// lye ſhewing furth yi praiſe.

Let them be clothed with shame and ignominy that thus swell against me.

Let them be glad and rejoice that favor my right- eousness, and make them to say, "The Lord ought ever be magnified," whom it has thus pleased to set His ser- vant at rest.

And my tongue also shall speak of Thy righteousness dai- ly, showing forth Thy praise.

Folio 73r

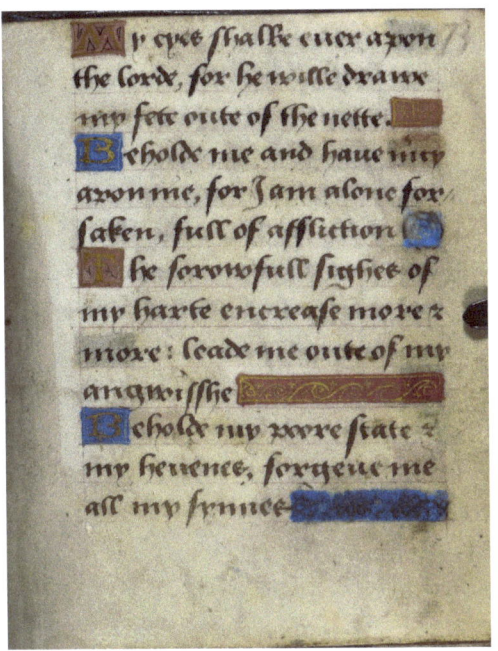

My eyes shall be ever upon
the Lord, for He will draw
my feet out of the net.

Behold me and have mercy
upon me, for I am alone, forsaken, full of affliction.

The sorrowful sights of
my heart increase more and
more. Lead me out of my
anguish.

Behold my poor state and
my heaviness. Forgive me
all my sins.

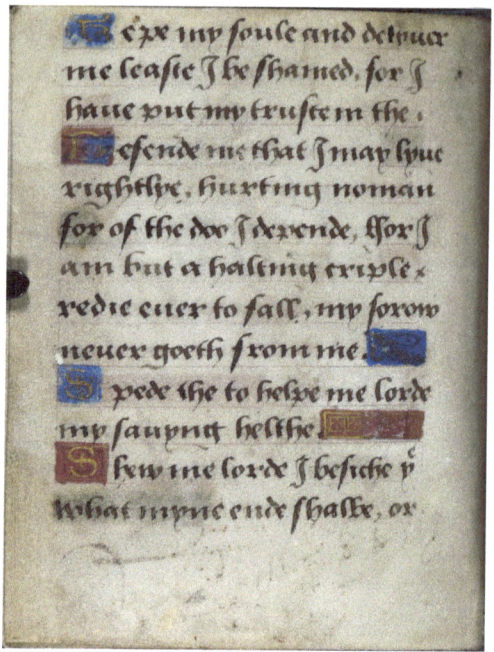

Kepe my ſoule and delyuer
me leaſte J be ſhamed, for J
haue put my truſte in the.
Defende me that J may lyue
rightlye, hurting noman
for of the doo J depende, ffor J
am but a halting criple x
redie euer to fall, my ſorow
neuer goeth frome me.
Spede the to helpe me lorde
my ſauyng helthe.
Shew me lorde J beſiche yᵉ
what myne ende ſhalbe, or

Keep my soul and deliver
me lest I be shamed, for I
have put my trust in Thee.
Defend me that I may live
rightly, hurting no man,
for of Thee do I depend, for I
am but a halting cripple
ready ever to fall. My sorrow
never goes from me.
Speed Thee to help me, Lord,
my saving health.
Show me, Lord, I beseech Thee,
what my end shall be, or

Folio 74r

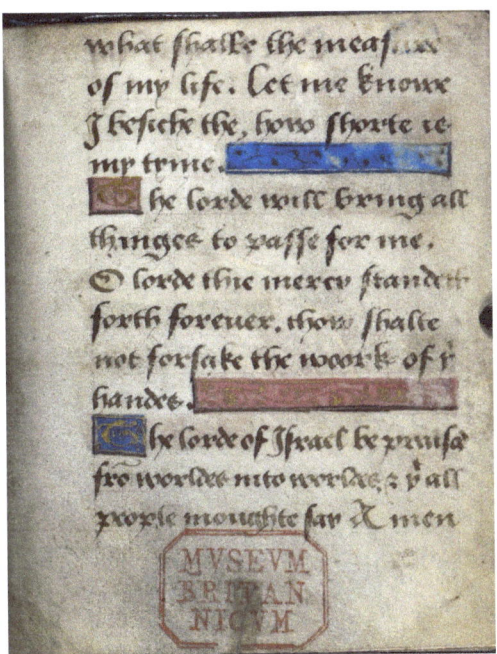

what fhalbe the meafure
of my life. let me knowe
J befiche the, how fhorte is
my tyme.
The lorde will bring all
thinges to paffe for me.
O lorde thie mercy ftandeth
forth foreuer. thow fhalte
not forfake the woork of y^i
handes.
The lorde of Jfrael be praifed
frõ worldes into worldes, & y^t all
people moughte fay Amen

what shall be the measure
of my life. Let me know,
I beseech Thee, how short is
my time.
The Lord will bring all
things to pass for me.
Oh Lord, Thy mercy stands
forth forever. Thou shall
not forsake the work of Thy
hands.
The Lord of Israel be praised
from worlds into worlds, and that all
people might say, "Amen."

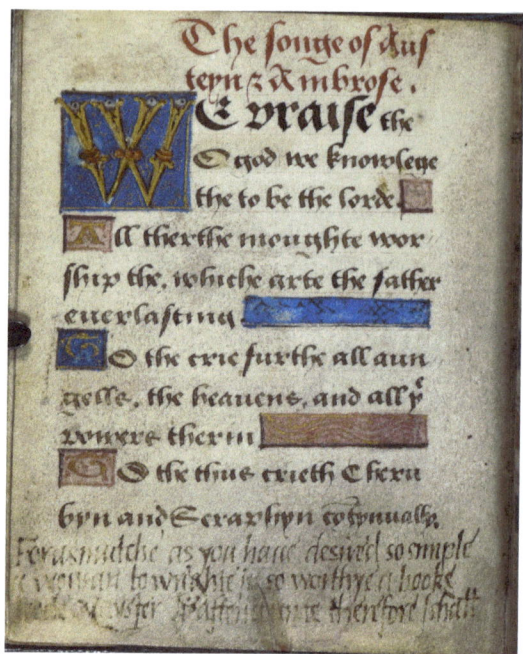

The ſonge of Auſ teyn & Ambroſe.

We praiſe the O god we knowlege the to be the lorde.
All therthe moughte wor‖ ſhip the, whiche arte the father euerlaſtng
To the crie furthe all aun‖ gelles, the heuens, and all yᵉ poweres therin.
To the thus crie Cheru byn and Seraphyn cõtynually.

Forasmutche as you haue desired so simple a woman to wrighte in so worthye a booke goode Mayster Leaftenaunte therefore J shall

The song of Austen and Ambrose.

We praise Thee, oh God, we acknowledge Thee to be the Lord.
All the Earth ought [to] wor- ship Thee, which are the Father everlasting.
To Thee cry forth all an- gels, the heavens, and all the powers therein.
To Thee thus cry cheru- bim and seraphim continually.

Forasmuch as you have desired so simple a woman to write in so worthy a book, good Master Lieutenant, therefore I shall

Folio 75r

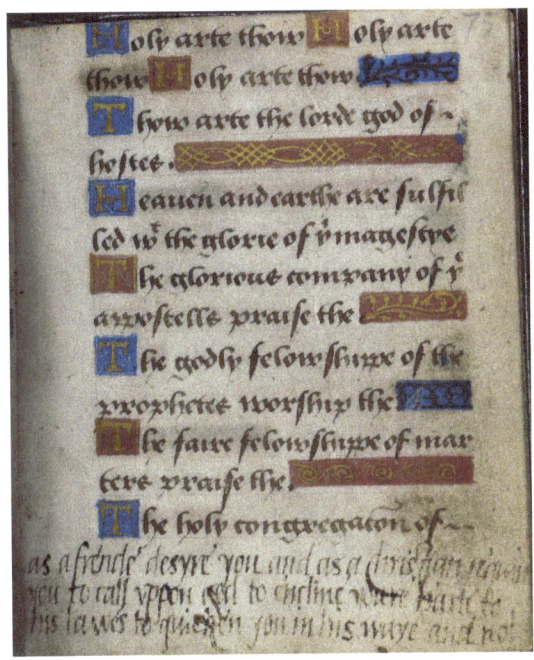

Holye arte thow, Holy arte thow Holy arte thow
Thow arte the lorde god of x hoftes.
Heauen and earthe are fulfilled wt the glorie of yⁱ mageftye
The glorious company of yᵉ appoftelles praife the
The godly felowfhippe of the prophetes worfhip the
The faire felowfhippe of mar// ters praife the.
The holy congregacõn of xx

as a frende defyre you and as a Christian require you to call vppon god to encline youre harte to his lawes to quicken you in his waye and not

Holy are Thou, Holy are Thou, Holy are Thou.
Thou are the Lord God of hosts.
Heaven and earth and fulfilled with the glory of Thy majesty.
The glorious company of the Apostles praise Thee.
The godly fellowship of the Prophets worship Thee.
The fair fellowship of martyrs praise Thee.
The holy congregation of

as a friend desire you and as a Christian require you to call upon God to incline your heart to His laws, to quicken you in His way, and not

Folio 75v

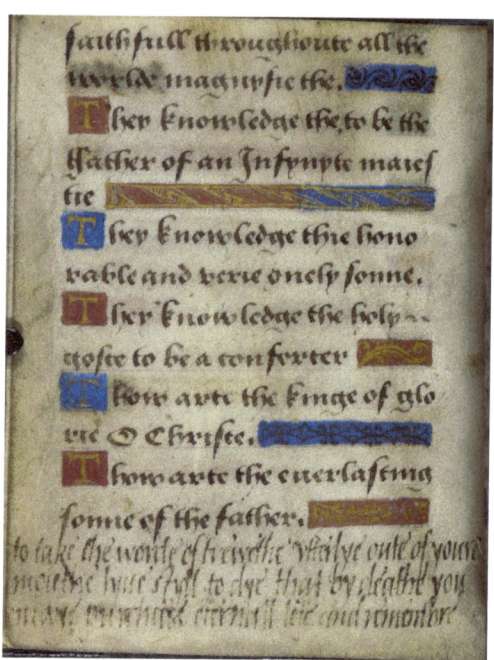

faithfull throughoute all the
worlde magnyfie the.
They knowledge the, to be the
ffather of an Jnfynyte maies/
tie
They knowledge thie hono//
rable and verie onely ſonne.
They knowledge the holy xx
goſte to be a conforter
Thow arte the kynge of glo//
rie O Chriſte.
Thow arte the euerlaſting
ſonne of the father.

to take the worde of trewethe vtterlye oute of youre
mouthe lyue ſtyll to dye that by deathe you
maye purchaſe eternall life and remembre

faithful throughout all the
world to magnify Thee.
They acknowledge Thee to be the
Father of an infinite majes-
ty.
They acknowledge Thy hono-
rable and very only Son.
They acknowledge the Holy
Ghost to be a comforter.
Thou are the King of Glo-
ry, oh Christ.
Thou are the everlasting
Son of the Father.

to take the word of truth utterly out of your
mouth. Live still to die, that by death you
may purchase eternal life. And remember

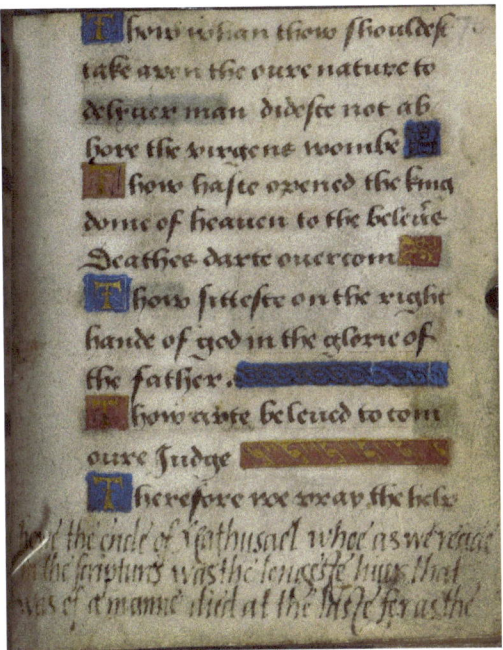

Thow whan thow ſhouldeſt
take apon the oure nature to
delyuer man didefte not ab//
hore the virgens wombe
Thow haſte opened the king
dome of heuen to the beleu^rs
Deathes darte ouercom
Thow fitteſte on the right
hande of god in the glorie of
the father.
Thow arte beleuved to com
oure Judge
Therefore we pray the help

howe the ende of Mathusael whoe as we reade
in the ſcriptures was the longeſte liver that
was of a manne died at the laſte for as the

Thou, when Thou should
take upon Thee our nature to
deliver man, did no ab-
hor the virgin's womb.
Thou have opened the Kingdom of Heaven to the believers,
death's dart overcome.
Thou sit on the right
hand of God in the glory of
the Father.
Thou are believed to [be]come
our judge.
Therefore we pray Thee help

how the end of Mathuselah, who as we read
in the Scriptures was the longest-lived that
was of a man, died at the last, for as the

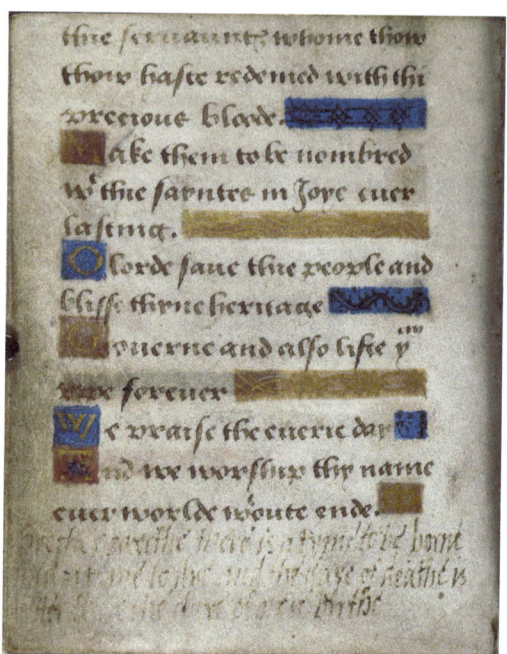

thie feruaunt*e* whome thow
thow hafte redemed with thi
precious bloode.
Make them to be nombred
w^t the fayntes in Joye euer
lafting.
O lorde faue thie people and
bliffe thyne heritage
Gouerne and alfo lifte y^m
vppe foreuer
We praife the euerie day
And we worfhip thy name
euer worlde w^toute ende.

Scriptures sayethe there is a tyme to be borne and a tyme to dye and the daye of deathe is better than the daye of oure byrthe

Thy servant whom Thou
Thou have redeemed with Thy
precious blood.
Make them to be numbered
with the saints in joy everlasting.
Oh Lord, save Thy people and
bless Thyne heritage.
Govern and also lift them
up forever.
We praise Thee every day.
And we worship Thy name
ever world without end.

Scriptures say, there is a time to be born and a time to die, and the day of death is better than the day of our birth

Folio 77r

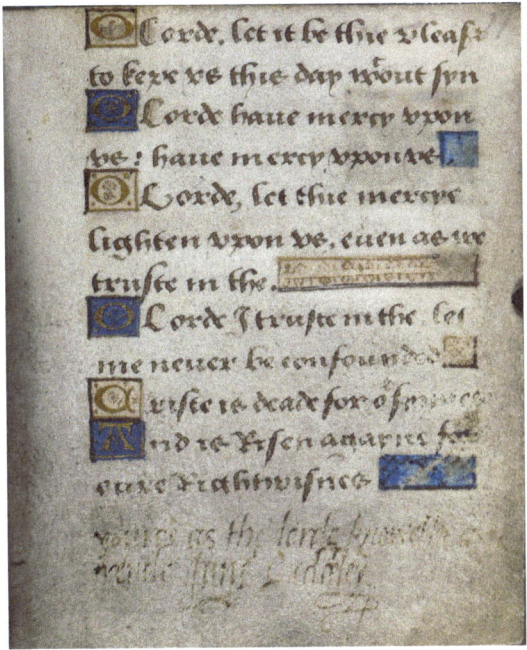

O Lorde, let it be thie pleas^r
to kepe vs this daye w^{t}out syn
O Lorde haue mercy vpon
vs: haue mercy vpon vs
O Lorde, let thie mercye
lighten vpon vs, euen as we
truſte in the.
O Lorde J truſte in the, let
me neuer be confounded
Criſte is deade for o^r fynnes
And is Riſen agayne for
oure Rightwiſnes

youres as the lorde knowethe as a
frende Jane Duddeley

O h Lord, let it be Thy pleasure
to keep us this day without sin.
O Lord, have mercy upon
us; have mercy upon us.
O Lord, let Thy mercy
lighten upon us, even as we
trust in Thee.
O Lord, I trust in Thee. Let
me never be confounded.
Christ is dead for our sins
And is risen again for
our righteousness.

Yours, as the Lord knows, as a
friend, Jane Dudley

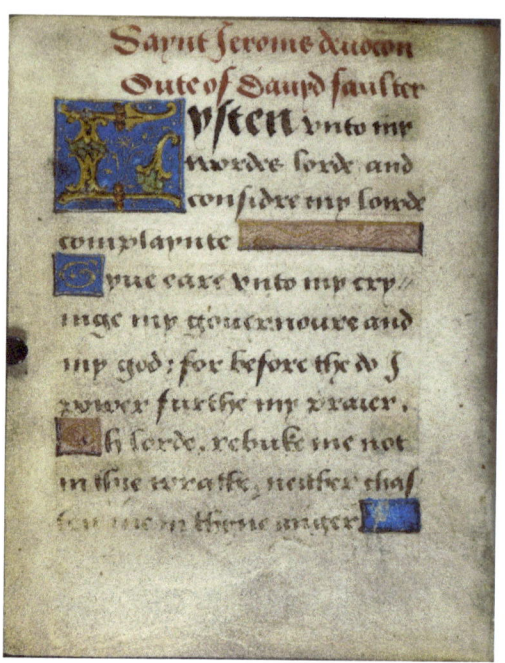

Saynt Jeroms deuocõn Oute of Davyd faulter

Lyften vnto my wordes lorde and confidre my lowde complaynte
Gyue care vnto my cry// inge my gouernoure and my god: for before the do J power furthe my praier.
Oh lorde, rebuke me not in thie wrathe, neither chaf/ ten me in thnyne anger

Saint Jerome's devotion out of David's Psalter

Listen unto my words, Lord, and consider my loud complaint.
Give care unto my cry- ing, my Governor and my God, for before Thee do I pour forth my prayer.
Oh Lord, rebuke me not in Thy wrath, neither chas- ten me in Thine anger,

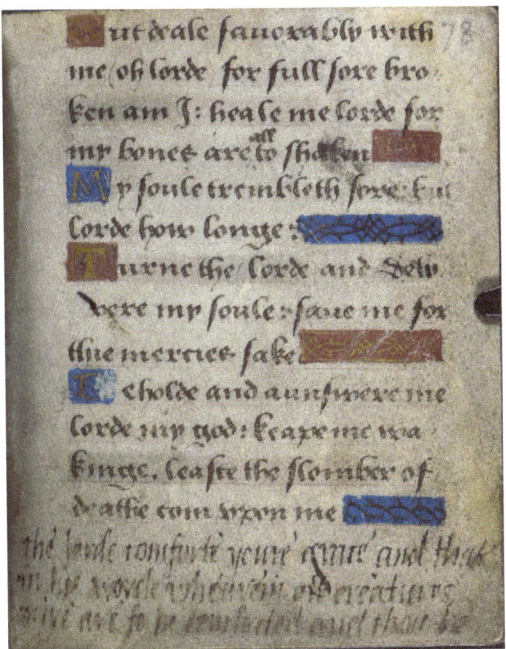

But deale fauorably with
me (oh lorde) for full fore bro//
ken am J: heale me lorde for
my bones are to fhaken (all)
My foule trembleth fore: but
lorde how longe:
Turne the (lorde) and Dely/
uere my foule: faue me for
thie mercies fake
Beholde and aunfwere me
lorde my god: keape me wa//
kinge, leafte the flombre of
deathe com vpon me
the lorde comforte youre grace and that
in his worde whearin all creatures
onlye are to be comforted and thoughe

* greatly

But deal favorably with
me, Oh Lord, for full sore broken am I. Heal me, Lord, for
my bones are all shaken.
My soul trembles sore,* but
Lord how long?
Turn Thee, Lord, and deliver my soul. Save me for
Thy mercy's sake.
Behold and answer me,
Lord my God. Keep me wa-
king, lest the slumber of
death come upon me.
The Lord comfort your Grace, and that
in His Word wherein all creatures
only are to be comforted. And though

Folio 78v

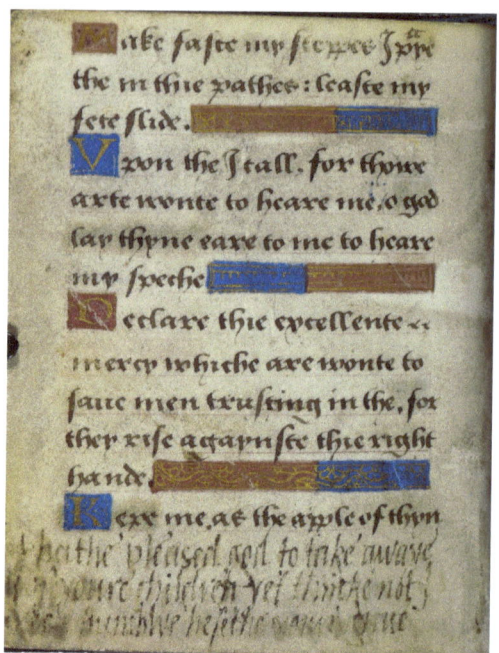

|M|ake faſte my steppes I p^aye the in thie pathes: leaſte my fete ſlide.
|V|pon the I call, for thowe arte wonte to heare me, (o god) lay thyne eare to me to heare my ſpeche
|D|eclare thie excellente xx mercy whiche are wonte to ſaue men truſting in the, for they riſe agaynſte thie right hand.
|K|epe me. as the apple of thyn
it hathe pleaſed god to take awaye ii of youre children yet thincke not I moſte humblye beſeche youre grace

|M|ake fast my steps, I pray Thee, in Thy paths, lest my feet slide.
|U|pon Thee I call, for Thou are wont* to hear me, oh God. Lay Thine ear to me to hear my speech.
|D|eclare Thy excellent mercy which are wont to save men trusting in Thee, for they rise against Thy right hand.
|K|eep me as the apple of Thine
it has pleased God to take away two of your children,† yet think not, I most humbly beseech your Grace,

* in the habit of   † i.e., daughter Jane and son-in-law Guildford

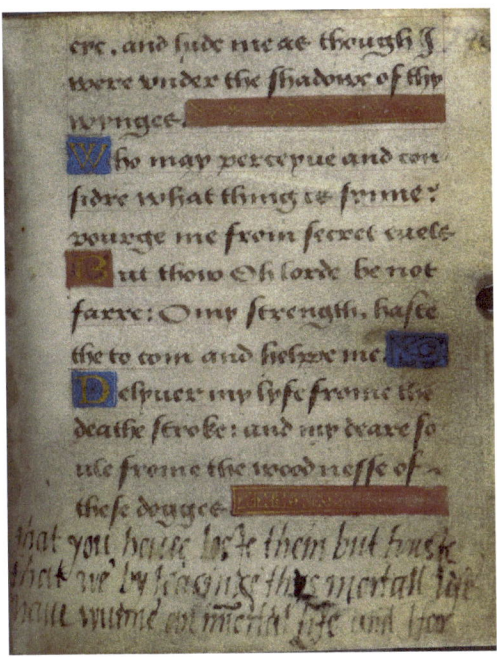

eye. and hide me as though J
were vnder the shadowe of thy
wynges.
Who may perceyue and con//
fider what thing is fynne?
pourge me from fecret euels
But thow (Oh lorde) be not
farre: O my ftrength, hafte
the to com and helppe me.
Delyuer my lyfe frome the
deathe ftroke: and my deare fo/
ule frome the woodneffe of x
thefe dogges

that you hauee loste them but truste
that we by leauing thys mortall life
haue wunne an imõrtal life and J for

eye, and hide me as though I
were under the shadow of Thy
wings.
Who may perceive and consider what thing is sin?
Purge me from secret evils.
But Thou, oh Lord, be not
far. Oh my strength, hasten
Thee to come and help me.
Deliver my life from the
death stroke, and my dear soul from the wildness of
these dogs.

that you have lost them, but trust
that we, by leaving this mortal life,
have won an immortal life. And I for

Folio 79v

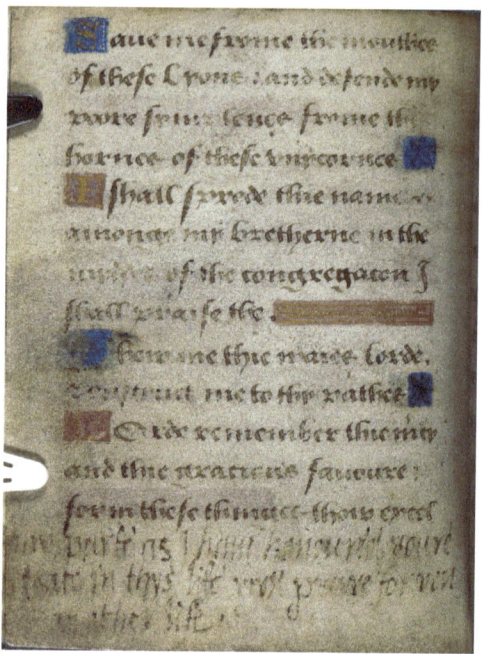

Saue me frome the mouthes of thefe Lyons: and defende my poore fymplenes frome the hornes of thefe vnycornes
I fhall fprede thie name xx amonge my bretherne in the myddes of the congregacõn J fhall praife the.
Shew me thie waies lorde, conftrict me to thy pathes
LOrde remember thie m^{r}cy and thie gracious fauoure: for in thefe thinges thow excel
for my partfe as J haue honoured youre grace in thys life will praye for you in another life.

Save me from the mouths of these lions, and defend my poor simplness from the horns of these unicorns.
I shall spread Thy name among my brethren in the midst of the congregation. I shall praise Thee.
Show me Thy ways, Lord. Constrict me to Thy paths.
Lord, remember Thy mercy and Thy gracious favor, for in these things Thou [have] excel-
for my part, as I have honored your Grace in this life, [I] will pray for you in another life.

Folio 80r

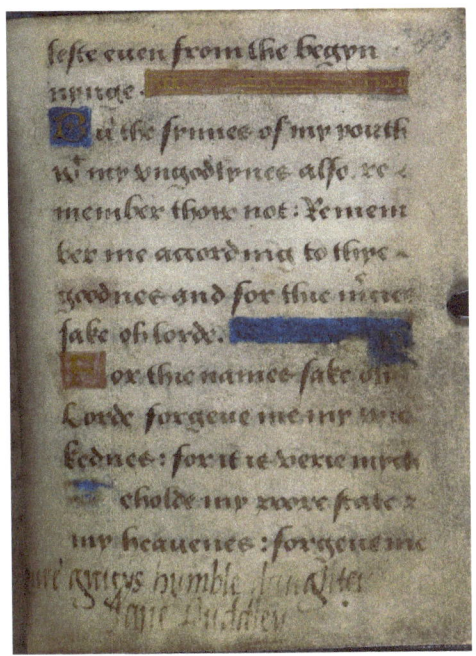

lefte euen from the begyn //
nynge.
  But the fynnes of my youth
w^t my vngodlynes alfo. re x
member thow not: Remem
ber me according to thye x
goodnes and for thie m^{r}cies
fake oh lorde.
  For thie names fake oh
Lorde forgeue me my wi
ckednes: for it is verie mych
  Beholde my poor state &
my heavenes: forgeue me
[y]oure gracys humble daughter
       Jane Duddley

led even from the begin-
ing.
  But the sins of my youth
with my ungodliness also, remember Thou not. Remem-
ber me according to Thy
goodness and for Thy mercy's
sake, oh Lord.
  For Thy name's sake, oh
Lord, forgive me my wi-
ckedness, for it is very much.
  Behold my poor state and
my heaviness. Forgive me
[y]our Grace's humble daughter,
       Jane Dudley

Folio 80v

all my sins.

Take not away my soul with the ungodly, neither yet my life with these bloody men.

Lord hear my voice. I call upon Thee. Have mercy upon me and answer me.

Turn not Thy face from me. Suffer not Thy servant to slide in Thy wrath. Hitherto have Thou been my helper. Caste me not now away, neither forsake me, oh God my

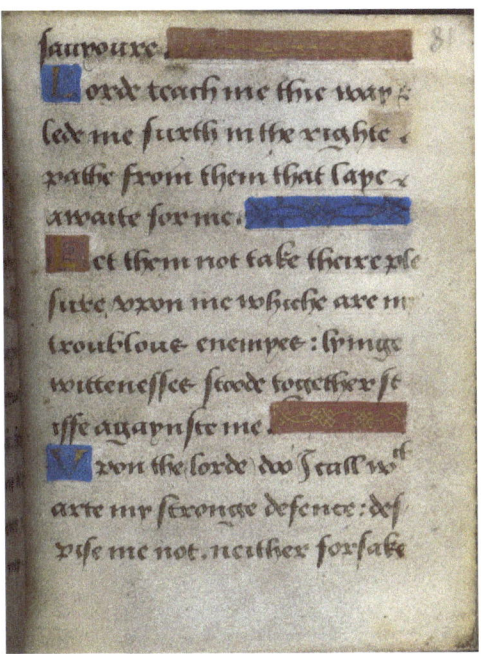

fauyoure).
Lorde teach me thie way &
lede me furth in the righte x
pathe from them that laye x
awaite for me.
Let them not take theire ple/
fure vpon me whiche are my
troublous enemyes: lyinge
wittenesses stoode together st//
iff agaynste me.
Vpon the (lorde) doo J call w^ch
arte my stronge defence: def//
pise me not, neither forsake

Savior.
Lord, teach me Thy way and
lead me forth in the right
path from them that lay
await for me.
Let them not take their pleasure upon me which are my
troublous enemies, lying
witnesses stood together st-
iff against me.
Upon me, Lord, do I call, which
are my strong defense. Despise me not, neither forsake

Folio 81v

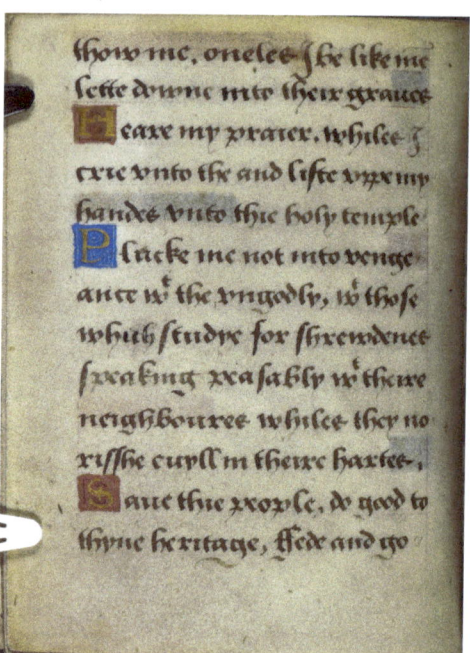

thow me, oneles J be like mē
lette downe into their graues
Heare my praier, whiles J
crie vnto the and lifte vppe my
handes vnto thie holy temple
Plucke me not into venge//
ance wt the vngodly, wt thofe
which ftudye for fhrewdenes
fpeaking peafably wt theire
neighboures whiles they no
riffhe euyll in theire hartes.
Saue thie people, do good to
thyne heritage, ffede and go//

Thou me, unless I be like men
let down into their graves.
Hear my prayer while I
cry unto Thee, and lift up my
hands unto Thy holy temple.
Pluck* me not into venge-
ance with the ungodly, with those
which study for shrewdness,
speaking peaceably with their
neighbors while they nou-
rish evil in their hearts.
Save Thy people. Do good to
Thine heritage. Feed and go-

* (obsolete) to bring a person forcibly into or out of a specified state or condition

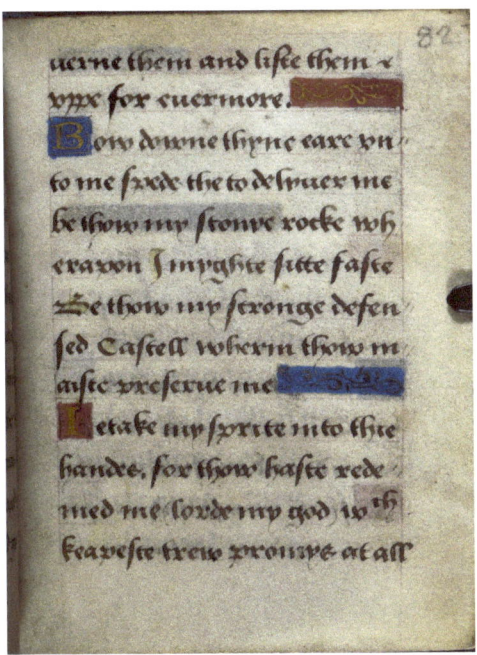

uerne them and lifte them x
vppe for euermore.
Bow downe thyne eare vn//
to me spede the to delyuer me
be thow my ftonye rocke wh//
erapon J myghte fitte fafte
Be thow my ftronge defen//
fed Caftell wherin thow m//
aifte preferue me
Betake my fprite into thie
handes, for thow hafte rede//
med me (lorde my god) w^ch
keapefte trew promys at all

vern them and lift them
up forevermore.
Bow down Thine ear unto me. Speed Thee to deliver me.
Be Thou my stony rock wh-
ereupon I might sit fast.
Be Thou my strong defen-
ded castle wherein Thou m-
ay preserve me.
Betake my spirit into Thy
hands, for Thou have redeemed me, Lord my God, which
keeps true promise at all

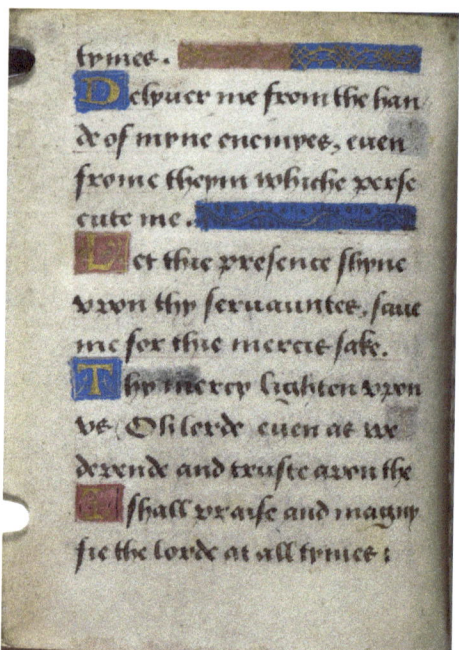

tymes.

Delyuer me from the han//
de of myne enemyes, euen
frome theym whiche perfe
cute me.

Let thie prefence fhyne
vpon thy feruauntes, faue
me for thie mercis fake.

Thy mercy lighten vpon
vs (Oh lorde) euen as we
depende and trufte apon the

I fhall praife and magny
fie the lorde at all tymes:

times.

Deliver me from the hands of my enemies, even
from them which perse-
cute me.

Let Thy presence shine
upon Thy sevants. Save
me for Thy mercy's sake.

Thy mercy alight upon
us, oh Lord, even as we
depend and trust upon Thee.

I shall praise and magnify the Lord at all times.

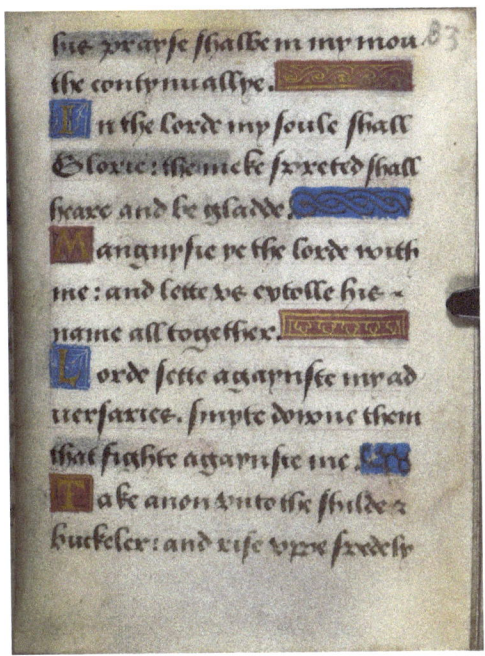

his prayſe ſhalbe in my mou/
the contynuallye.
In the lorde my ſoule ſhall
Glorie: the meke ſpreted ſhall
heare and be gladde.
Mangnyfie ye the lorde with
me: and lette vs extolle his
name all together.
Lorde ſette agaynſte my ad/
uerſaries. ſmyte downe them
that fighte agaynſte me.
Take anon vnto the ſhilde &
buckeler: and riſe vppe ſpedely

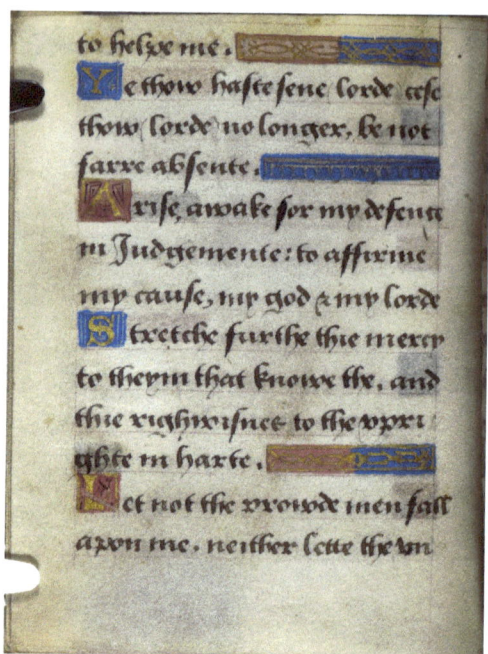

to helpe me.
Ye thow hafte fene (lorde) cefe thow (lorde) no longer, be not farre abfente.
Arife, awake for my defence in Judgemente: to affirme my caufe, my god & my lorde
Stretche furthe thie mercy to theym that knowe the, and thie rightwisnes to the vpri// ghte in harte.
Let not the prowde men fall apon me, neither lette the vn//

to help me.
Yea, Thou have seen, Lord; cease Thou, Lord, no longer. Be not far absent.
Arise, awake for my defense in judgment, to affirm my cause, my God and Lord.
Stretch forth Thy mercy to them that know Thee, and Thy rigteousness to the upri- ght in heart.
Let not the proud men fall upon me, neither let the un-

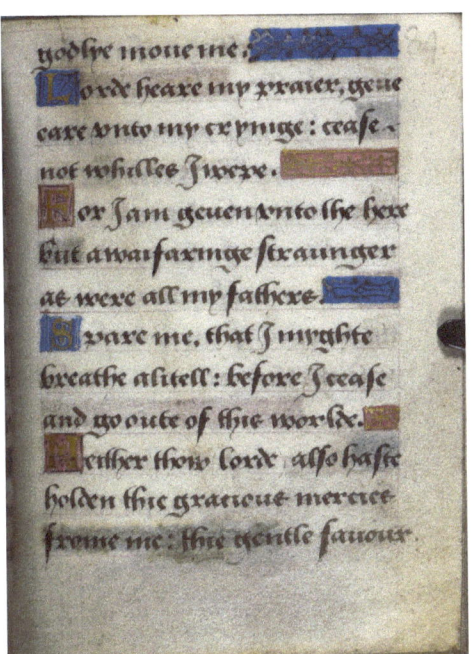

godlye moue me.
Lorde heare my praier, geue
care vnto my cryinge: ceafe x
not whilles J wepe.
For J am geuen vnto the here
but awaifaringe ftraunger
as were all my fathers.
Spare me, that J myghte
breathe alitell: before J ceafe
and go oute of this worlde.
Neither thow (lorde) alfo hafte
holden thie gracious mercies
frome me: thie gentle fauour

godly move me.
Lord hear my prayer. Give
care unto my crying. Cease
not while I weep.
For I am given unto Thee here
but a wayfaring stranger,
as were all my fathers.
Spare me, that I might
breathe a little before I cease
and go out of this world.
Neither Thou, Lord, also have
held Thy gracious mercies
from me.* Thy gentle favor

* in modern syntax: "Neither also, Lord, [should] Thou withhold Thy gracious mercies from me."

Folio 84v

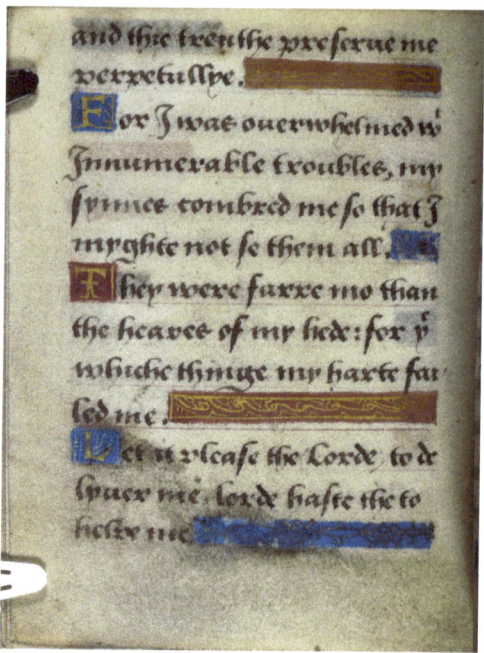

and thie treuthe preserue me
perpetallye.
For J was ouerwhelmed wt
Jnnumerable troubles, my
synnes combred me so that J
myghte not se them all.
They were farre mo than
the heaves of my hede: for ye
whiche thinge my harte fai‐
led me.
Let it pleafe the (Lorde) to de
lyuer me, lorde haste the to
helpe me.

and Thy truth preserve me
perpetually.
For I was overwhlemed with
innumerable troubles. My
sins encumbered me so that I
might not see them all.
They were far mo[re] than
the hairs of my head, for the
which thing my heart fai‐
led me.
Let it please Thee, Lord, to de‐
liver me. Lord, hasten Thee to
help me.

Folio 85r

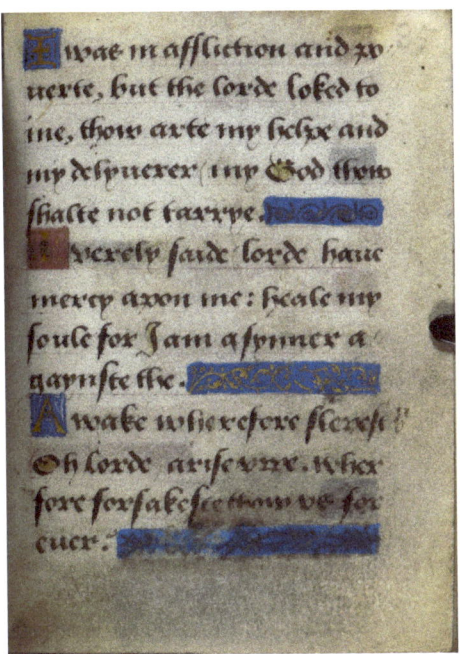

I was in affliction and po//
uerte, but the lorde loked to
me, thow arte my helpe and
my delyuerer (my God) thow
fhalte not tarrye.
I verely faide (lorde) haue
mercy apon me: heale my
foule for J am a fynner a//
gaynfte the.
A wake wherefore flepeste
(Oh lorde) arife vppe. wher
fore forfakefte thow vs for
euer?

I was in affliction and po-
verty, but the Lord looked to
me. Thou are my help and
my deliverer, my God. Thou
shall not tarry.
I verily said, "Lord, have
mercy upon me. Heal my
soul, for I am a sinner a-
gainst Thee.
A wake, wherefore* sleep,
oh Lord? Arise up. Where-
fore forsake Thou us for-
ever?

* why

Folio 85v

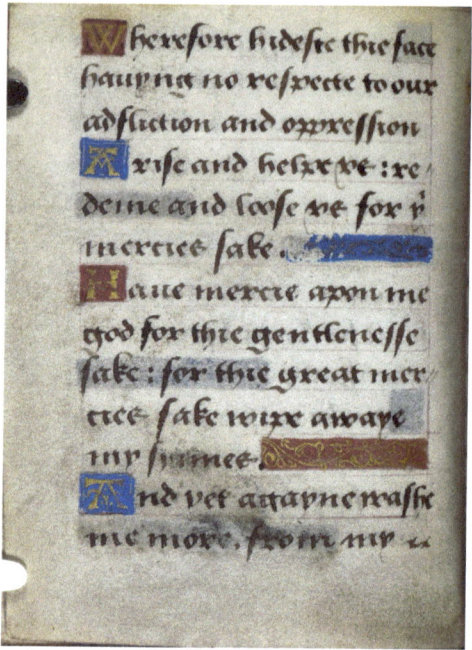

<u>W</u>herefore hideſte thie face hauynge no reſpecte to our adfliction and oppreſſion <u>A</u>riſe and helpe vs: re⁄⁄deme and looſe vs for yⁱ mercies ſake. <u>H</u>aue mercie apon me god for thie gentleneſſe ſake: for thie great mer⁄⁄cies ſake wipe awaye my ſynnes. <u>A</u>nd yet agayne waſhe me more, from my xx

Wherefore hide Thy face, having no respect to our affliction and oppression? Arise and help us. Redeem and loose us for Thy mercy's sake. Have mercy upon me, God, for Thy gentleness' sake. For Thy great mercy's sake, wipe away my sins. And yet again wash me more, from my

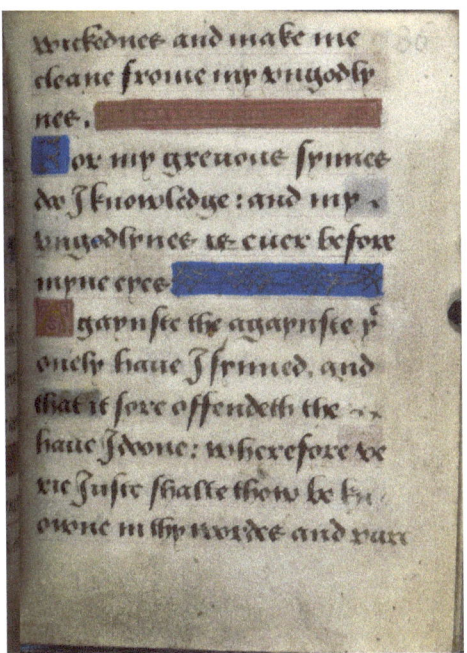

wickedness and make me
clean from my ungodli-
ness,
F or my grievous sins
do I acknowledge, and my
ungodliness is ever before
my eyes.
A gainst Thee, against Thee
only have I sinned and
that it sore offends Thee
have I done. Wherefore verily just shall Thou be known in Thy words and pure

Folio 86v

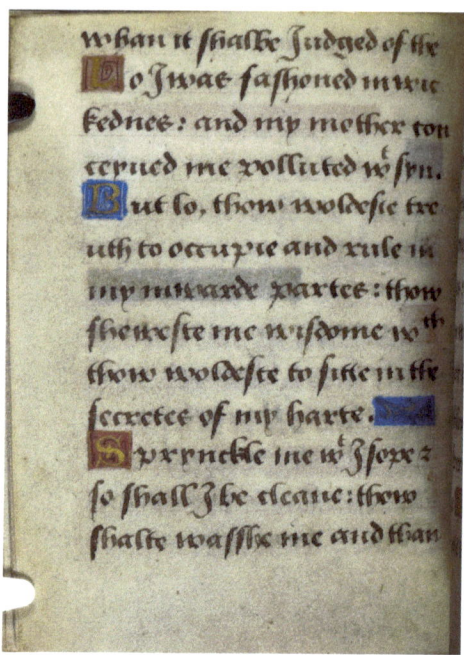

whan it fhalbe Judged of the Lo J was fafhoned in wic kednes: and my mother con ceyued me polluted wt fyn. But lo, thow woldefte tre/uth to occupie and rule in my inwarde partes: thow shewefte me wifdom wch thow woldefte to fitte in the fecretes of my harte. Sprynkle me wt Ifope & fo fhall I be cleane: thow fhalte wafshe me and than

when it shall be judged of Thee. Lo, I was fashioned in wickedness, and my mother conceived me polluted with sin. But lo, Thou would [have] truth to occupy and rule in my inward parts. Thou showed me wisdom which Thou would [have] to sit in the secrets of my heart. Sprinkle me with hyssop* and so shall I be clean. Thou shall wash me and then

* A plant named in the Old Testament for use in ceremonial purifications, variously conjectured to have been a species of *Satureia*, Marjoram (*Origanum*), or (with more probability) the Thorny Caper (*Capparis spinosa*).

Folio 87r

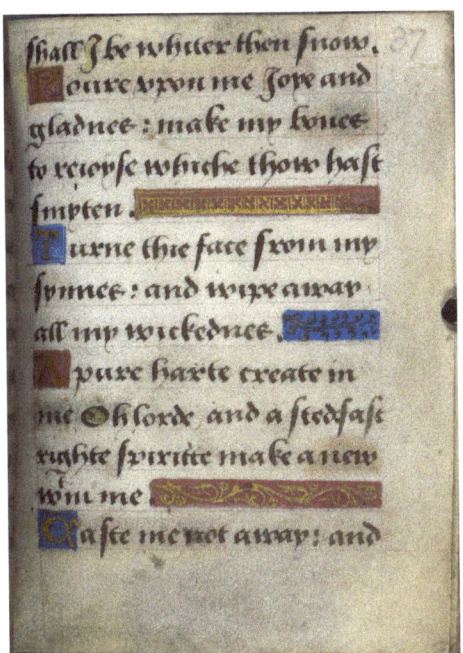

ſhall J be whiter then ſnow.
P oure vpon me Joye and
gladnes: make my bones
to reioyſe which thow haſt
ſmyten.
T urne thie face from my
ſynnes: and wipe away
all my wickednes.
A pure harte create in
me (Oh lorde) and a ſtedfaſte
righte ſpiritte make a new
w^tin me.
C aſte me not away: and

shall I be whiter than snow.
P our upon me joy and
gladness. Make my bones
to rejoice which Thou have
smitten.
T urn Thy face from my
sins and wipe away
all my wickedness.
A pure heart create in
me, oh Lord, and a steadfast
right spirit make anew
within me.
C aste me not away, and

Folio 87v

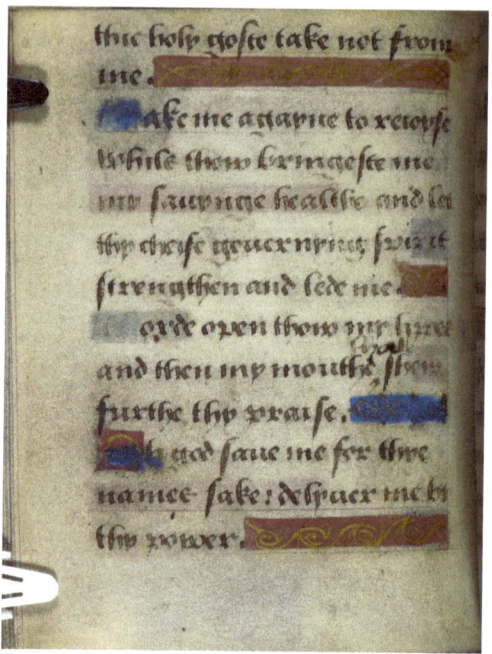

thie holy goſte take not from
me.
Make me agayne to reioyſe
whils thow bringeſte me
my ſauinge healthe and let
thy cheife gouernyng ſpirit
ſtrengthen and lede me.
    orde open thow my lippes
and then my mouthe ſhall ſhew
furthe thy praiſe.
Oh god ſaue me for thye
names ſake: delyuer me by
thy power.

Thy Holy Ghost not from
me.
Make me again to rejoice
while Thou bring me
my saving health, and let
Thy chief governing spirit
strengthen and lead me.
[L]ord,* open Thou my lips
and then my mouth shall show
forth Thy praise.
Oh God, save me for Thy
name's sake. Deliver me by
Thy power.

---

* As at Folio 16r, the artist who decorated the manuscript failed to add a decorated L, though in this instance the scribe also failed to include one as a guide.

Folio 88r

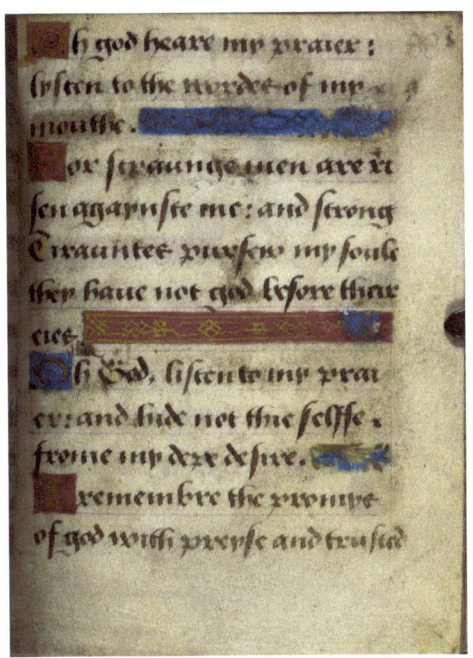

Oh god heare my praier:
lyften to the wordes of my x
mouthe.
For ftraunge men are ri
fen agaynfte me: and ftrong
Tirauntes purfew my foule
they haue not god before their
eies.
Oh God, liften to my prai
er: and hide not thie felffe x
frome my depe defire.
I remembre the promys
of god with preyfe and trufted

Oh God, hear my prayer.
Listen to the words of my
mouth,
For strange men are risen against me, and strong
tyrants pursue my soul.
They have not God before their
eyes.
Oh God, listen to my prayer and hide not Thyself
from my deep desire.
I remember the promise
of God with praise and trusted

Folio 88v

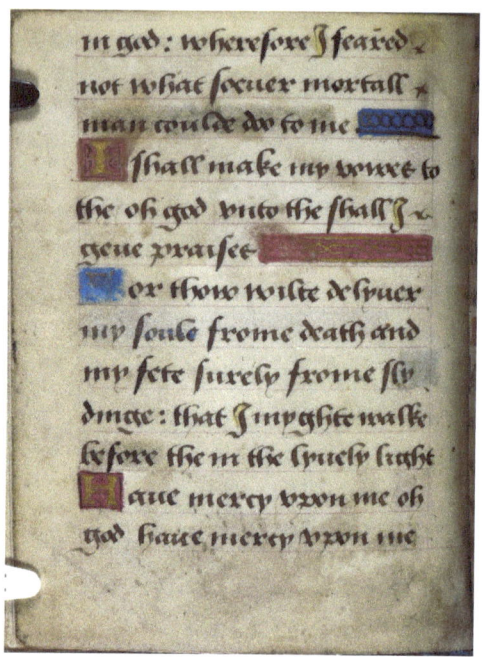

in god: wherefore J feared x
not what soeuer mortall x
man coulde doo to me.
   I ſhall make my vowes to
the (oh god) vnto the ſhall J x
geue praiſes
   For thow wilte delyuer
my ſoule from death and
my fete ſurely frome fly//
dinge: that J myghte walke
before the in the lyuely light
   Haue mercy vpon me (oh
god) haue mercy vpon me

in God, therefore I feared
not whatsoever mortal
man could do to me.
   I shall make my vows to
Thee, oh God; unto Thee shall I
give praises.
   For Thou will deliver
my soul from death and
my feet surely from sli-
ding, that I might walk
before Thee in the lively light.
   Have mercy upon me, oh
God, have mercy upon me,

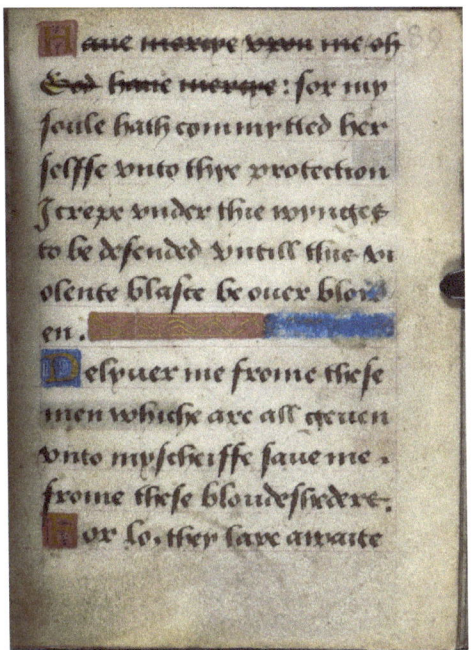

~~Haue mercye vpon me (oh God) haue mercye~~: for my
foule hath commytted her
felffe vnto thy protection
J crepe vnder thie wynges
to be defended vntil this vi
olente blafte be ouer blow//
en.

Delyuer me frome thefe
men whiche are all geuen
vnto myfcheiffe faue me x
frome thefe bloudefheders.
For lo, they laye awaite

for my
soul has committed her-
self unto Thy protection.
I creep under Thy wings
to be defended until this violent blast be over-blow-
n.

Deliver me from these
men which are all given
unto mischief. Save me
from these blood-shedders.
For lo, they lie await

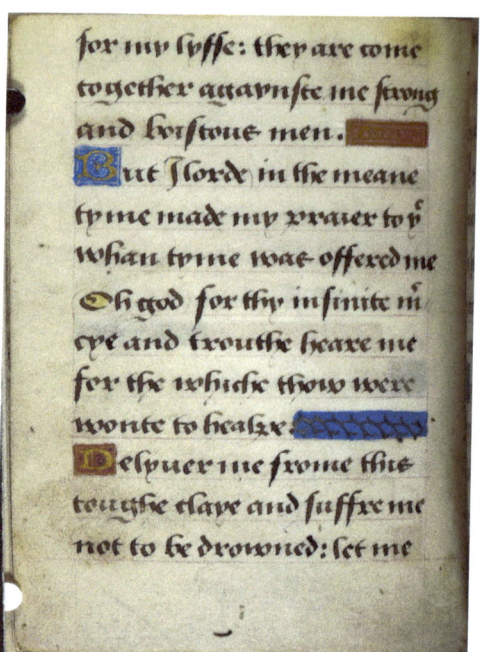

for my lyffe: they are come
together agaynſte me ſtrong
and boiſtous men.
But J (lorde) in the meane
tyme made my praier to yᵉ
whan tyme was offered me
(Oh god) for thy infinite mʳ⁄⁄
cye and trouthe heare me
for the whiche thow were
wonte to healpe.
Delyuer me frome this
toughe claye and ſuffre me
not to be drowned: let me

for my life. They are come
together against me, strong
and boisterous men.
But I, Lord, in the mean-
time, made my prayer to Thee
when time was offered [to] me.
Oh God, for Thy infinite mercy and truth, hear me,
for the which Thou were
accustomed to help.
Deliver me from this
tough clay and suffer me
not to be drowned. Let me

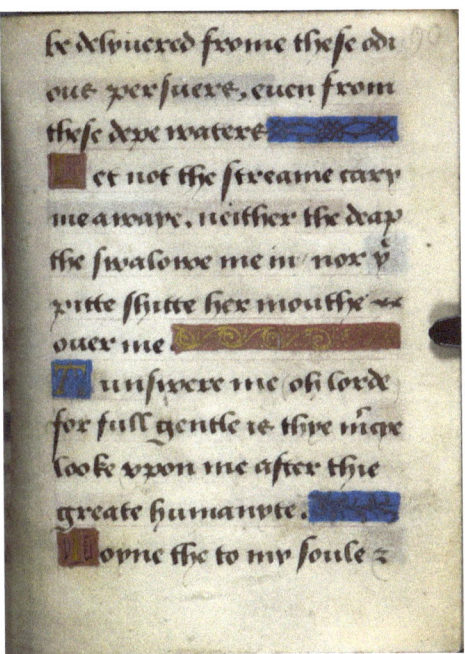

be delyuered frome thefe odi/
ous perfuers, euen from
thefe depe waters

Let not the ftreame cary
me awaye, neither the deap
the fwalowe me in/ nor yᵉ
pitte fhitte her mouthe xx
ouer me.

Aunfwere me (oh lorde)
for full gentle is thie mʳcye
looke vpon me after thie
greate humanyte.

Ioyne the to my foule &

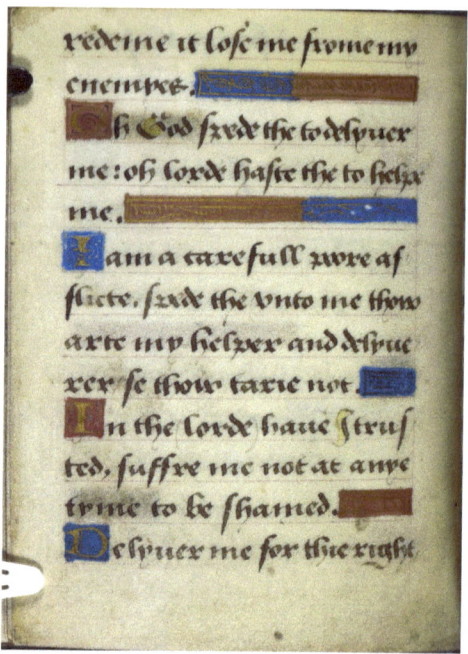

redem it lofe me frome my
enemyes
Oh God fpede the to delyuer
me: oh lorde hafte the to helpe
me.
I am a carefull poore af//
flicte. fpede the vnto me thow
arte my helper and delyue//
rer/ fe thow tarie not.
In the (lorde) haue J truf//
ted, fuffre me not at anye
tyme to be fhamed.
Delyuer me for thie right//

redeem it. Loose me from my
enemies.
Oh God, speed Thee to deliver
me. Oh Lord, hasten Thee to help
me.
I am a care-full poor af-
flicted. Speed Thee unto me. Thou
are my helper and delive-
rer. See Thou tarry not.
In Thee, Lord, have I trusted. Suffer me not at any
time to be shamed.
Deliver me for Thy right-

Folio 91r

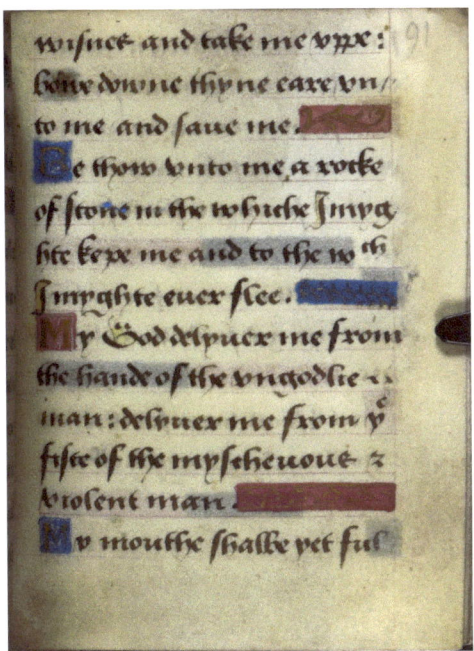

wiſenes and take me vppe:
bowe downe thyne eare vn//
to me and ſaue me.
Be thow vnto me a rocke
of ſtone in the whiche I myg//
hte kepe me and to the w^{ch}
I myghte euer flee.
My God delyuer me from
the hande of the vngodlie xx
man: delyuer me from y^e
fiſte of the myſcheuous &
violent man.
My mouthe ſhalbe yet ful

eousness and take me up.
Bow down Thine ear un-
to me and save me.
Be Thou unto me a rock
of stone, in the which I might keep me and to the which
I might ever flee.
My God, deliver me from
the hand of the ungodly
man. Deliver me from the
fist of the mischievous and
violent men.
My mouth shall be yet full

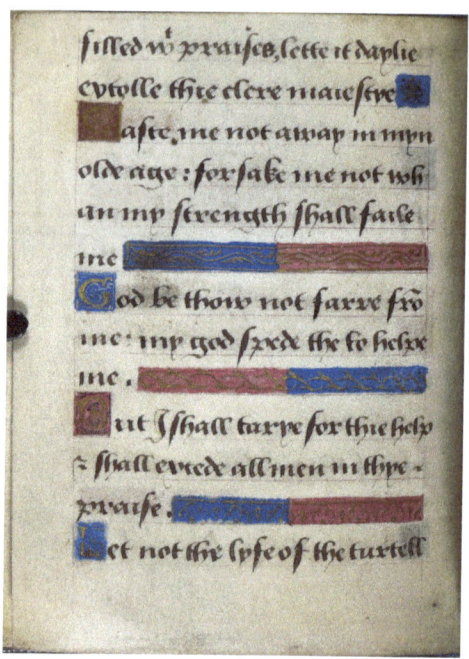

filled with praises. Let it daily extol Thy clear majesty.

Caste me not away in my old age. Forsake me not when my strength shall fail me.

God, be Thou not far from me. My God, speed Thee to help me.

But I shall tarry for Thy help and shall exceed all men in Thy praise.

Let not the life of the turtle-

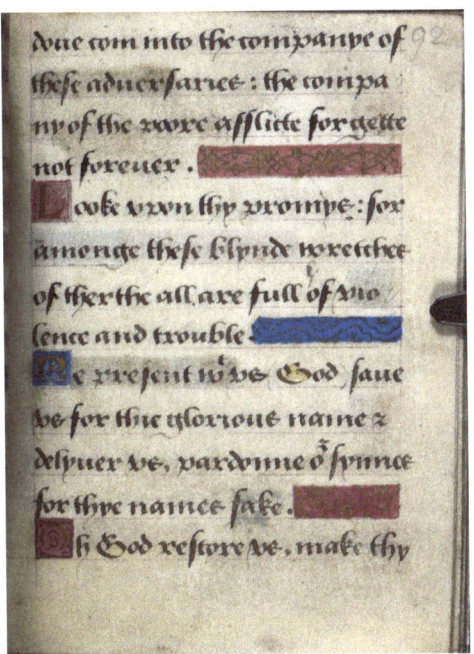

doue com into the companye of
thefe aduerſaries: the compa//
ny of the poore afflicte forgette
not foreuer.

Looke vpon thy promys: for
amonge thefe blynde wretches
of therth all are full of vio//
lence and trouble.

Be prefent w^t vs (God) faue
vs for thie glorious name &
delyuer vs, pardonne o^r fynnes
for thye names fake.

Oh God reſtore vs, make thy

dove come into the company of
these adversaries. The company of the poor afflicte[d] forget
[Thee] not forever.

Look upon Thy promise, for
among these blind wretches
of the Earth all are full of violence and trouble.

Be present with us, God. Save
us for Thy glorious name and
deliver us. Pardon our sins
for Thy name's sake.

Oh God, restore us. Make Thy

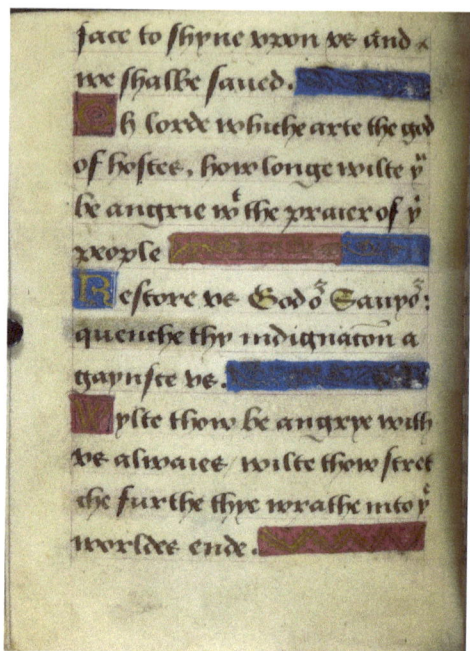

face to fhyne vpon vs and x
we fhalbe faued.
Oh lorde whiche arte the god of hoftes, how longe wilte y{u} be angrie wt the praier of y{i} people
Reftore vs God o{r} Sauyo{r}: quenche thy indignacõn a// gaynfte vs.
Wylte thow be angrye with vs alwaies/ wilte thow ftret che furthe thye wrathe into ye worldes ende.

face to shine upon us and we shall be saved.
Oh Lord, which are the God of hosts, how long will Thou be angry with the prayer of Thy people?
Restore us, God our Savior. Quench Thy indignation against us.
Will Thou be angry with us always? Will Thou stretch forth Thy wrath unto the world's end?

Folio 93r

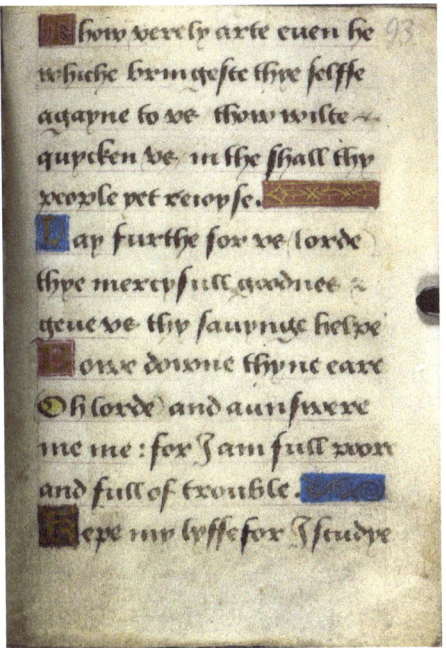

Thow verely arte euen he
whiche bringeſte thye felffe
agayne to vs/ thow wilte xx
quycken vs/ in the fhall thy
people yet reioyfe.
Lay furthe for vs (lorde)
thye mercyfull goodnes &
geue vs thy sauynge helpe
Bowe downe thyne eare
(Oh lorde) and aunfwere
me me: for J am full poore
and full of trouble.
Kepe my lyffe for J ftudye

Thou verily are even He
which brings Thyself
again to us. Thou will
quicken us. In Thee shall Thy
people yet rejoice.
Lay forth for us, Lord,
Thy merciful goodness and
give us Thy saving help.
Bow down Thine ear,
oh Lord, and answer
me, for I am fully poor
and full of trouble.
Keep my life, for I study

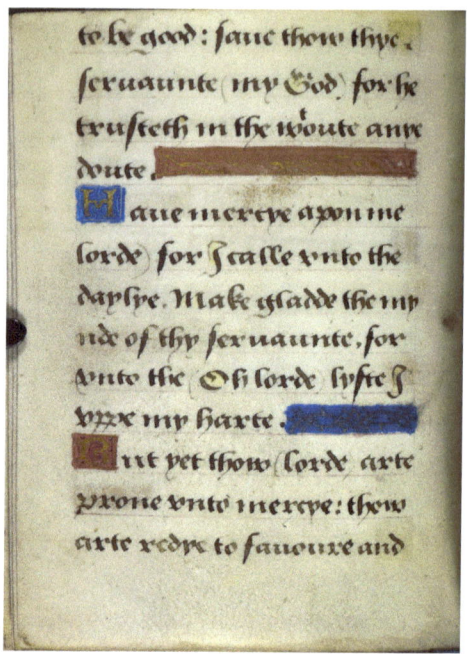

to be good: faue thow thye x feruaunte (my God) for he trufteth in the wᵗoute anye doute.

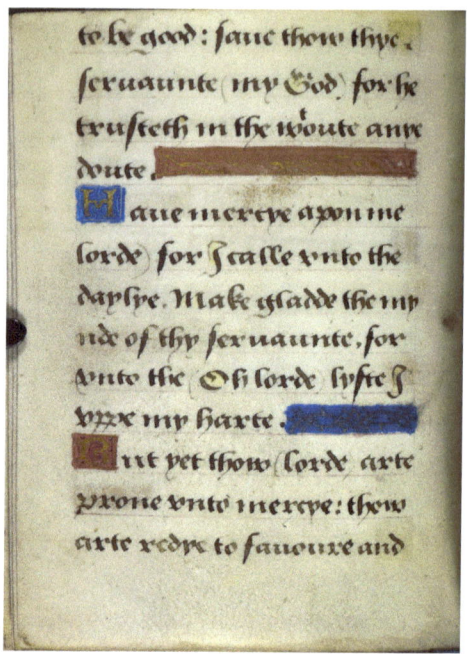 aue mercye apon me (lorde) for J calle vnto the daylye. Make gladde the mynde of thy feruaunte, for vnto the (oh lorde) lyfte I vppe my harte.

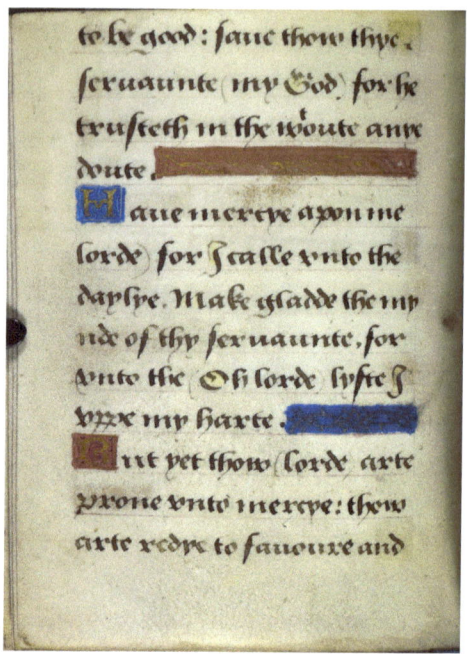 ut yet thow (lorde) arte prone vnto mercye: thow arte redye to fauoure and

to be good. Save Thou Thy servant, my God, for he trusts in Thee without any doubt.

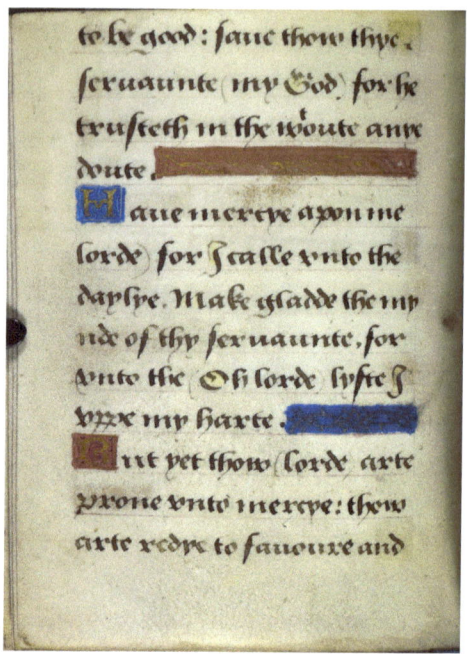 ave mercy upon me, Lord, for I call unto Thee daily. Make glad the mind of Thy servant, for unto Thee, oh Lord, lift I up my heart.

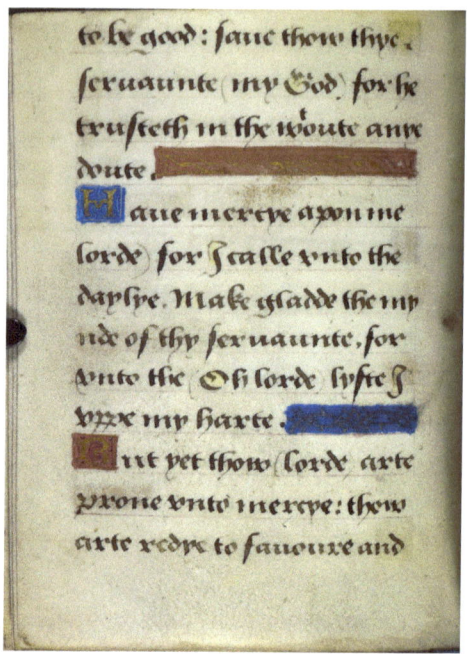 ut yet Thou, Lord, are prone unto mercy. Thou are ready to favor and

Folio 94r

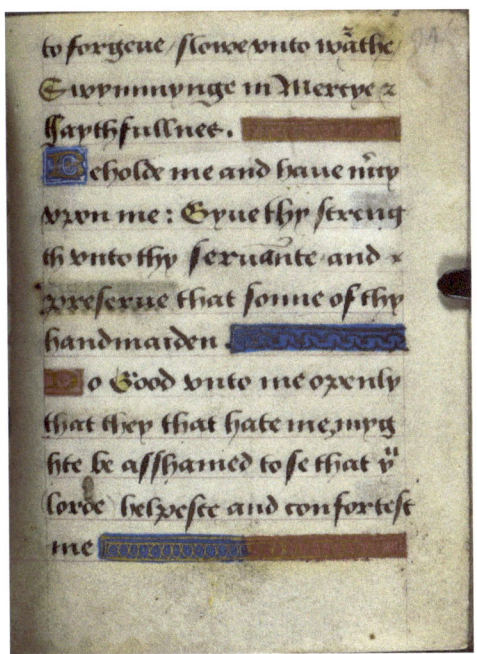

to forgeue / flowe vnto wrathe/ Swymmynge in Mercye & ffaythfullnes.

Beholde me and haue m͏ʳcy vpon me: Gyue thy ſtreng/th vnto thy ſeruãnte/ and x preſerue that ſonne of thy handmaiden.

Do Good vnto me openly that they that hate me, myg//hte be aſſhamed to ſe that yᵘ (lorde) helpeſte and conforteſt me

---

to forgive, slow unto wrath, swimming in mercy and faithfulness.

Behold me and have mercy upon me. Give Thy strength unto Thy servant, and preserve that son of Thy handmaiden.

Do good unto me openly [so] that they that hate me might be ashamed to see that Thou, Lord, help and comfort me.

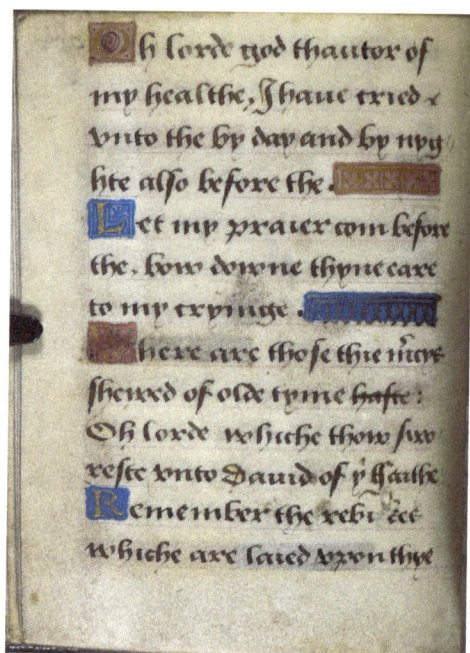

<table>
<tr><td>

:O:h lorde god thautor of
my healthe, J haue cried x
vnto the by daye/and by nyg//
hte alſo before the.
:L:et my praier com before
the, bowe downe thyne eare
to my crynge.
:W:here are thoſe thie m^rcys
ſhewed of olde tyme ~~haſte~~:
(Oh lorde) whiche thow ſwo/
reſte vnto David of y^i ffaithe
:R:emember the rebukes
whiche are laied vpon thye

</td><td>

:O:h Lord God, author of
my health, I have cried
unto Thee by day and by nig-
ht also before Thee.
:L:et my prayer come before
Thee. Bow down Thine ear
to my crying.
:W:here are those Thy mercies
showed of old time,
oh Lord, which Thou swo-
re unto David of Thy faith?
:R:emember the rebukes
which are laid upon Thy

</td></tr>
</table>

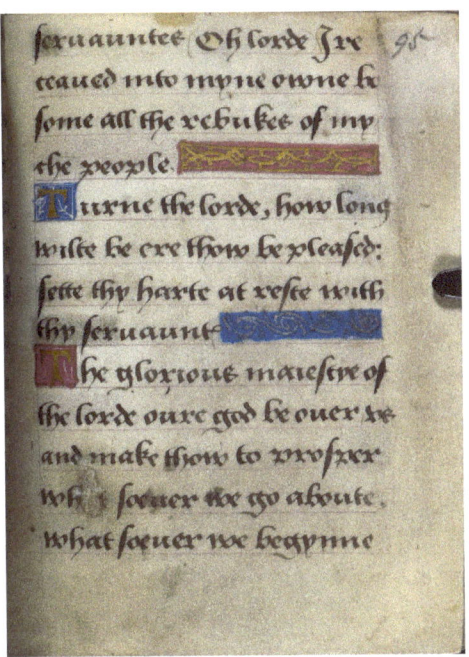

ſeruauntes (oh lorde) J re
ceaued into myne owne bo
ſome all the rebukes of my//
che people.

Turne the lorde, how long
wilte be ere thow be pleaſed:
ſette thy harte at reſte with
thy ſeruauntₑ

The glorious maieſtye of
the lorde oure god be ouer vs
and make thow to proſper
what foeuer we go aboute,
what foeuer we begynne

servants, oh Lord. I re-
ceived into my own bo-
som all the rebukes of much people.

Turn Thee, Lord; how long
will [it] be err Thou be pleased?
Set Thy heart at rest with
Thy servants.

The glorious majesty of
the Lord our God be over us,
and make Thou to prosper
whatsoever we go about.
Whatsoever we begin,

Folio 95v

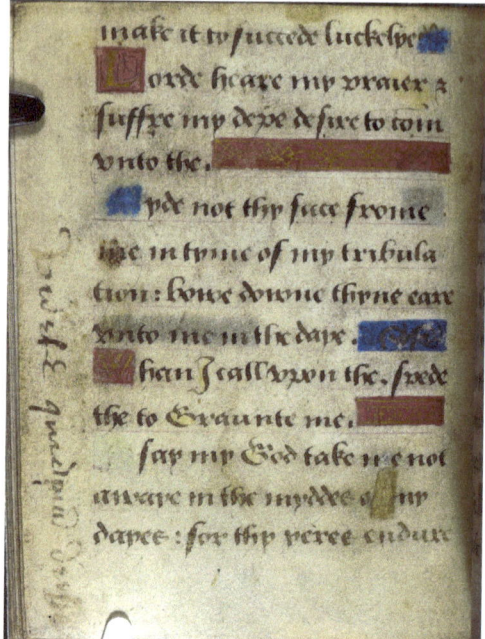

make it to succeed luckily.
Lord hear my prayer and
suffer my deep desire to come
unto Thee.
Hide not Thy face from
me in time of my tribula-
tion. Bow down Thine ear
unto me on that day.
When I call upon Thee, speed
Thee to grant me.
   * say my God, take me not
away in the midst of my
days, for Thy years endure

---

* As before at Folios 16r and 87v, a decorated initial is entirely missing here. The Latin marginal note in a 17th- or 18th-Century hand, "Videte quidpiam deeste," ("Look, something is missing") alludes to the omission.

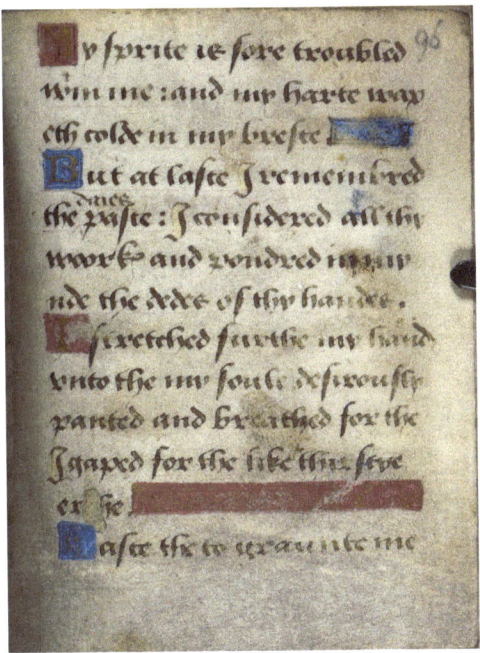

My sprite is sore troubled w^tin me: and my harte wax// eth colde in my breste.
But at laste J remembred the paste: (daies) J considered all thy woork_ℓ and pondred in my// nde the dedes of thy handes.
I stretched furthe my hand vnto the my soule desirously panted and breathed for the J gaped for the like thirstye erthe.
Haste the to graunte me

My spirit is sore troubled within me, and my heart waxes cold in my breast.
But at last I remembered the days past. I considered all Thy works and pondered in mind the deeds of Thy hands.
I stretched forth my hand unto Thee. My soul desirously panted and breathed for Thee. I gaped for Thee like thirsty earth.
Hasten Thee to grant me,

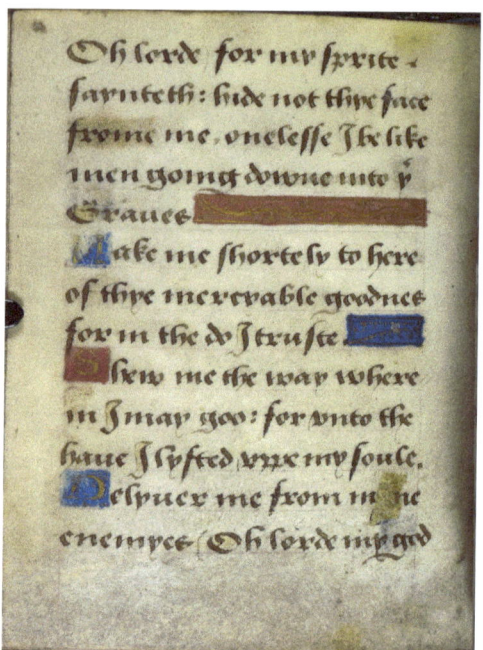

(Oh lorde) for my fprite x
faynteth: hide not thye face
frome me, oneleffe J be like
men going downe into yr
Graues.

Make me fhortely to here
of thye mercyable goodnes
for in the do J trufte.

Shew me the way where//
in J may goo: for vnto the
haue J lyfted vppe my foule.

Delyuer me frome myne
enemyes (oh lorde my god)

oh Lord, for my spirit
faints. Hide not Thy face
from me, unless I be like
men going down into their
graves.

Make me shortly to hear
of Thy merciable goodness,
for in Thee do I trust.

Show me the way wherein I may go, for unto Thee
have I lifted up my soul.

Deliver me from my
enemies, oh Lord my God,

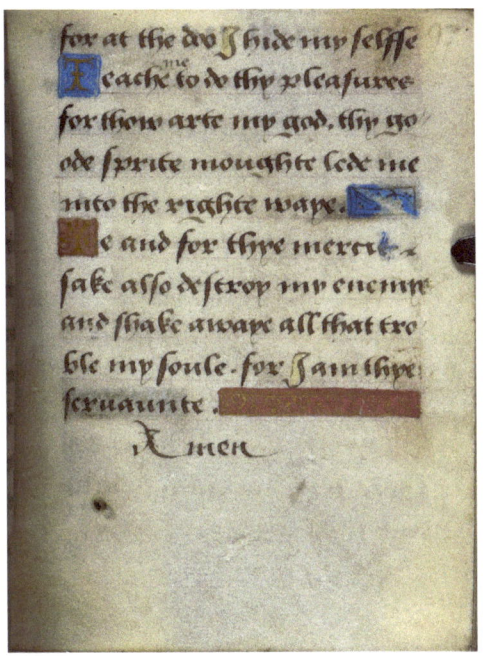

for at Thee do I hide myself.
Teach me to do Thy pleasures,
for Thou are my God. Thy good spirit might lead me
into the right way.
Yea, and for Thy mercy's
sake also, destroy my enemies
and shake away all that trouble my soul, for I am Thy
servant.

        Amen.

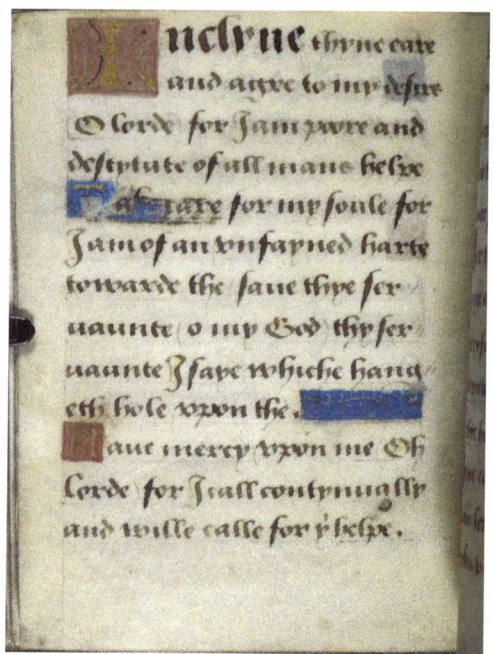

Inclyne thyne eare and agre to my defire (O lorde) for J am poore and deftytue of all mans helpe **T**ake care for my foule for J am of an vnfayned harte toward the/ faue thye fer// uaunte (o my God) thy fer// uaunt J faye whiche hang// eth hole vpon the. **H**aue mercy vpon me (Oh lorde) for J call contynually and wille calle for y[i] helpe.

Incline Thine ear and agree to my desire, oh Lord, for I am poor and desitute of all men's help. **T**ake care for my soul, for I am of an unfained heart toward Thee. Save Thy servant, oh my God, Thy servant, I say, which hangs whole upon Thee. **H**ave mercy upon me, oh Lord, for I call continually and will call for Thy help.

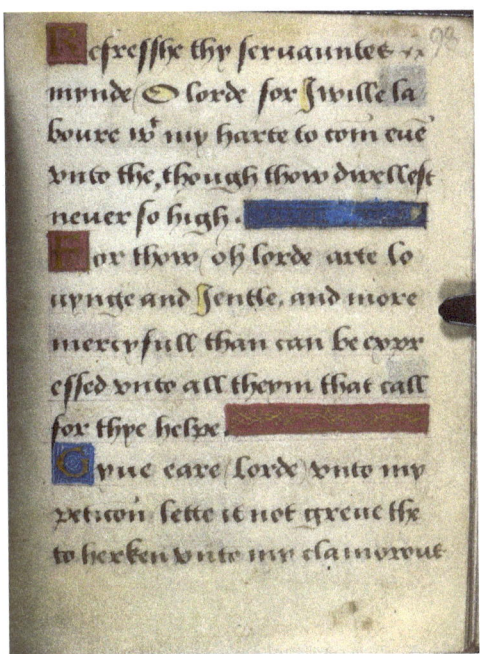

Refreffhe thy feruauntes xx mynde (O lorde) for J will la// boure wt my harte to cõm euẽ vnto the, though thow dwelleft neuer fo high.

For thow (oh lorde) arte lo// uynge and Jentle, and more mercyfull than can be expr effed vnto all theym that call for thye helpe.

Gyue eare (Lorde) vnto my peticõn/ lette it not greue the to herken vnto my clamorous

Folio 98v

praiers.

As often as anye aduerſite happeneth vnto me/ J ſhall call for thye helpe, truſting in tyme to come that thowe wilte graunte me the thing whiche thowe ſhalte thyncke moſte for my proffet

There is not one of theym that wicked men take for god// des to be compared vnto the (O lorde) neither can anye

prayers.

As often as any adversity happens unto me, I shall call for Thy help, trusting in time to come that Thou will grant me the thing which Thou shall think most for my profit.

There is not one of them that wicked men take for god-s to be compared unto Thee, oh Lord, neither can any

Folio 99r

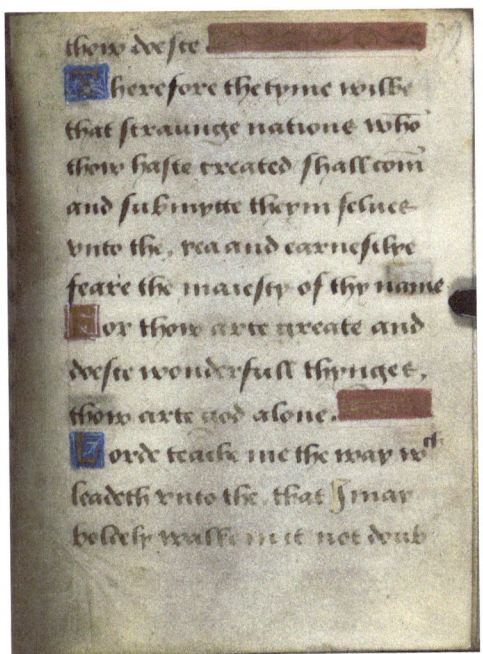

thow doeſte.
Therefore the tyme wilbe
that ſtraunge nations whõ
thow haſte created/ ſhall cõm
and ſubmytte theym ſelues
vnto the, yea and earneſtlye
feare the maieſty of thy name
For thow arte greate and
doeſte wonderfull thinges,
thow arte god alone.
Lorde teache me the way w^ch
leadeth vnto the, that J may
boldely walke in it not doub//

Thou do.
Therefore the time will be
that strange nations whom Thou
have created shall come
and submit themselves
unto Thee, yea, and earnestly
fear the majesty of Thy name.
For Thou are great and
do wonderful things.
Thou are God alone.
Lord, teach me the way which
leads unto Thee, that I may
boldly walk in it, not doub-

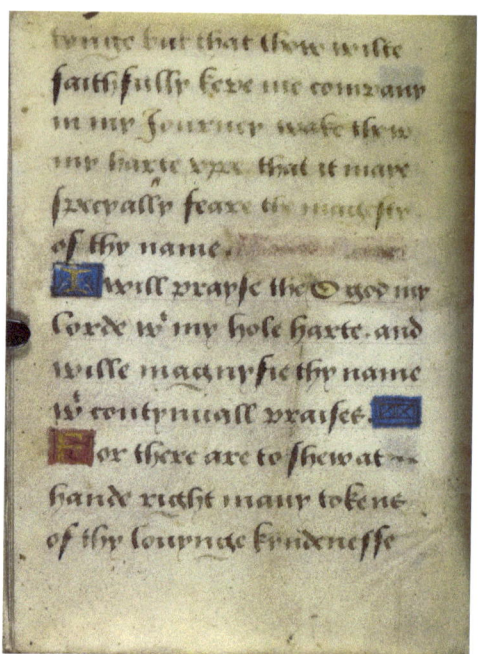

tynge but that thow wilte
faithfully kepe me company
in my Journey wake thow
my harte vppe that it maye
fpecyally feare the magefty
of thy name.

I will prayfe the (O god my
lorde) wt my hole harte. and
wille magnyfie thy name
wt contynuall praifes.

F or there are to fhew at
hande right many tokens
of thy louynge kyndeneffe

Folio 100r

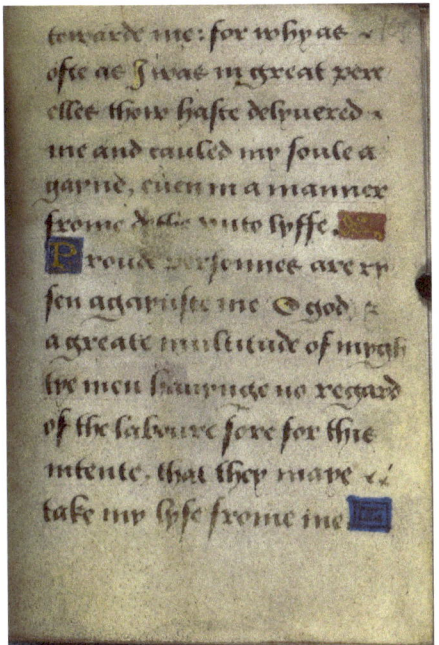

towarde me: for why as
ofte as J was in great pere//
elles/ thow haste delyuered
me and caused my soule a//
gayne, euen in a manner
frome dethe vnto lyffe.
Proude persones are ry//
sen agaynste me (O god) &
a greate multitude of mygh
tye men hauynge no regard
of the laboure sore for this
intente, that they maye
take my lyfe frome me.

toward me, for why as
often as I was in great perils, Thou have delivered
me and called my soul a-
gain, even in a manner
from death unto life.
Proud persons are ri-
sen against me, oh God, and
a great multitude of mighty men having no regard
of Thee labor sore for this
intent, that they may
take my life from me.

But thow (o lorde god) arte mercyfull and good, flowe vnto wrathe/ but merue// lous prone vnto kyndeneffe and kepinge of thy promyffes **B**ehold me and haue m︢cy apon me, geue ftrengthe vnto thy feruanute, and preferve the fonne of thye handmaiden.
Shew fome token of thy loue towarde me that my enemyes may fe and be

But Thou, oh Lord God, are merciful and good, slow unto wrath, but marvelous prone unto kindness and keeping of Thy promises. **B**ehold me and have mercy upon me. Give strength unto Thy servant, and preserve the son of Thy handmaiden.
Show some token of Thy love toward me that my enemies may see and be

Folio 101r

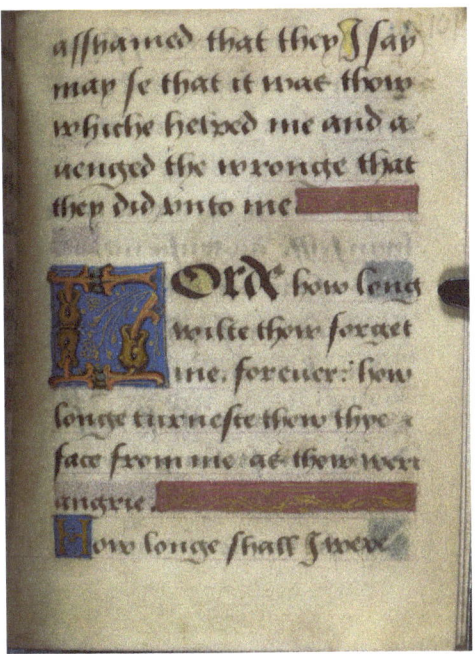

affhamed that they (J fay) may fe that it was thow whiche helped me and a/ uenged the wrong that they did vnto me.

L**Orde** how long wilte thow forget me. foreuer? how longe turnefte thow thye x face from me as thow wert angrie.
How longe fhall J wepe

ashamed that they, I say, may see that it was Thou which helped me and a- venged the wrong that they did unto me.

L**ord**, how long will Thou forget me? Forever? How long turn Thou Thy face from me as [though] Thou were angry?
How long shall I weep

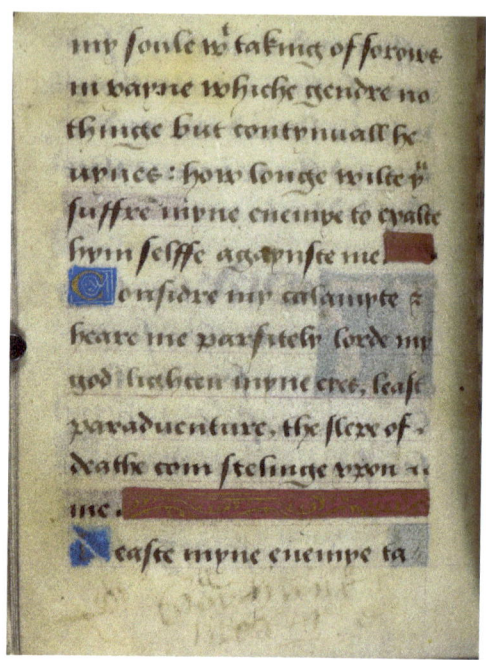

my foule wt taking of forows
in vayne whiche gendre no//
thinge but contynuall he//
uynes: how longe wilte yu
fuffre myne enemye to exalte
hym felffe agaynste me.
Confidre my calamyte &
heare me parfitely lorde my
god lighten myne eyes, leaft
paraduenture, the flepe of
deathe com ftelinge vpon
me.
Leafte myne enemye ta//

my soul with taking of sorrows
in vain which engender nothing but continual he-
aviness? How long will Thou
suffer my enemy to exalt
himself against me?
Consider my calamity and
hear me perfectly, Lord my
God. Enlighten my eyes lest
peradventure the sleep of
death come stealing upon
me,
Lest my enemy ta-

N.B. Additional writing added in later centuries by a differnt hand is faintly visible in the lower margin of this page, but it is largely illegible.

kinge courage, faye: J haue
ouercom hym and my ene//
myes reioife if J myfcarie
As for me J haue put all
my trufte in thye goodnes/
wherefore J doubte not but
the tyme fhall com that my
harte fhall reioyfe for the hea//
lthe that thow hafte brought
me and that I fhall haue oc
cafion, to finge the prayfes
of the lorde when he fhall x
haue auenged the wronge y^t

king courage, say, "I have
overcome him and my ene-
mies rejoice if I miscarry."
As for me, I have put all
my trust in Thy goodness,
therefore I doubt not but [that]
the time shall come that my
heart shall rejoice for the health that Thou have brought
me, and that I shall have occasion to sing the praises
of the Lord when He shall
have avenged the wrong that

Folio 102v

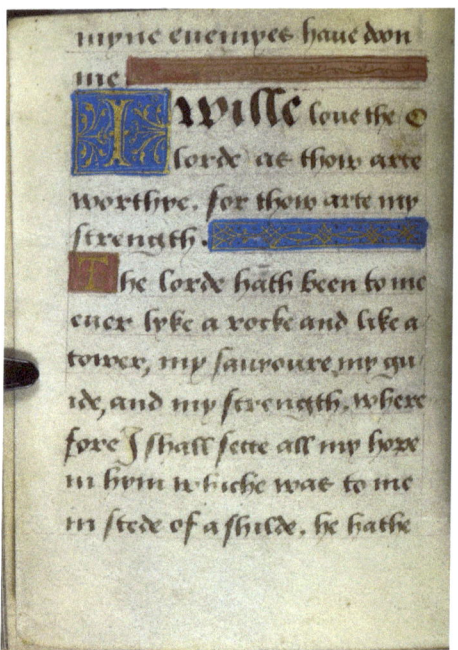

myne enemyes haue doon me.

I wille loue the (O lorde) as thow arte worthy, for thow arte my ſtrength.

The lorde hathe been to me euer lyke a rocke and like a// tower, my ſauyoure, my gu// ide, and my ſtrength, wher// for J ſhall lette all my hope in hym whiche was to me in ſtede of a ſhilde. he hathe

my enemies have done me.

I will love Thee, oh Lord, as Thou are worthy, for Thou are my strength.

The Lord has been to me ever like a rock and like a tower, my Savior, my gu-ide, and my strength, there-fore I shall let* all my hope in Him, which was to me instead of a shield. He has

* to leave undisturbed, to allow to remain

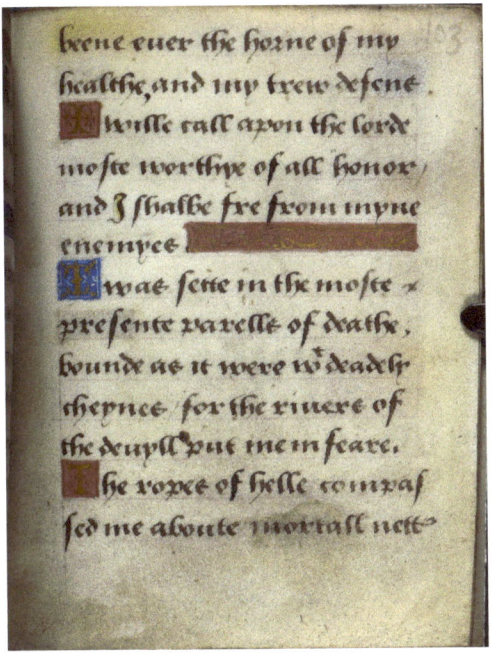

been euer the horne of my
health, and my trew defens
I wille call apon the lorde
moſte worthye of all honor/
and J ſhalbe fre from myne
enemyes.
I was ſette in the moſte x
preſente parelles of deathe,
bounde as it were w^t deadely
cheynes/ for the riuers of
the deuyll put me in feare.
T he ropes of helle compaſ
ſed me aboute mortall nett

been ever the horn of my
health and my true defense.
I will call upon the Lord,
most worthy of all honor,
and I shall be free from my
enemies.
I was set in the most
present perils of death,
bound as it were with deadly
chains, for the rivers of
the Devil put me in fear.
T he ropes of Hell compas-
sed* me about; [a] mortal net

* surrounded, encircled, enclosed

Folio 103v

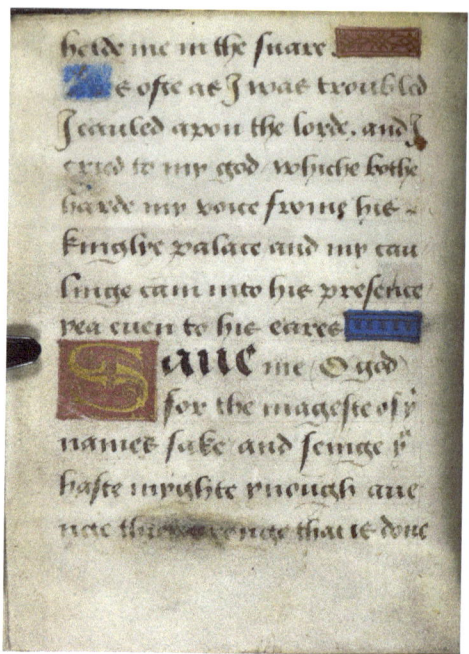

helde me in the fnare.
As ofte as J was troubled
J cauled apon the lorde and J
cried to my god/ whiche bothe
harde my voice frome his x
kinglye palace/ and my cau//
linge cãm into his prefence/
yea euen to his eares
Saue me(o god)
for the magefte of y^i
names fake/ and feinge y^u
hafte myghte ynough aue
nge this wronge that is done

held me in the snare.
As often as I was troubled,
I called upon the Lord and I
cried to my God, which both
heard my voice from His
kingly palace, and my calling came into His presence,
yea, even to His ears.
Save me, oh God,
for the majesty of Thy
name's sake. And seeing [that] Thou
have might enough, ave-
nge this wrong that is done

Folio 104r

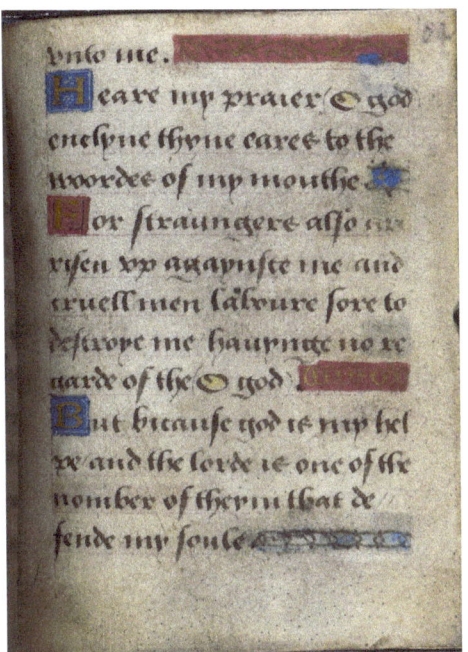

vnto me.

Heare my praier (o god) enclyne thine eares to the woordes of my mouthe

For ftraungers alfo are rifen vp agaynfte me and cruell men laboure fore to deftroye me hauynge no regarde of the (o god).

But bicuafe god is my helpe/ and the lorde is one of the nomber of theym that de// fende my foule.

unto me.

Hear my prayer, oh God. Incline Thine ears to the words of my mouth,

For strangers also are risen up against me, and cruel men labor sore to destroy me, having no regard of Thee, oh God.

But because God is my help, and the Lord is one of the number of them that defend my soul.

Folio 104v

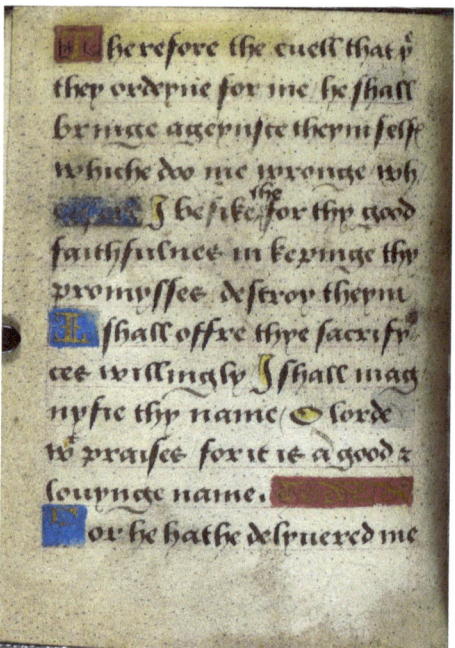

Therefore the euell that yᵉ
they ordeyne for me/ he fhall
brynge ageynfte theym felf₍ₑ₎
whiche doo me wronge/ wh//
erfore J befike for thy good
faithfulnes in kepinge thy
promyffes/ deftroy theym
　I fhall offre thye facrify//
ces willingly J fhall mag//
nyfie thy name (O lorde)
wᵗ praifes/ for it is a good &
louynge name.
　F or he hathe delyuered me

Therefore the evil that the*
they ordain for me, He shall
bring against themselves,
which do me wrong. Th-
erefore I beseech Thee for Thy good
faithfulness in keeping Thy
promises, destroy them.
　I shall offer Thy sacrifices willingly. I shall magnify Thy name, oh Lord,
with praises, for it is a good and
loving name.
　F or He has delivered me

* The scribe appears to have mistakenly added an extraneous "the" to the text.

Folio 105r

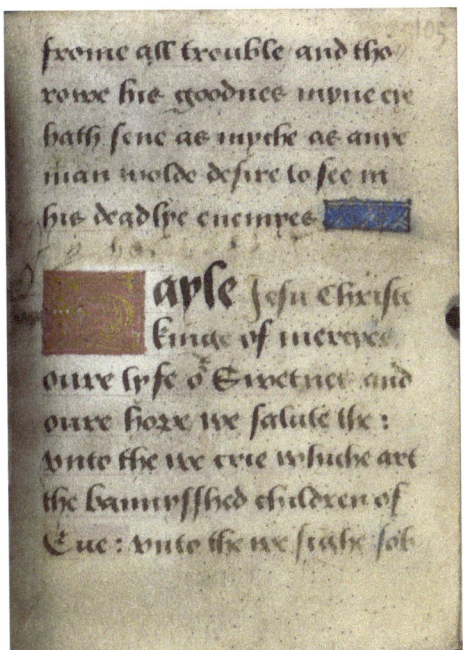

frome all trouble/ and tho//
rowe his goodnes myne eye
hathe ſene as myche as anye
man wolde deſire to ſee in
his deadlye enemyes.

Hayle Jeſu Chriſte
kinge of mercyes
oure lyfe oᣴ Swetenes and
oure hope/ we ſalute the:
vnto the we crie whiche art
the bannyſſhed children of
Eue: vnto the we figh ſob//

Hail, Jesus Christ,
king of mercies,
our life, our sweetness, and
our hope. We salute Thee.
Unto Thee we cry, which are
the banished children of
Eve. Unto Thee we sigh sob-

from all trouble, and th-
rough His goodness my eye
has seen as much as any
man would desire to see in
his deadly enemies.

* Writing in a different and later hand has again been added to the page, in this instance
between the two prayers, and is again illegible.

binge and wepinge in xx
this vaile of wretchednes
haſte the therefore oʳ med//
atoure: turne vnto vs x
thoſe thy mercyful eyes.
O Jeſu all prayſe worthy
ſhew vs the preſence of yⁱ
father after this outelaw//
rye. O gentle, O mercy//
full O ſwete Jeſu Chriſte
Jn all oure trouble and
heuynes O Jeſu oʳ healthe
& glorie ſocoure vs
      Amen
	bing and weeping in
	this veil of wretchedess.
	Hasten Thee therefore, our med-
	iator. Turn unto us
	those Thy merciful eyes.
	Oh Jesus, all praiseworthy,
	show us the presence of Thy
	Father after this outlaw-
	ry. Oh gentle, oh merci-
	ful, oh sweet Jesus Christ,
	in all our trouble and
	heaviness, oh Jesus, our health
	and glory, succor us.
	      Amen.

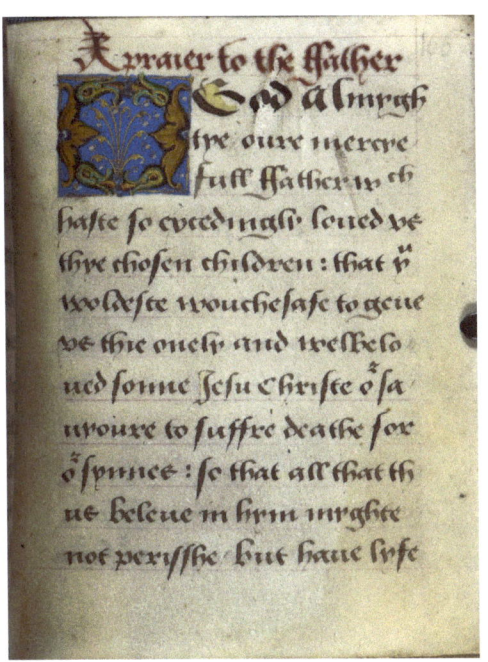

A praier to the ffather

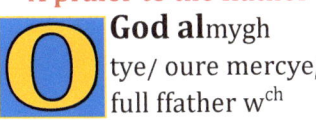

God almygh
tye/ oure mercye//
full ffather w^{ch}
haſte ſo exceedingly loued vs
thye choſen children: that y^u
woldeſte wouchſafe to geue
vs thie onelye and welbe//
loued ſonne Jeſu Chriſte o^r ſa/
uyoure to ſuffre deathe for
o^r ſynnes: ſo that all that th
us beleue in hym myghte
not periſſhe/ but haue lyfe

A prayer to the Father

God Almigh-
ty, our merci-
ful Father which
has so exceedingly loved us,
Thy chosen children, that Thou
would vouchsafe to give
us Thy only and well-be-
loved Son, Jesus Christ our Savior, to suffer death for
our sins, so that all that thus believe in Him might
not perish, but have life

Folio 106v

euerlaftine: We befiche
the for thye abountaunte
mercye/ and for that inefty
mable loue/ which thow
barefte to thy fonne Chrifte
oure fauyoure, Geue vs of
thye grace/ and power thy
fauoure into o^r hartes, that
we may beleue. feale and x
knowe parfitely that thow
onelye arte o^r god, o^r father &
to vs an almyghtye helper,
delyuerer, and a fauyo^r from

everlasting. We beseech
Thee for Thy abundant
mercy, and for that inestimable love which Thou
bear to Thy Son Christ
our Savior, give us of
Thy grace, and pour Thy
favor into our hearts, that
we may believe. Feel and
know perfectly that Thou
only are our God, our Father, and
to us an almighty helper,
deliverer, and savior from

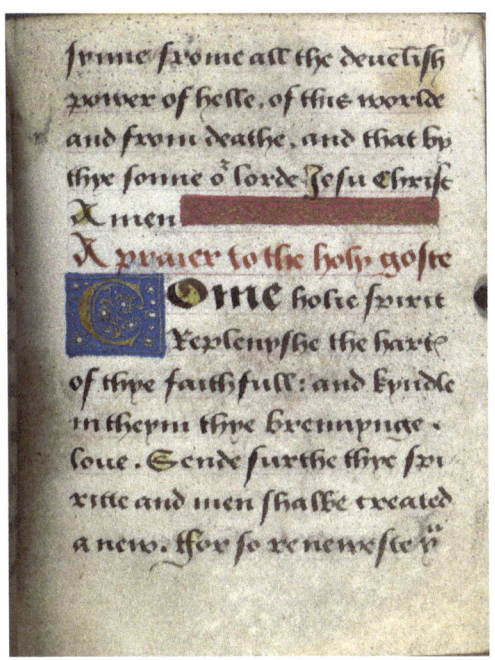

ſynne/ frome all the deueliſh power of helle, of this worlde and from deathe, and that by thye ſonne o^r lorde Jeſu Chriſt Amen

A praier to the holy goſte

Ome holie ſpirit Replenyſhe the hart*ℓ* of thye faithfull: and kyndle in theym thye brennynge x loue. Sende furthe thy ſpi// ritte and men ſhalbe created a new. ffor ſo renewſte y^u

sin, from all the devilish power of Hell, of this world, and from death, and that by Thy Son our Lord Jesus Christ. Amen.

A prayer to the Holy Ghost

Ome Holy Spirit, replenish the hearts of Thy faithful, and kindle in them Thy burning love. Send forth Thy spirit and men shall be created anew, for so renew Thou

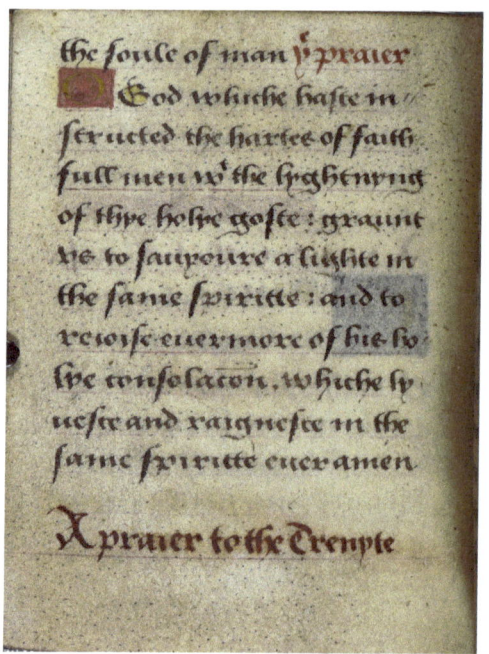

the foule of man y^e praier
🟧God whiche hafte in//
ftructed the hartes of faith//
full men w^t the lyghtnyng
of thye holye gofte: graunt
vs to favyoure a light in
the fame fpiritte: and to
reioice euermore for his ho//
lye confolacõn, which ly
uefte and raignefte in the
fame fpiritte euer amen

A praier to the Trenyte

the soul of man the prayer.
🟧h God which has in-
structed the hearts of faithful men with the lightening*
of Thy Holy Ghost, grant
us to favor a light in
the same spirit, and to
rejoice evermore for his holy consolation, which li-
ves and reigns in the
same spirit ever. Amen.

A prayer to the Trinity

* enlightenment

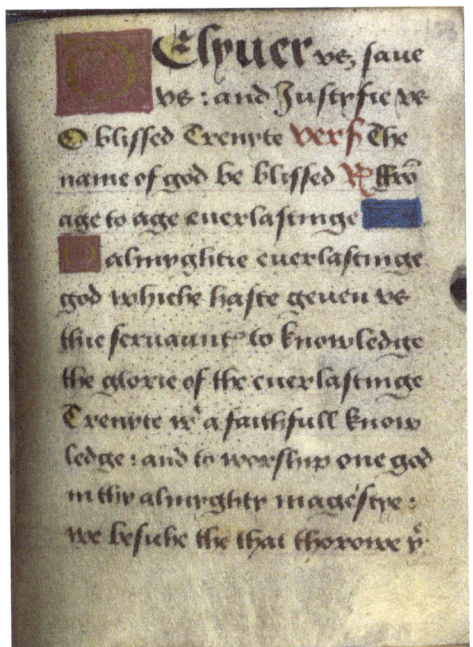

D**Elyuer** vs, ſaue
vs: and Juſtyfie vs
O blyſſed Trenyte **Verſ** The
name of god be bliſſed **R**ℓ ffrõ
age to age euerlaſtinge
O almyghtie euerlasſtinge
god whiche haſte geuen vs
thie ſeruaunt‿ to knowledge
the glorie of the euerlaſtinge
Trenyte wᵗ a faithfull know
ledge: and to worſhip one god
in thy almyghty mageſtye:
we beſiche the that thorowe yᵉ

D**Eliver** us, save
us, and justify us,
oh blessed Trinity. **Verse:*** The
name of God be blessed. **Response:**† From
age to age everlasting.
Oh almighty, everlasting
God which has given us,
Thy servants, to acknowledge
the glory of the everlasting
Trinity with a faithful knowledge, and to worship on God
in Thy almighty majesty,
we beseech Thee that through the

* "Verse" indicates a phrase to be uttered by the celebrant of a Roman Catholic Mass or by the priest/preacher in a reform worship service.
† The "Response" is voiced by the congregation in answer to the Verse.

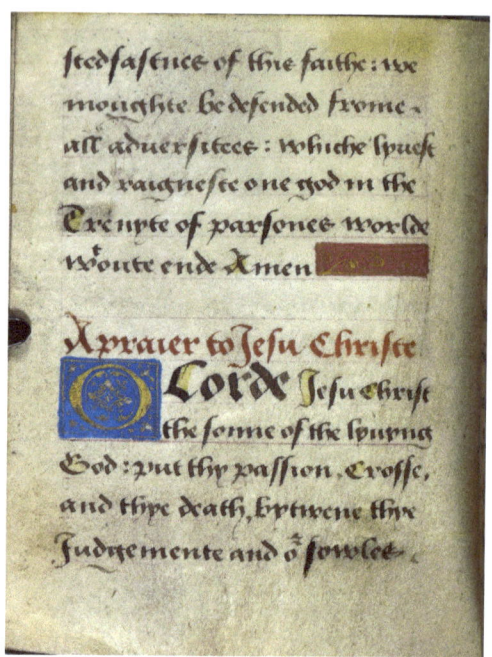

ſtedfaſtnes of thie faithe: we
moughte be defended frome x
all adverſitees: whiche lyueſt
and raigneſte one god in the
Trenyte of parſones worlde
w^toute ende Amen

A praier to Jeſu Chriſte

O Lorde Jeſu Chriſt
The ſonne of the lyuyng
God: put thy paſſion, Croſſe,
and thye death, bytwene thye
Judgemente and o^r ſowles

steadfastness of Thy faith, we
might be defended from
all adversities, which lives
and reigns, one God in the
Trinity of persons, world
without end. Amen.

A prayer to Jesus Christ

O Lord Jesus Christ,
the son of the living
God, put Thy Passion, Cross,
and Thy death between Thy
judgment and our souls,

nowe and in the owre of deathe
and graunte vs whilles we
lyue mercye and grace to them
that departe forgeuenes and x
refte: vnto thy holy churche xx
geue peace and concorde and to
vs that are fynners lyfe and x
euerlaftinge glorie whiche ly∥
uefte and reignefte wᵗ the father
and wᵗ the holye gofte euer

The Glorious Paffion of oʳ
lorde Jefu Chrifte/ delyuer vs
frome forowfull heuynes and

Folio 109v

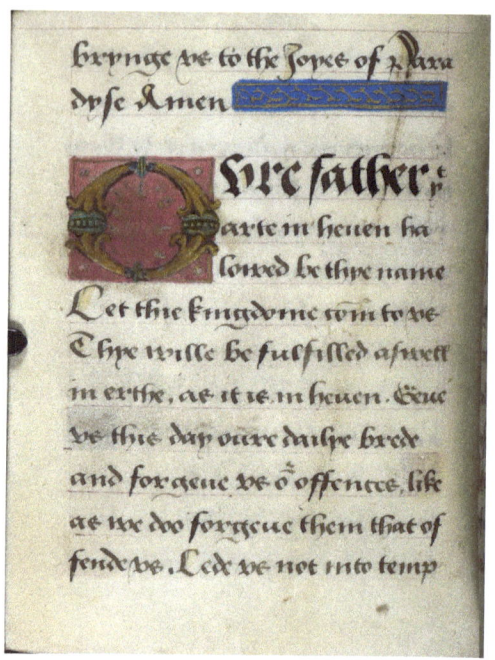

brynge vs to the Joyes of Para
dyſe Amen

Oure father yᵗ
arte in heuen ha//
lowed be thye name
Let thie kingdome cõm to vs
Thye wille be fulfilled aſwell
in erthe, as it is in heuen. Geue
vs this day oure dailye brede
and forgeue vs oʳ offences, like
as we doo forgeue them that of
fende vs. Lede vs not into temp/

bring us the joys of Para-
dise. Amen.

Our Father that
is in heaven, ha-
llowed be Thy name.
Let Thy Kingdom come to us.
Thy will be fulfilled as well
in Earth as it is in Heaven. Give
us this day our daily bread,
and forgive us our offenses, like
as we do forgive them that offend us. Lead us not into temp-

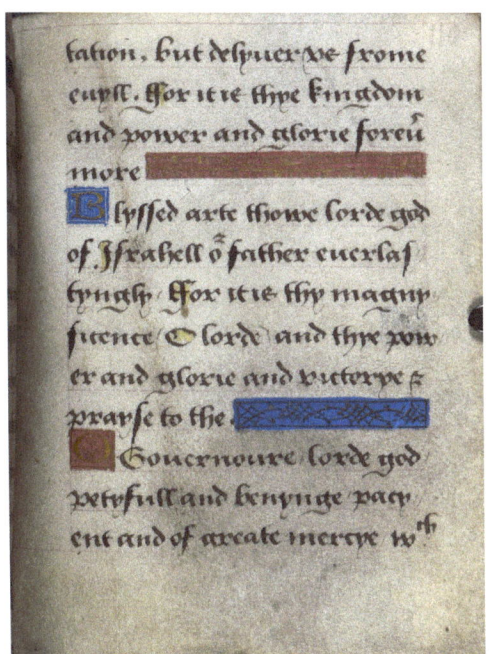

tation, but delyuer vs frome
euyll. ffor it is thye kingdom
and power and glorie foreu^r
more

Blyffed arte thow lorde god
of Jfrahell o^r father euerlaf//
tyngly/ ffor it is thy magny//
ficence (O lorde) and thy pow//
er and glorie and victorye &
prayfe to the.

O Gouernoure/ lorde god/
petyfull and benygne/ pacy//
ent and of greate mercye/ w^{ch}

taion, but deliver us from
evil, for it is Thy Kingdom
and power and glory forever
more.

Blessed are Thou, Lord God
of Israel, our Father everlastingly, for it is Thy magni-
ficence, oh Lord, and Thy power and glory and victory, and praise
to Thee.

Oh Governor, Lord God,
pitiful and benign, pati-
ent, and of great mercy, which

doefte extende thy mercye vnto thowfandes/ whiche takeft away wickednes/ myfchefe and fynne/ and none of hym felffe is inno// cente before the. J befiche the y^t thow wilte take away oure xx wickednes and fynne

I befiche the lorde god of he// uen/ ftronge/ myghty and ter// rible/ whiche kepefte conue// naunte and mercie w^t fuche as loue the and obferue thye commaundement₽. Let thyn

do extend Thy mercy unto thousands, which takes away wickedness, mischief and sin, and none of himself is inno- cent before Thee, I beseech Thee that Thou will take away our wickedness and sin.

I beseech Thee Lord God of He- aven, strong, mighty, and ter- rible, which keeps cove- nant and mercy with such as love Thee and observe Thy commandments, let Thy

eares be harkenynge/ and y{i}
eyes open that thow mayeſte x
here the prayer of thye ſ{u}ant
O lorde whiche arte pacient
and of greate mercie and ta//
keſte away o{r} Inyquyte & myſc//
cheife, forgeue (J beſiche the)
the fynne of this thy people af//
ter the gretnes of thye m{r}cy
L orde god, do not deſtroye y{i}
people/ and thyne enheritãnce
whiche thow haſte boughte thr//
ough thye power

ears be harkening and Thy
eye open that Thou may
hear the prayer of Thy servant.
O h Lord, which is patient
and of great mercy and take away our iniquities and mischief, forgive, I beseech Thee,
the sin of this Thy people after the greatness of Thy mercy.
L ord God, do not destroy Thy
people and Thine inheritance
which Thou have brought through Thy power

Folio 111v

Thow hafte beene guyde in thye mercye to the people which thowe hafte redemed.
Forgeue thow thye people though they be fynners, for y^u arte my god. Let thyne eyes (J befiche the) be open and thyne eares intentyffe vnto the prayer that is made in this place
O lorde thow arte o^r father and we are but claye thow arte our creatoure and all we but the work$_\ell$ of thyne handes (O lorde)

Thou have been [a] guide in Thy mercy to the people which Thou have redeemed.
Forgive Thou Thy people though they be sinners, for Thou are my God. Let Thine eyes, I beseech Thee, be open and Thine ear intent unto the prayer that is made in this place.
Oh Lord, Thou are our Father, and we are but clay. Thou are our Creator and all we but the works of Thine hands, oh Lord.

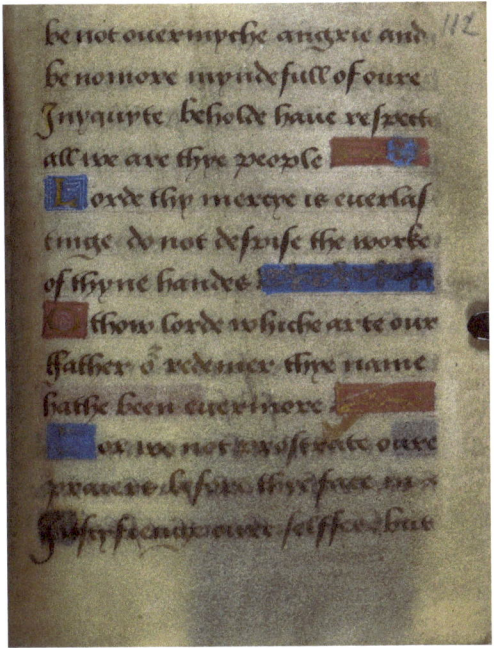

be not overmyche angrie and
be nomore myndefull of oure
Jnyquyte/ beholde haue respecte
all we are thye people.
Lorde thy mercye is euerlas//
tinge/ do not despise the worke
of thyne handes.
O thow lorde whiche arte our
ffather/ oʳ redemer/ thye name
hathe been euermore.
F or we not prostrate oure
praiers before thye face in x
Juſtyfienge oure ſelffes, but

be not overmuch angry, and
be no more mindful of our
iniquity. Behold, have respect;
all we are Thy people.
Lord, Thy mercy is everlasting. Do not despise the work
of Thine hands.
Oh Thou, Lord, which are our
Father, our Redeemer, Thy name
has been evermore,
For we not prostrate our
prayers before Thy face in
justifying ourselves, but

in trufte of the grete mercye/ her//
ken lorde/ be pleafed/ oh lorde at//
tende/ and doo/ be not flakke (my
god) for thyne owne fake/ for y^i
name hathe been cauled vpon
this Cetye and vpon the people.
Lorde god here the clamoure
of this people and open vnto x
them thie treafure/ the well of
the water of lyfe
Let all that knowe thye nãm
lorde trufte in the for thow hafte
not forfaken them that feke y^e

in trust of the great mercy. Harken, Lord, be pleased. Oh Lord, at-
tend, and do. Be not slack, my
God, for Thine own sake, for Thy
name has been called upon
this city and upon the people.
Lord God, hear the clamour
of this people and open unto
them Thy treasure, the well of
the water of life.
Let all that know Thy name,
Lord, trust in Thee, for Thou have
not forsaken them that seek Thee.

Folio 113r

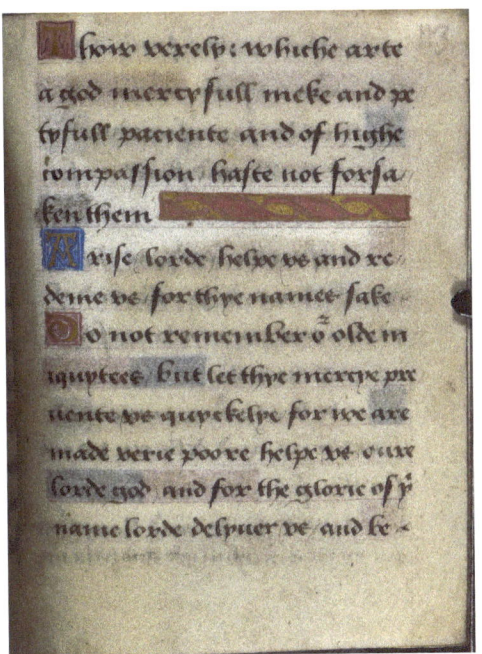

Thow verely: whiche arte
a god mercyfull meke and pe//
tyfull/paciente and of highe
compaffion/ hafte not forfa//
ken them
Arife (lorde) helpe vs and re//
deme vs/ for thye names fake
Do not remember oʳ olde in//
iquytees/ but let thye mercye pre//
uente vs quyckelye / for we are
made verie poore helpe vs (oure
lorde god) and for the glorie of yⁱ
name lorde delyuer vs/ and be x

Thou verily, which are
a God merciful, meek, and pitiful, patient, and of high
compassion, have not forsaken them.
Arise, Lord, help us and redeem us, for Thy name's sake.
Do not remember our old iniquities, but let Thy mercy prevent us quickly, for we are
made very poor. Help us, our
Lord God, and for the glory of Thy
name, Lord, deliver us, and be

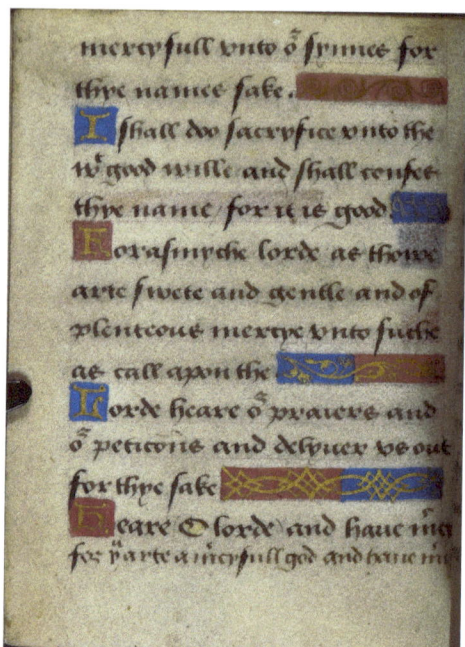

mercyfull vnto o^r fynnes for
thye names sake.
I fhall doo facryfice vnto the
w^t good wille/ and fhall confes
thye name/ for it is good.
F orafmyche lorde as thowe
arte fwete and gentle and of
plenteous mercye vnto fuche
as call apon the
L orde heare o^r praiers and
o^r peticõns and delyuer vs out
for thye fake
H eare (O lorde) and haue m^{r}ci
for y^u arte a m^{r}cyfull god and haue m^{r}cy

merciful unto our sins for
Thy name's sake.
I shall do sacrifices unto Thee
with good will and shall confess
Thy name, for it is good,
F orasmuch, Lord, as Thou
are sweet and gentle and of
plenteous mercy unto such
as call upon Thee.
L ord hear our prayers and
our petitions and deliver is out
for Thy sake.
H ear, oh Lord, and have mercy,
for Thou are a merciful God and have mercy

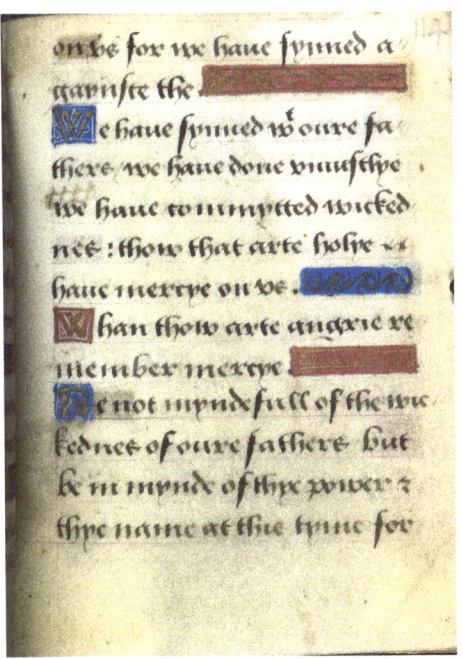

on vs for we haue ſynned a//
gaynſte the.

We haue ſynned wᵗ oure fa//
thers/ we haue done vniuſtlye
we haue commytted wicked//
nes: thow that arte holye xx
haue mercye on vs.

Whan thow arte angrie re//
member mercye.

Be not myndefull of the wic//
kednes of oure fathers/ but
be in mynde of thye power &
thye name at thie tyme for

on us, for we have sinned a-
gainst Thee.

We have sinned with our fathers. We have done unjustly.
We have committed wicked-
ness. Thou are holy;
have mercy on us.

When Thou are angry, remember mercy.

Be not mindful of the wick-
kedness of our fathers, but
be in mind of Thy power and
Thy name at Thy time, for

Folio 114v

thow arte oure lorde god.
Let albe gladde that trufte
in the/ they fhall reioyfe euer//
more and thow fhalte dwell
in them/ and all that loue y^i
name fhall glorie in the
Thow arte rightwis (O lorde)
and all thye Jugement$_\ell$ are
trew and all thye waies m^{r}cy
treuth & Jugemente.
Blyffed is thye name O god
of o^r fathers whiche in thye xx
wrathe doefte fhew mercye &

Thou are our Lord God.
Let all be glad that trust
in Thee. They shall rejoice evermore, and Thou shall dwell
in them, and all that love Thy
name shall glory in Thee.
Thou are righteous, oh Lord,
and all Thy judgments are
true, and all Thy ways mercy,
truth, and judgment.
Blessed is Thy name, oh God
of our fathers, which in Thy
wrath do show mercy and

Folio 115r

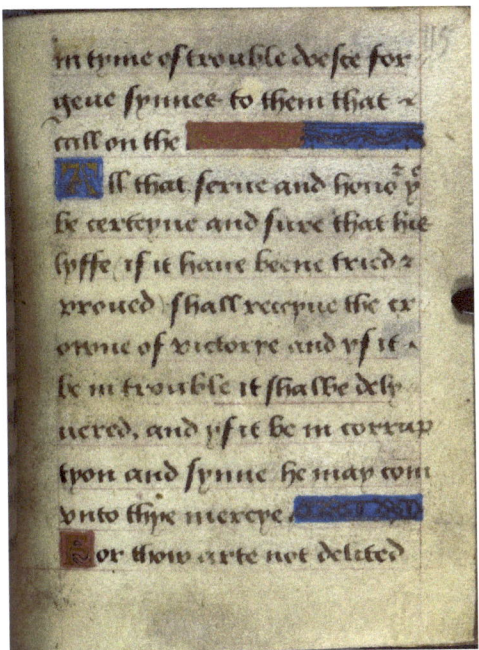

in tyme of trouble doeſte for//
geue ſynnes to them that x
call on the
All that ſerue and honor yͤ
be certeyne and ſure that his
lyffe (if it haue beene tried &
proued) ſhall receyue the cr//
owne of victorye and yf it x
be in trouble it ſhalbe dely//
uered, and yf it be in corrup/
tyon and ſynne he may com
vnto thye mercye.
For thow arte not delited

in time of trouble do forgive sins to them that
call on Thee.
All that serve and honor Thee
be certain and sure that his
life, if it have been tried and proved,
shall receive the cr-
own of victory, and if it
be in trouble it shall be delivered, and if it be in corrup-
tion and sin he may come
unto Thy mercy,
For Thou are not delighted

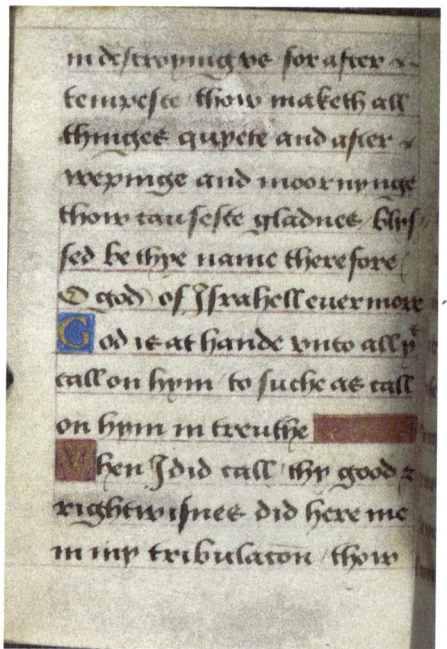

in deſtroying vs/ for after x
tempeſte/ thow maketh all
thinges quyete and after x
wepinge and moornynge
thow cauſeſte gladnes/ blyſ//
ſed be thye name therefore (
O god) of Jſrahell euermore
God is at hande vnto all yt
call on hym/ to fuche as call
on hym in treuthe
When J did call thy good &
rightwiſnes did here me
in my tribulacõn/ thow

in destroying us, for after [the]
tempest Thou make all
things quiet, and after
weeping and mourning
Thou cause gladness. Blessed be Thy name therefore,
oh God of Israel, evermore.
God is at hand unto all that
call upon Him, to such as call
on Him in truth.
When I did call Thy good and
righteousness, [Thou] did hear me
in my tribulation. Thou

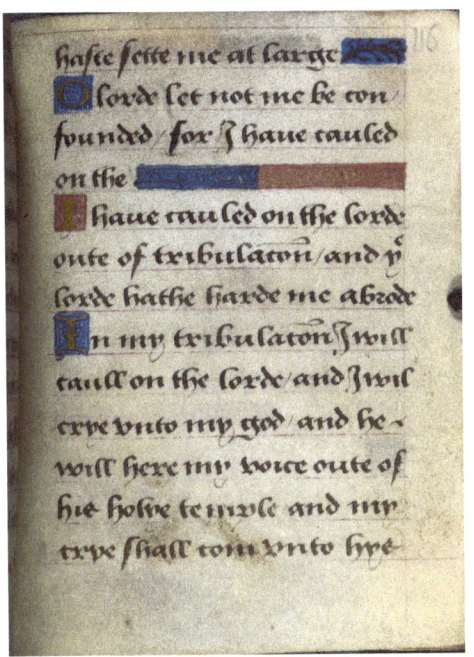

haſte ſette me at large
O lorde let me not be con//
founded for J haue cauled
on the.

I haue cauled on the lorde
oute of tribulacõn/ and yᵉ
lorde hathe harde me abrode

In my tribulacõn J will
caul on the lorde/ and J will
crye vnto my god/ and he x
will here my voice oute of
his holye temple/ and my
crye ſhall com vnto hys

have set me at large.
Oh Lord, let me not be confounded, for I have called
on Thee.

I have called on the Lord
out of tribulation, and the
Lord has heard me abroad.

In my tribulation I will
call on the Lord, and I will
cry unto my God, and He
will hear my voice out of
His holy temple, and my
cry shall come unto His

Folio 116v

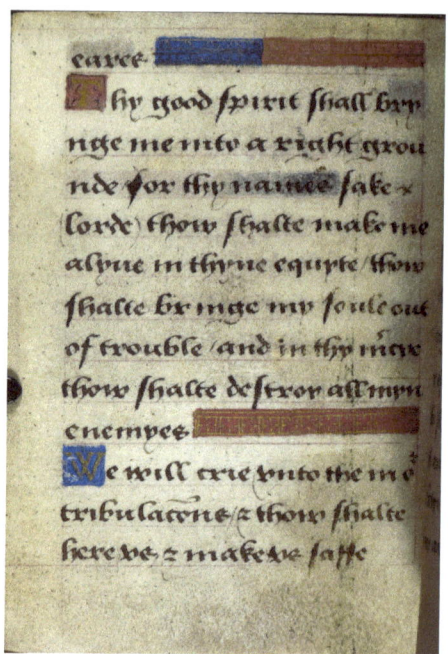

eares
Thy good ſpirit ſhall bry
nge me into a right grou
nde for thy names ſake x
(lorde) thow ſhalt make me
alyue in thyne equyte/ thow
ſhalte bringe my ſoule out
of trouble/ and in thy m͡rcye
thow ſhalte deſtroy all myn
enemyes
We will crie vnto the in o͞r
tribulacõns/ & thow ſhalte
here vs & make vs ſaffe

ears.
Thy good spirit shall bring me into a right grou-
nd* for Thy name's sake,
Lord. Thou shall make me
alive in Thine equity. Thou
shall bring my soul out
of trouble, and in Thy mercy
Thou shall destroy all my
enemies.
We will cry unto Thee in our
tribulations, and Thou shall
hear us and make us safe.

* path or footing

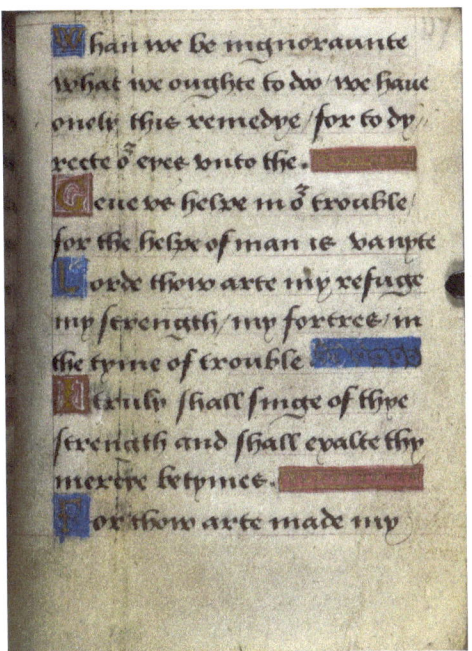

Whan we be ingnoraunte
what we oughte to doo/ we haue
onely this remedye/ for to dy//
recte oʳ eyes vnto the.
Geue vs helpe in oʳ trouble/
for the helpe of man is vanyte
Lorde thow arte my refuge
my ſtrength/ my fortres/ in
the tyme of trouble.
I truly ſhall fynge of thye
ſtrength and ſhall exalte thy
mercye betymes.
For thow arte made my

When we be ignorant [of]
what we ought to do, we have
only this remedy: for to direct our eyes unto Thee.
Give us help in our trouble,
for the help of man is vanity.
Lord, Thou are my refuge,
my strength, my fortress in
the time of trouble.
I truly shall sing of Thy
strength and shall exalt Thy
mercy betimes,*
For Thou are made my

* forthwith, immediately

Folio 117v

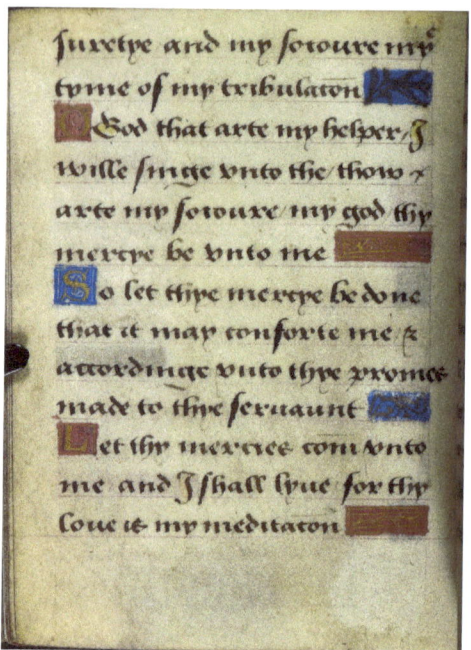

ſuretye and my ſucoure in yᵉ
tyme of my tribulacõn
O God that arte my helper/ J
wille ſynge vnto the/ thow ˣ
arte my ſucoure (my god) thy
mercye be vnto me
S o let thye mercye be done
that it may conforte me/ &
accordinge vnto thye promes
made to thye ſeruaunt
L et thy mercye com vnto
me/ and J ſhall lyue/ for thy
loue is my meditacõn

surety and my succor in the
time of my tribulation.
O h God that is my helper, I
will sing unto Thee. Thou
are my succor, my God, Thy
mercy be unto me.
S o let Thy mercy be done
that it may comfort me,
and according to the promise
made to Thy servant.
L et Thy mercy come unto
me, and I shall live, for Thy
love is my meditation.

Folio 118r

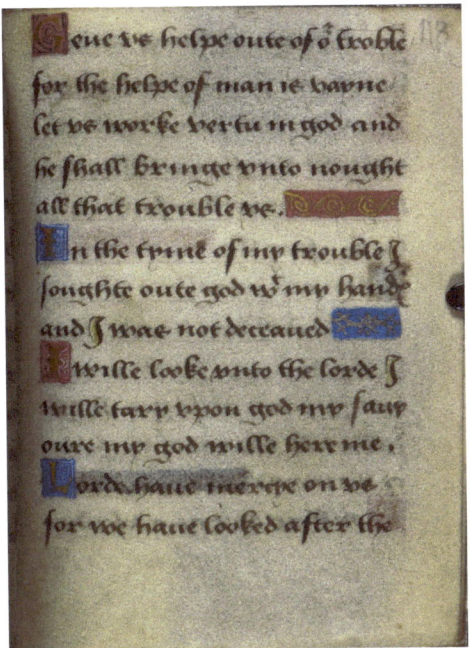

Geue vs helpe oute of oʳ troble/
for the helpe of man is vayne/
let vs worke vertu in god/ and
he ſhall bringe vnto nought
all that trouble vs.
In the tyme of my trouble J
foughte oute god wᵗ my handₑ
and J was not deceaued
I wille looke vnto the lorde J
will tary vpon god my ſauy
oure my god wille here me.
Lorde haue mercye on vs/
for we haue looked after the

Give us help out of our trouble,
for the help of man is vain.
Let us work virtue in God, and
He shall bring unto naught
all that troubles us.
In the time of my trouble I
sought out God with my hands,
and I was not deceived.
I will look unto the Lord. I
will tarry upon God my Savi-
or. My God will hear me.
Lord have mercy on us,
for we have looked after Thee.

Folio 118v

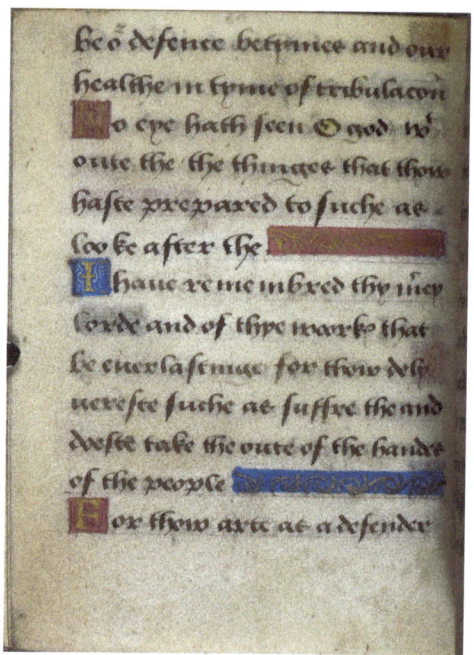

be oʳ defence betymes and our
healthe in tyme of tribulacõn
No eye hathe feen (O god) wᵗ
oute the/ the things that thow
hafte prepared to fuche as
looke after the.
I haue remembred thy mʳcye
lorde and of thye woorkₑ that
be euerlaftinge for thow dely//
uerfte fuche as fuffre the and
doefte take the oute of the handes
of the people
For thow arte as a defender

be our defense betimes* and our
health in time of tribulation.
No eye has seen, oh God, with-
out Thee the things that Thou
have prepared to such as
look after me.
I have remembered Thy mercy,
Lord, and of Thy works that
be everlasting, for Thou deli-
ver such as suffer Thee, and
do take Thee out of the hands
of the people,
For Thou are as a defender

* in due course (here used differently than on Folio 117r)

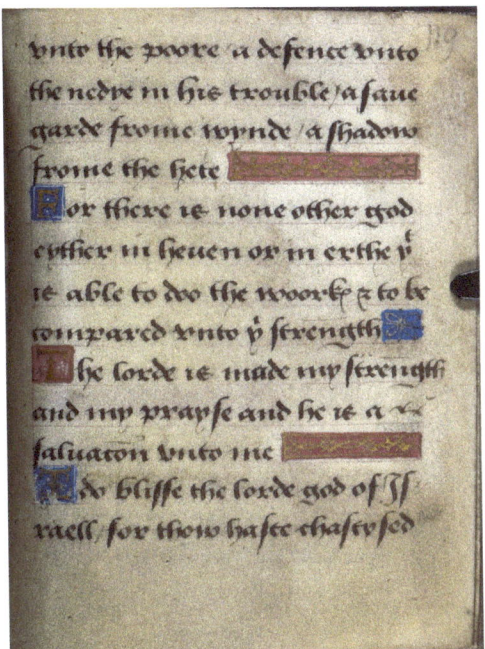

vnto the poore/ a defence vnto
the nedye in his trouble/ a ſaue
guarde frome wynde/ a ſhadow
frome the hete

For there is none other god
eyther in heuen or in erthe y^t
is able to doo the woorkₑ & to be
compared vnto y^i ſtrength

The lorde is made my ſtrength
and my prayſe and he is a xx
ſaluacõn vnto me

I do bliſſe the lorde god of Jſ//
raell/ for thow haſte chaſtyſed

unto the poor, a defense unto
the needy in his trouble, a safeguard from wind, a shadow
from the heat.

For there is none other God,
either in Heaven or in Earth, that
is able to do the works and to be
compared unto Thy strength.

The Lord is made my strength
and my praise, and He is a
savlation unto me.

I do bless the Lord God of Israel, for Thou have chastised

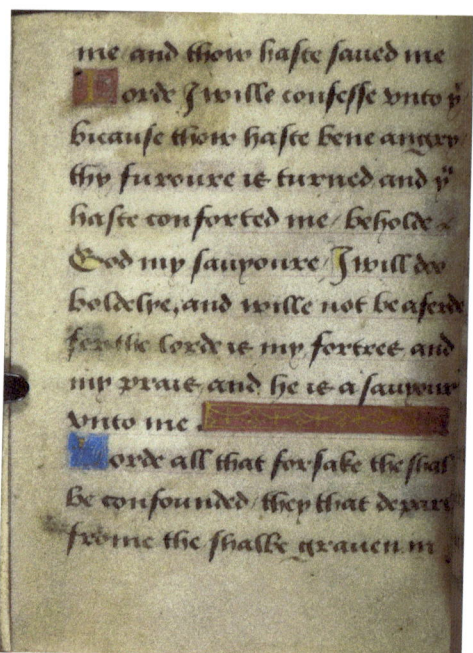

me/ and thow hafte faued me
Lorde J wille confeffe vnto y^e/
bicaufe thow hafte bene angry/
thy furoure is turned/ and y^u
hafte conforted me/ beholde x
God my fauyoure/ J will doo
boldelye, and wille not be afered
for the lorde is my fortres/ and
my prais/ and he is a fauyour
vnto me.
Lorde all that forfake the fhal
be confounded/ they that depart
frome the/ fhalbe grauen in

me, and Thou have saved me.
Lord, I will confess unto Thee
because Thou have been angry.
Thy furor is turned, and Thou
have comforted me. Behold,
God my Savior, I will do
boldly, and will not be afraid,
for the Lord is my fortress and
my praise, and He is a Savior
unto me.
Lord, all that forsake Thee shall
be confounded. They that depart
from Thee shall be graven* in

* buried

Folio 120r

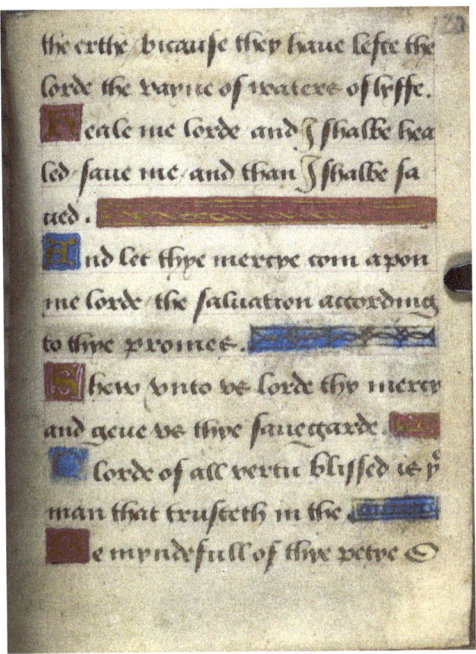

the erthe/ bicaufe they haue lefte the lorde the rayne of waters of lyffe.

Heale me lorde/ and J fhalbe healed/ faue me/ and than J fhalbe fa// ued.

And let thye mercye com apon me lorde/ the faluation according to thye promes.

Shew vnto vs lorde thy mercy and geue vs thye fauegarde.

O lorde of all vertu bliffed is yᵉ man that trufteth in the.

Be myndefull of thye petye O

the Earth because they have left the Lord, the rain of the waters of life.

Heal me, Lord, and I shall be healed. Save me, and then I shall be saved.

And let Thy mercy come upon me, Lord, the salvation according to Thy promise.

Show unto us, Lord, Thy mercy and give us Thy safeguard.

Oh Lord of all virtue, blessed is the man that trusts in Thee.

Be mindful of Thy pity, oh

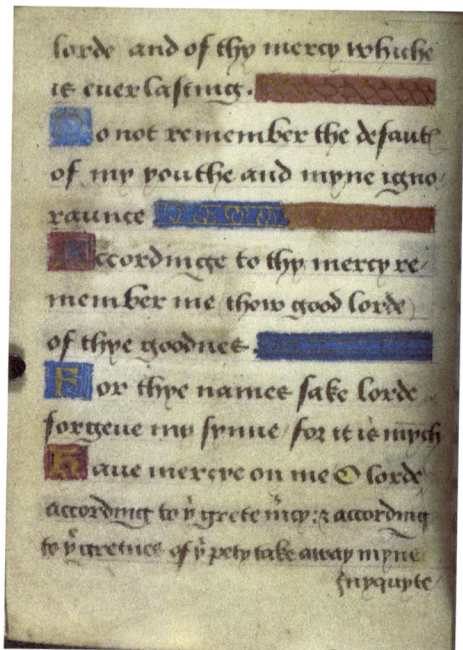

lorde and of thy mercy whiche
is euerlaſting.
Do not remember the defautℓ
of my youthe and myne igno//
raunce
Accordinge to thy mercy re/
member me (thow good lorde)
of thye goodnes.
For thye names ſake lorde
forgeue my ſynne/ for it is mỹch
Haue mercye on me (O lorde)
according to y¹ grete mᵣcy: & according
to yᵉ gretnes of yⁱ pety take away myne
Jnyquyte/

Lord and of Thy mercy which
is everlasting.
Do not remember the defaults
of my youth and my igno-
rance.
According to Thy mercy, remember me, Thou good Lord,
of Thy goodness.
For Thy name's sake, Lord,
forgive my sin, for it is much.
Have mercy on me, oh Lord,
according to Thy great mercy, and according
to the greatness of Thy pity, take away my
iniquity.

Folio 121r

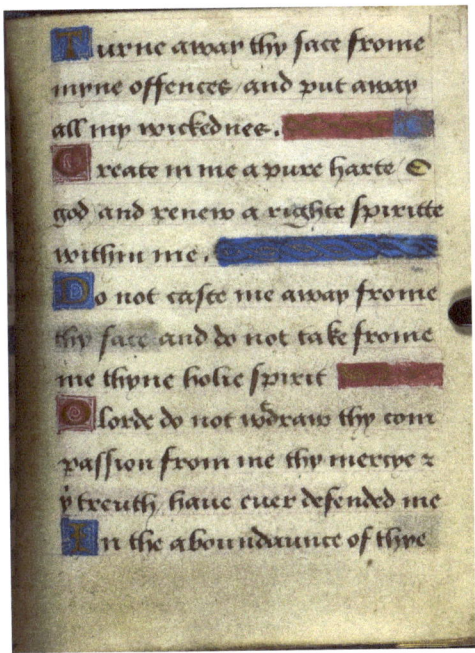

Turne away thy face frome
myne offences/ and put away
all my wickednes.
Create in me a pure harte (O
god) and renew a right fpiritte
within me.
Do not cafte me away frome
thy face and do not take frome
me thyne holie fpirit
O lorde do not w{t}draw thy com//
paffion from me/ thy mercye &
y{i} treuth/ haue euer defended me
In the aboundaunce of thye

Turn away Thy face from
my offenses and put away
all my wickedness.
Create in me a pure heart, oh
God, and renew a right spirit
within me.
Do not cast me away from
Thy face and do not take from
me Thy Holy Spirit.
Oh Lord do not withdraw Thy com-
passion from me. Thy mercy and
Thy truth have ever defended me.
In the abundance of Thy

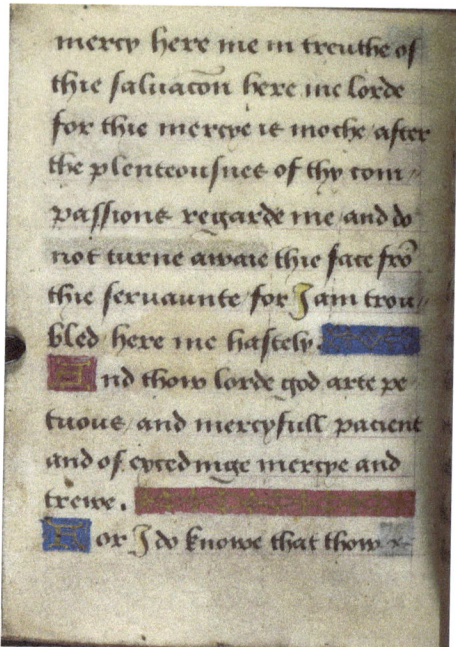

mercy here me in treuthe of
thie falvacõn here me lorde
for thie mercye is moche/ after
the plenteoufnes of thy com//
paffions regarde me/ and do
not turne awaie thie face frõ
thie feruaunte/ for J am trou//
bled/here me haftely.
   And thow lorde god arte pe//
tuous/ and mercyfull pacient
and of excedinge mercye and
trewe.
   For J do knowe that thow xx

mercy, hear. In truth of
Thy salvation, hear me Lord,
for Thy mercy is much. After
the plenteousness of Thy com-
passions, regard me and do
not turn away Thy face from
Thy servant, for I am troubled. Hear me hastily.
   And Thou, Lord God, are piteous and merciful, patient
and of exceeding mercy, and
true,
   For I do know that Thou

Folio 122r

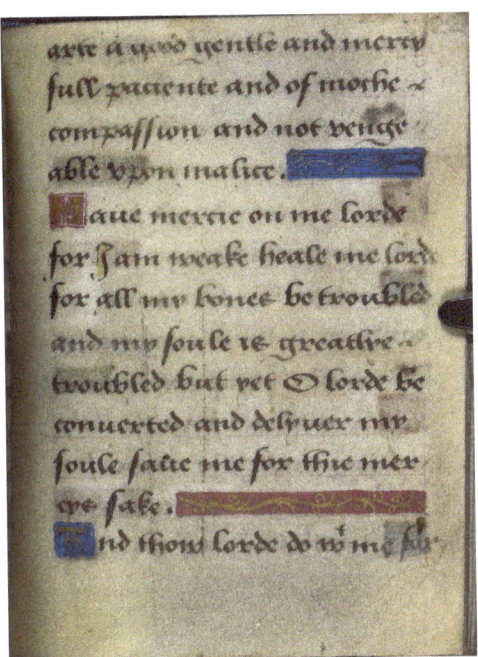

arte a good gentle and mercy full paciente and of moche x compaffion and not venge// able vpon malice.

Haue mercie on me lorde for J am weake heale me lorde for all my bones be troubled and my foule is greatlye x trobled/ but not yet O lorde be conuerted/ and delyuer my foule/ faue me for thie mer// cys fake.

And thow lorde do w^t me for

are a good, gentle, and merciful, patient, and of much compassion, and not vengeful upon malice.*

Have mercy on me, Lord, for I am weak. Heal me, Lord, for all my bones be troubled and my soul is greatly troubled. But not yet, oh Lord, be converted, and deliver my soul. Save me for Thy mercy's sake.

And Thou, Lord, do with me for

---

* and not vengeful solely for reasons of malice.

Folio 122v

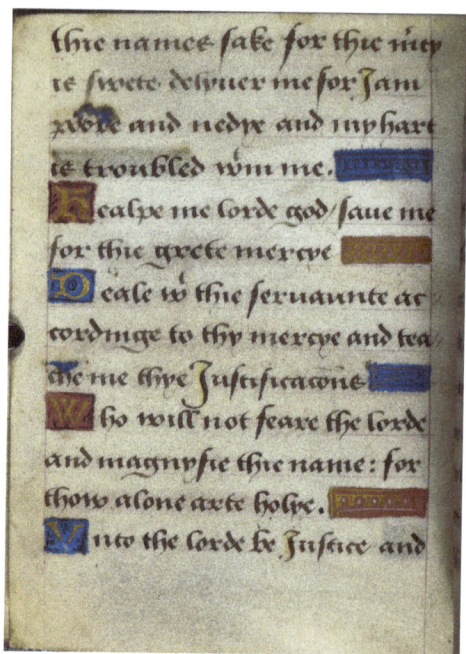

thie names fake/ for thie m^rcy
is fwete. delyuer me for J am
poore and nedye and my harte
is troubled w^tin me.
Healpe me lorde god/ faue me
for thie grete mercye
Deale w^t thie feruaunte ac//
cordinge to thy mercye and tea//
che me thye Juftificacõns
Who will not feare the lorde
and magnyfie thie name: for
thow alone arte holye.
Vnto the lorde be Juftice and

Thy name's sake, for Thy mercy
is sweet. Deliver me, for I am
poor and needy and my heart
is troubled within me.
Help me, Lord God, save me
for Thy great mercy.
Deal with Thy servant according to Thy mercy and teach
me Thy justifications.
Who will not fear Thee, Lord,
and magnify Thy name? For
Thou alone are holy.
Unto Thee, Lord, be justice and

Folio 123r

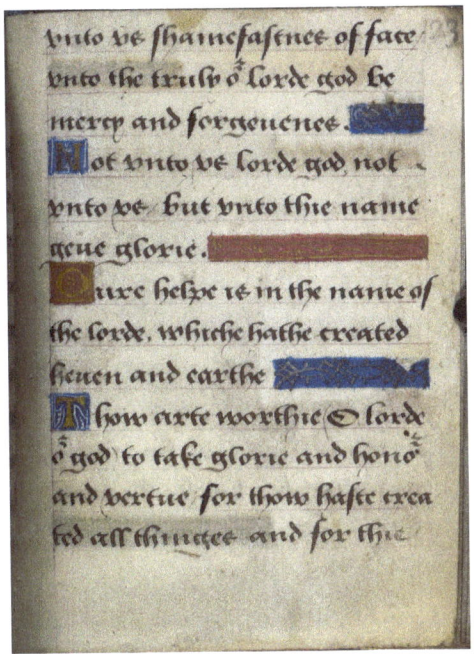

vnto vs fhamefaſtnes of face/
vnto the truly oʳ lorde god be
mercy and forgeuenes.

[N]ot vnto vs lorde god, not
vnto vs/ but vnto thie name
geue glorie.

[O]ure helpe is in the name of
the lorde, whiche hathe created
heuen and earthe

[T]how arte worthie (O lorde
oʳ god) to take glorie and honor
and vertue/ for thow haſte crea//
ted all thinges and for thie

unto us shamefastness of face.
Unto Thee, truly our Lord God, be
mercy and forgiveness.

[N]ot unto us, Lord God, not
unto us, but unto Thy name
give glory.

[O]ur help is in the name of
the Lord, which has created
Heaven and Earth.

[T]hou are worthy, oh Lord
our God, to take glory and honor
and virtue, for Thou have created all things, and for Thy

Folio 123v

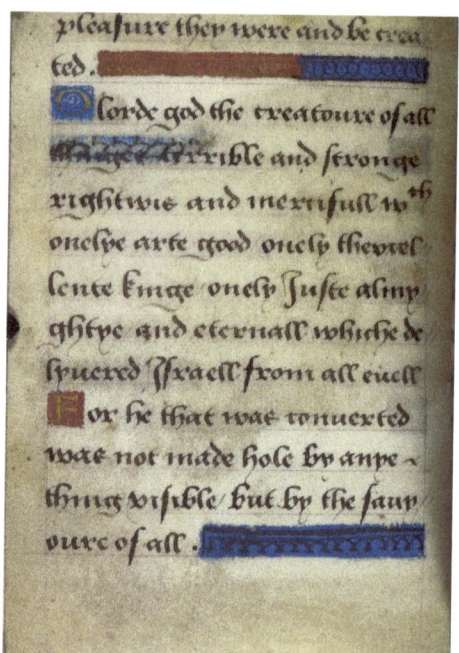

pleasure they were and be created.

Oh Lord God, the creator of all things terrible and strong, righteous and merciful, which only are good, only the excellent king, only just, almighty, and eternal, which delivered Israel from all evil.

For he that was converted was not made holy by anything visible, but by the Savior of all.

Folio 124r

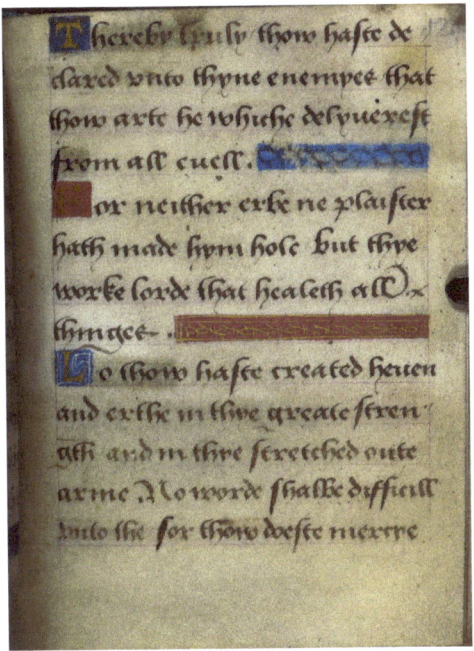

Thereby truly/ thow hafte de//
clared vnto thyne emeyes that
thow arte he whiche deliuereft
from all euell.
   For neither erbe ne plaifter
hathe made hym hole/ but thye
worke lorde that healeth all x
thinges.
   Lo thow hafte created heuen
and erthe in thye greate ftren//
gth/ and in thye ftretched oute
arme. No worde fhalbe difficill
vnto the/ for thow doefte mercye

Thereby truly Thou have declared unto Thine enemies that
Thou are He which delivers
from all evil,
   For neither herb nor plaster*
has made him whole, but [it is] Thy
work, Lord, that heals all
things.
   Lo, Thou have created Heaven
and Earth in Thy great strength, and in Thy stretched out
arm. No word shall be difficult
unto Thee, for Thou do mercy

* bandages

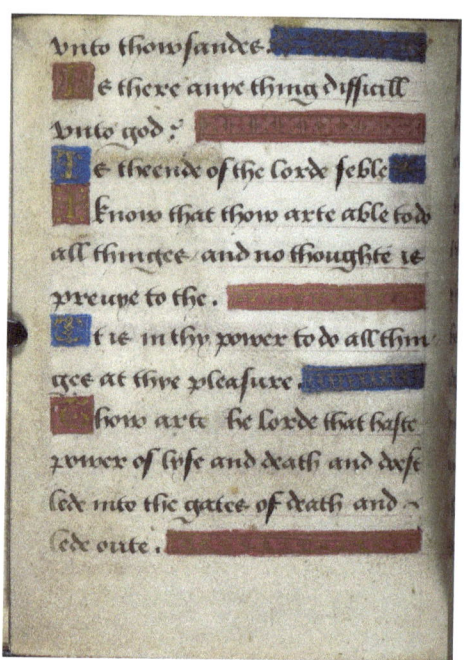

vnto thowſandes.
I s there anye thing difficill vnto god?
I s theende of the lorde feble
I know that thow arte able to do all thinges/ and no thoughte is preuye to the.
I t is in thy power to do all thin//ges at thye pleaſure.
T how arte he lorde that haſte power of lyfe and death and doeſt lede into the gates of death/ and x lede oute.

unto thousands.
I s there anything difficult unto God?
I s the end of the Lord feeble?
I know that Thou are able to do all things, and no thought is privy* to Thee.
I t is in Thy power to do all things at Thy pleasure.
T hou are [t]he Lord that has power of life and death and does lead into the gates of death and lead out.

* private, hidden

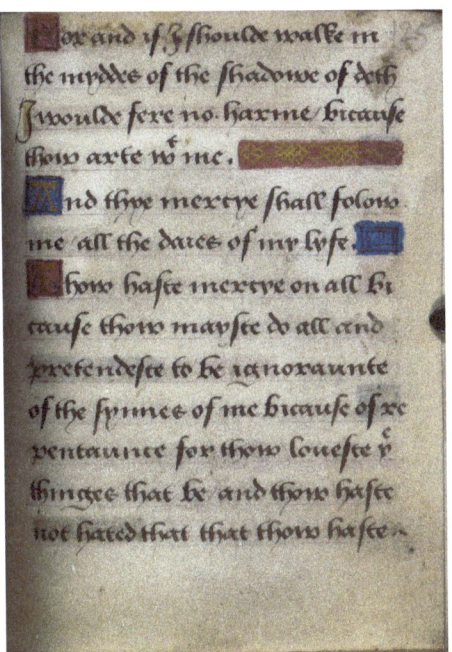

For and if J fhoulde walke in the myddes of the fhadowe of deth J woulde fere no harme/ bicaufe thow arte wt me.

And thye mercye fhall folow me/ all the daies of my lyfe.

Thow hafte mercye on all bicaufe thow mayfte do all and pretendefte to be ignoraunte of the fynnes of me bicaufe of repentaunce for thow louefte ye thinges that be/ and thow hafte not hated that that thow hafte x

For and if I should walk in the midst of the shadow of death, I would fear no harm, because Thou are with me,

And Thy mercy shall follow me all the days of my life.

Thou has mercy on all because Thou may do all and pretend to be ignorant of the sins of me because of repentance, for Thou loves the things that be, and Thou have not hated that that Thou have

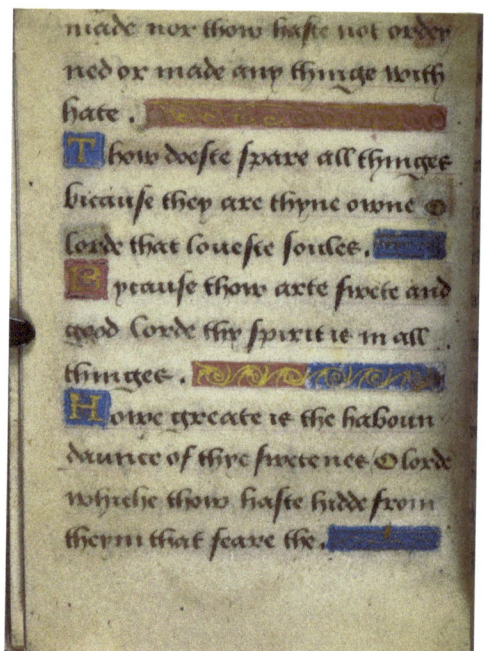

made nor thow haſte not ordey//
ned or made any thinge with
hate.
Thow doeſte ſpare all thinges
bicauſe they are thyne owne O
lorde that loueſte ſoules.
Bycauſe thow arte ſwete and
good lorde thy ſpirit is in all
thinges.
Howe greate is the haboun//
daunce of thye ſwetenes (O lorde)
whiche thow haſte hidde from
theym that feare the.

made, nor Thou have not ordained or made anything with
hate.
Thou do spare all things
because they are Thine own, oh
Lord that loves souls.
Because Thou are sweet and
good, Lord, Thy spirit is in all
things.
How great is the abundance of Thy sweetness, oh Lord,
which Thou have hidden from
them that fear Thee.

Folio 126r

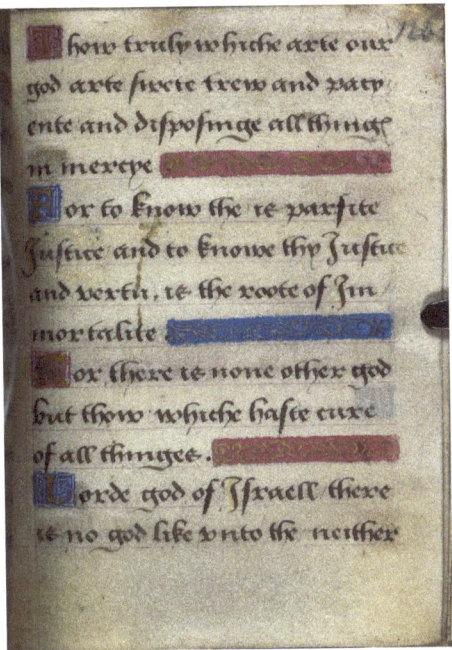

T how truly whiche arte our god arte fwete trew and pacy/ ene and difpofinge all thingₑ in mercye

F or to know the is parfite Juftice/ and to knowe thy Juftice and vertu, is the roote of Jm// mortalite.

F or there is none other god but thow/ whiche hafte cure of all thinges.

L orde god of Jfraell/ there is no god like vnto the/ neither

T hou truly, which are our God, are sweet, true, and patient and disposing [of] all things in mercy.

F or to know Thee is perfect justice, and to know Thy justice and virtue is the root of immortality.

F or this is none other God but Thou, which has sure of all things.

L ord God of Israel, there is no God like unto Thee, neither

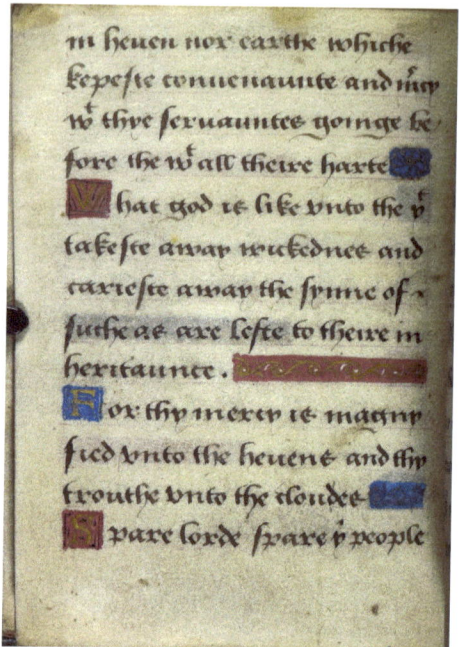

in heuen nor earthe whiche
kepefte conuenaunte/ and mrcy
wt thye feruauntes goinge be//
fore the wt all theire harte
What god is like vnto the yt
takefte away wickednes and
cariefte away the fynne of x
fuche as are lefte to theire in//
heritaunce.
For thy mercy is magny//
fied vnto the heuens and thy
trouthe vnto the cloudes
Spare lorde fpare yi people

in Heaven nor Earth which
keeps covenant and mercy
with Thy servants going before Thee with all their heart.
What god is like unto Thee that
takes away wickedness and
carries away the sin of
such as are left to their inheritance?
For Thy mercy is magnified unto the Heavens and Thy
truth unto the clouds.
Spare, Lord, spare Thy people

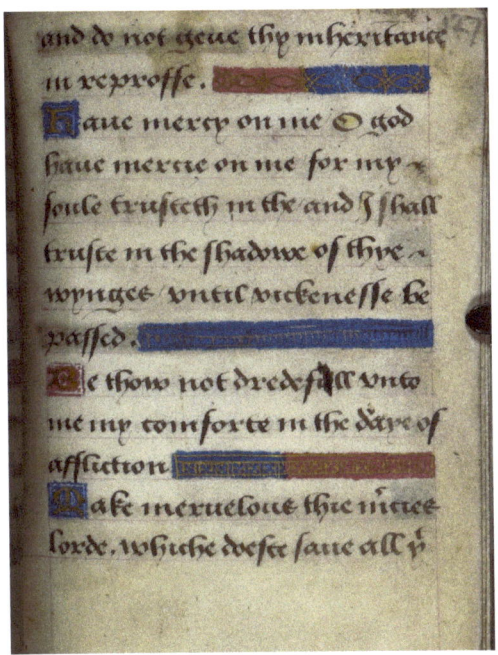

and do not geue thy inheritãce in reproffe.

Haue mercy on me/ O god haue mercie on me/ for my soule trusteth in the/ and J shall truste in the shadowe of thye wynges/ vntil vickenesse be passed.

Be thow not dredefull vnto me my comforte in the daye of affliction

Make meruelous thie m^{r}cies lorde, whiche doeste saue all y^t

and do not give Thy inheritance in reproof.

Have mercy on me, oh God, have mercy on me, for my soul trusts in Thee, and I shall trust in the shadow of Thy wings until wickedness be passed.

Be Thou not dreadful unto me, my comfort in the day of affliction.

Make marvelous Thy mercies, Lord, which do save all that

Folio 127v

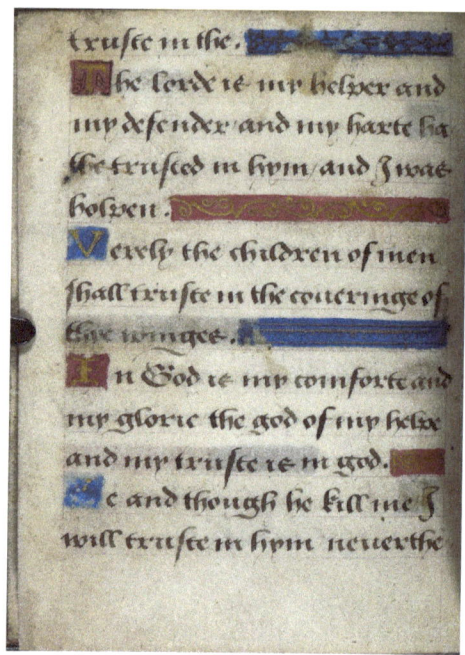

truſte in the.
The lorde is my helper and my defender/ and my harte ha// the truſted in hym/ and J was holpen.
Verely the children of men ſhall truſte in the coueringe of thye winges.
In God is my comforte and my glorie/ the god of my helpe and my truſte is in god.
Ye and though he kill me J will truſte in hym/ neuerethe//

trust in Thee.
The Lord is my helper and my defender, and my heart has trusted in Him, and I was helped.
Verily, the children of men shall trust in the covering of Thy wings.
In God is my comfort and my glory, the God of my help, and my trust is in God.
Yea, and though He kill me, I will trust in Him, neverthe-

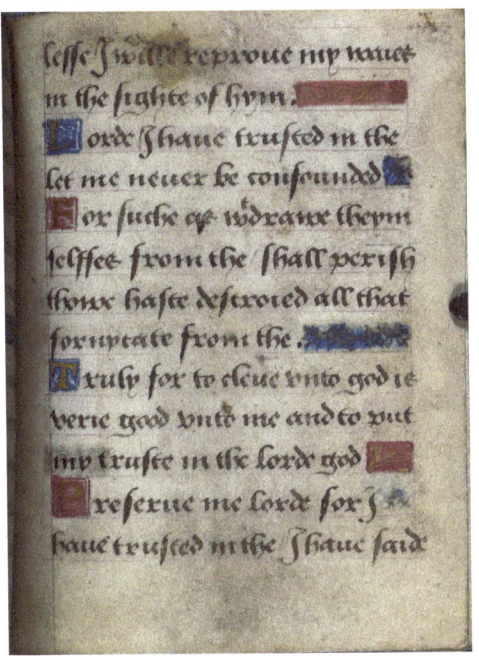

leffe J wille reproue my waies
in the fighte of hym.

Lorde J haue trufted in the/
let me neuer be confounded

For fuche as w^tdrawe theym
felffes from the/ fhall perifh
thowe hafte deftroied all that
fornycate from the.

Truly for to cleue vnto god is
verie good vnto me and to put
my trufte in the lorde god

Preferue me lorde for J xx
haue trufted in the/ J haue faide

less, I will reprove my ways
in the sight of Him.

Lord, I have trusted in Thee,
let me never be confounded,

For such as withdraw themselves from Thee shall perish.
Thou have destroyed all that
fornicate* against Thee.

Truly for to cleave unto God is
very good unto me, and to put
my trust in the Lord God.

Preserve me, Lord, for I
have trusted in Thee. I have said

---

* used here in the figurative and non-sexual sense of forsaking God for idols

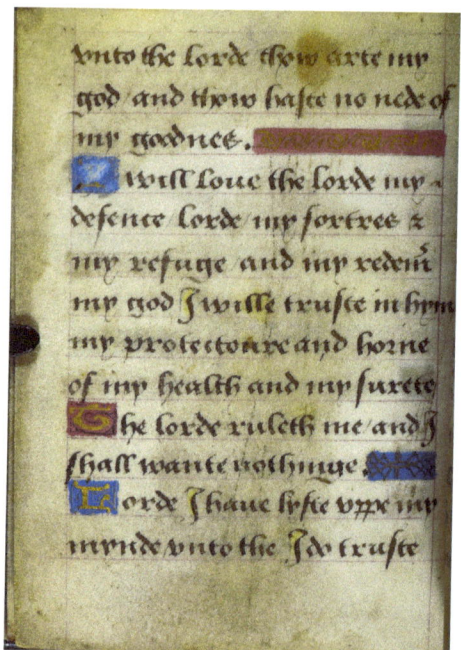

vnto the lorde thow arte my
god/ and thow hafte no nede of
my goodnes.
I will loue the lorde my x
defence/ lorde/ my fortres &
my refuge/ and my redem r
my god J will trufte in hym
my protectoure and horne
of my health and my furete
The lorde ruleth me/ and J
fhall wante nothinge.
Lorde J haue lyfte vppe my
mynde vnto the/ J do trufte

unto the Lord, Thou are my
God, and Thou has no need of
my goodness.
I will love Thee, Lord, my
defense, Lord, my fortress and
my refuge and my redeemer.
My God, I will trust in Him,
my protector and horn
of my health and my surety.
The Lord rules me, and I
shall want for nothing.
Lord, I have lift[ed] up my
mind unto Thee. I do trust

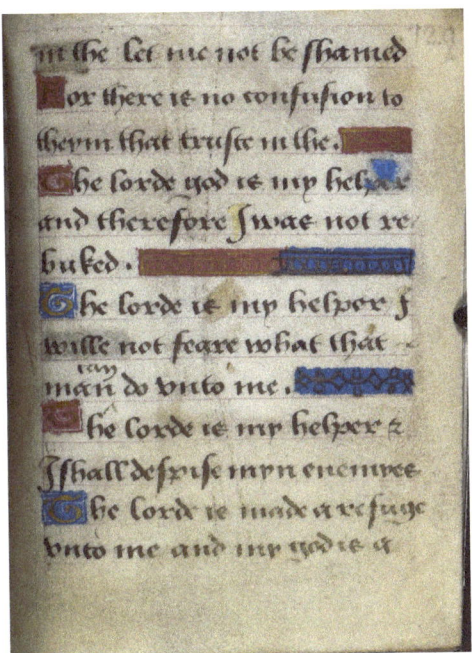

in the let me not be fhamed
For there is not confufion to
theym that trufte in the.
The lorde god is my helper
and therefore J was not re//
buked.
The lorde is my helper/ J
wille not feare what that x
man do vnto me. (can)
The lorde is my helper &
J fhall defpife myne enemyes
The lorde is made a refuge
vnto me/ and my god is a

in Thee, let me not be shamed,
For there is not confusion to
them that trust in Thee.
The Lord God is my helper,
and therefore I was not re-
buked.
The Lord is my helper. I
will not fear what that
man can do unto me.
The lord is my helper, and
I shall despise my enemies.
The Lord is made a refuge
unto me, and my God is a

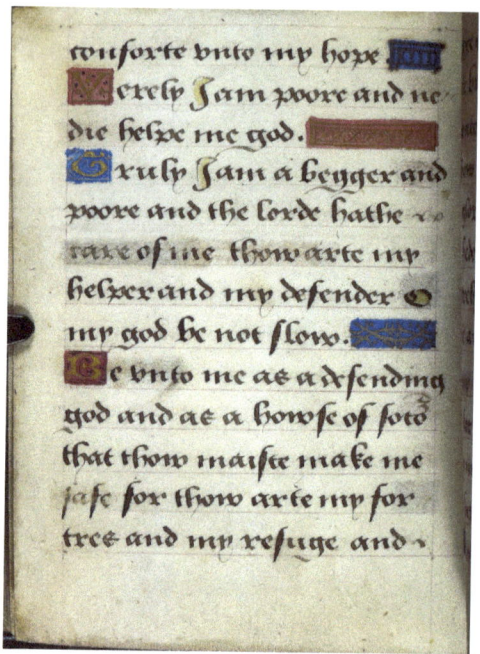

conforte vnto my hope.

Verely J am poore and ne//
die helpe me god.

Truly J am a begger and
poore and the lorde hathe xx
care of me thow arte my
helper and my defender/ O
my god be not flow.

Be vnto me as a defending
god and as a howfe of foco^r
that thow maiefte make me
fafe for thow arte my for
tres and my refuge and x

comfort unto my hope.

Verily, I am poor and needy; help me God.

Truly I am a beggar and
poor, and the Lord has
care of me. Thou are my
helper and my defender. Oh
my God, be not slow.

Be unto me as a defending
God and as a house of succor,
that Thou may make me
safe, for Thou are my fortres and my refuge and

Folio 130r

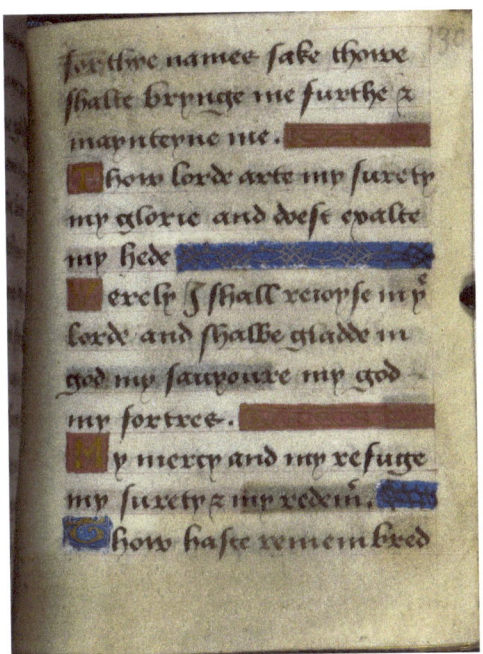

for thye names fake thowe
fhalte brynge me furthe &
maynteyne me.
T how lorde arte my furety
my glorie and doefte exalte
my hede
V erely J fhall reioyfe in yᵉ
lorde/ and fhalbe gladde in
god my fauyoure my god x
my fortres.
M y mercy and my refuge
my furety & my redemʳ.
T how hafte remembred

for Thy name's sake Thou
shall bring me forth and
maintain me.
T hou, Lord, are my surety,
my glory, and do exalt
my head.
V erily, I shall rejoice in the
Lord and shall be glad in
God my Savior, my God,
my fortress,
M y mercy and my refuge,
my surety and my redeemer.
T hou have remembered

Folio 130v

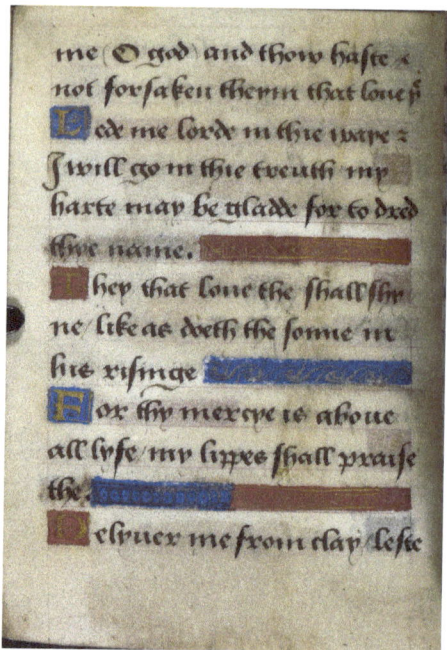

me (o god) and thow haſte x
not forſake theym that loue yᵉ
Lede me lorde in thie waye &
J will go in thie treuth/ my
harte may be gladde for to dred
thye name.
They that loue the ſhall ſhy//
ne/ lyke as doeth the ſonne in
his riſinge
For thy mercye is aboue
all lyfe/ my lippes ſhall praiſe
the.
Delyuer me from clay leſte

me, oh God, and Thou have
not forsaken them that love Thee.
Lead me, Lord, in Thy way, and
I will go in Thy truth. My
heart may be glad for to dread
Thy name.
They that love Thee shall shi-
ne like as does the sun in
his rising,
For Thy mercy is above
all life. My lips shall praise
Thee.
Deliver me from clay lest

Folio 131r

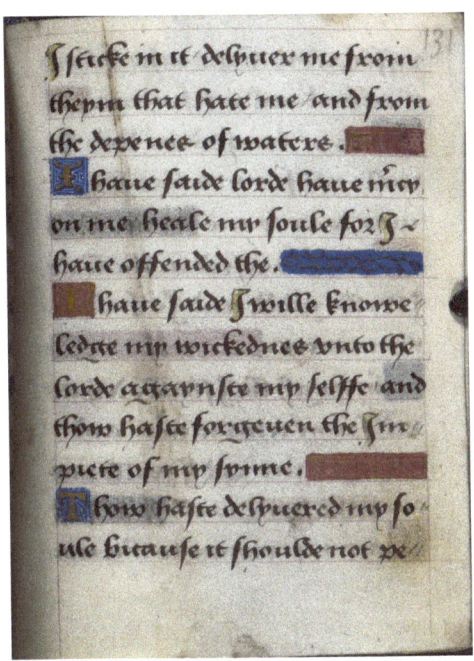

J fticke in it/ delyuer me from theym that hate me/ and from the depenes of waters.

I haue faide lorde haue m͡rcy on me/ heale my foule for J x haue offended the.

I haue said J wille knowe// ledge my wickednes vnto the lorde agaynfte my felffe/ and thow hafte forgeuen the Jm// piete of my fynne.

T how hafte delyuered my fo// ule bicaufe it fhoulde not pe//

I stick in it. Deliver me from them that hate me and from the deepness of waters.

I have said, "Lord have mercy on me. Heal my soul for I have offended Thee,

I have said, "I will acknowledge my wickedness unto Thee, Lord, against myself." And Thou have forgiven the impiety of my sin.

Thou have delivered my soul because it should not pe-

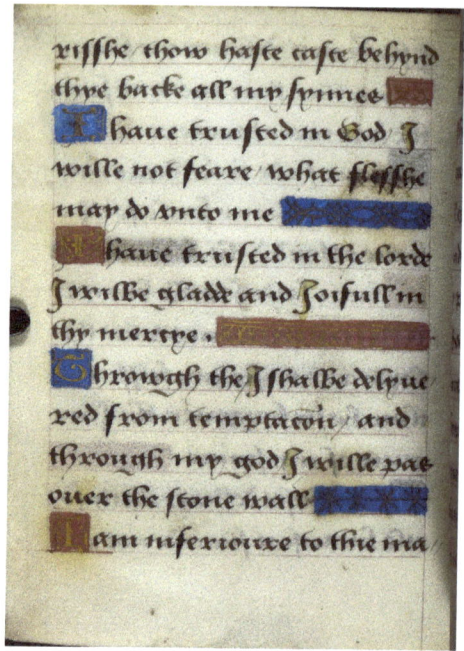

riſſhe/ thow haſte caſte behynd
thye backe all my fynnes
I haue truſted in God/ J
wille not feare/ what fleſſhe
may do vnto me
I haue truſted in the lorde
I wilbe gladde and Joifull in
thy mercye.
Throwgh the J ſhalbe delyue//
red from temptacõn/ and
throught my god J wille pas
ouer the ſtone wall
I am inferioure to thie ma//

rish. Thou have caste behind
Thy back all my sins.
I have trusted in God; I
will not fear what flesh
may do unto me.
I have trusted in Thee, Lord;
I will be glad and joyful in
Thy mercy.
Through Thee I shall be delive-
red from temptation, and
through my God I will pass
over the stone wall.
I am inferior to Thy ma-

Folio 132r

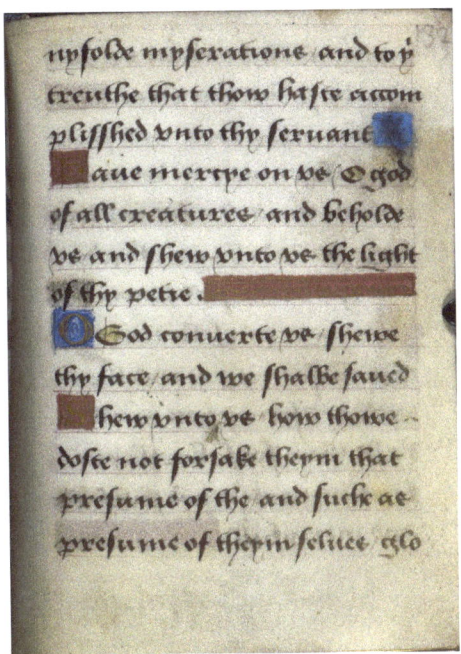

nyfolde myferations/ and for yⁱ
treuthe that thow hafte accom
pliffhed vnto thy feruant
Haue mercye on vs god (O god
of all creatures) and beholde
vs and fhew vnto vs the light
of thy petie.
O God conuerte vs/ fhewe
thy face/ and we fhalbe faued
Shew vnto vs how thowe ~
dofte not forfake theym that
prefume of the/and fuche as
prefume of theym felues/ glo

nifold miserations, and for Thy
truth that Thou have accom-
plished unto Thy servant.
Have mercy on us God, oh God
of all creatures, and behold
us and show unto us the light
of Thy pity.
Oh God, convert us. Show
Thy face, and we shall be saved.
Show unto us how Thou
do not forsake they that
presume of Thee, and such as
presume of themselves, glo-

rieng in theire owne vertu x
thow doeſte bringe lowe.
Remember lorde/ and ſhew
thye ſelfe vnto vs in tyme of oʳ
tribulacõn/ and geue me com//
forte (O lorde king of godes
and of vnyuerſall power
In the manyfolde mercies
thow haſte not created them
vnto conſumption/ neither
haſte thow forſaken theym/
for thow arte a god pitefull
and mercyfull.

rying in their own virtue,
Thou do bring low.
Remember, Lord, and show
Thyself unto us in time of our
tribulation, and give me comfort, oh Lord King of Gods
and of universal power.
In the manifold mercies,
Thou have not created them
unto consumption. Neither
have Thou forsake them, for
Thou are a God pitiful*
and merciful.

* i.e., full of pity

Folio 133r

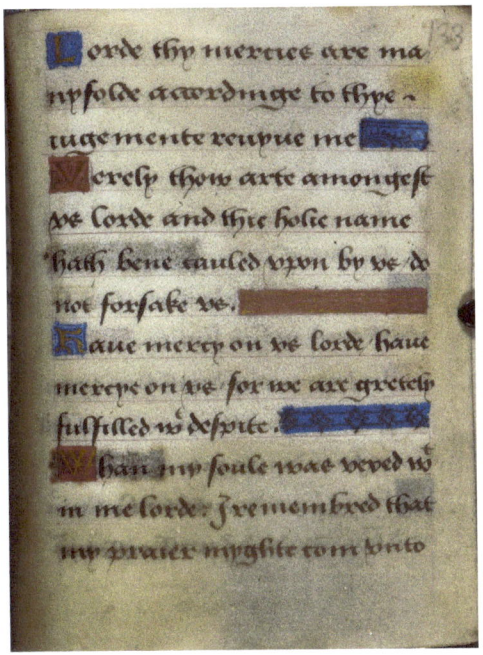

Lorde thy mercies are ma//
nyfolde accordinge to thye x
iugemente reuyue me
Verely thow arte amongeſt
vs lorde and thie holy name
hathe bene cauled vpon by vs/ do
not forſake vs.
Haue mercy on vs lorde/ haue
mercye on vs for we are gretely
fulfilled w^t deſpite.
Whan my ſoule was vexed w^t
in me lorde: J remembred that
my praier myghte com vnto

Lord, Thy mercies are manifold according to Thy
judgment. Revive me.
Verily, Thou are among
us, Lord, and Thy holy name
has been called upon by us. Do
not forsake us.
Have mercy on us, Lord, have
mercy on us for we are greatly
fulfilled* with despite.†
When my soul was vexed within me, Lord, I remembered that
my prayer might come unto

* i.e., entirely filled

† contempt, hatred, malice

the euen vnto thye holy temple
Troubles do oppreffe me on eue//
ry parte but it is better for me
to falle into the handes of the lorde
(for his petye is greate) then into
the handes of men.
The lorde wille do that/ that fe//
meth good in his fighte.
The forowes of deathe haue com//
paffed me and the perelles of hell
haue founde me oute.
I haue founde oute tribulacõn
and forowe/ and J will calle vpõ

Folio 134r

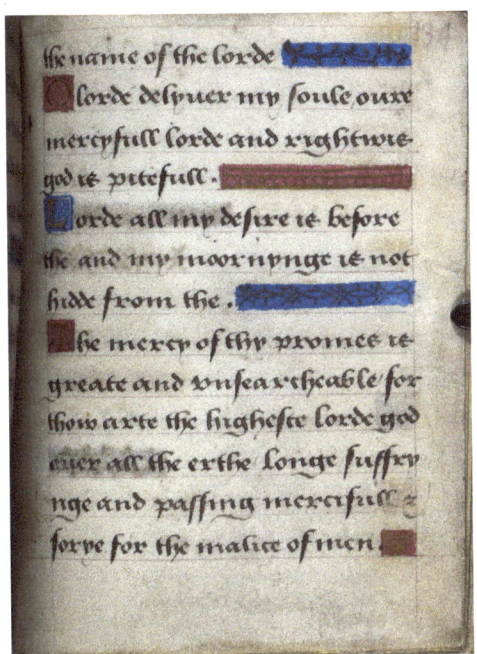

the name of the lorde
O lorde delyuer my foule oure mercyfull lorde and rightwis god is pitefull.
L orde all my defire is before the and my moornynge is not hidde from the.
T he mercy of thy promes is greate and vnfearcheable/ for thow arte the highefte lorde god euer all the erthe/ longe fuffry// nge and paffing mercifull & forye for the malice of men.

the name of the Lord.
O h Lord, deliver my soul. Our merciful Lord and righteous God is pitiful.
L ord, all my desire is before Thee, and my mourning is not hidden from Thee.
T he mercy of Thy promise is great and unsearchable, for Thou are the highest Lord God over all the Earth, long-sufferi- ng and passing merciful and sorry for the malice of men.

Folio 134v

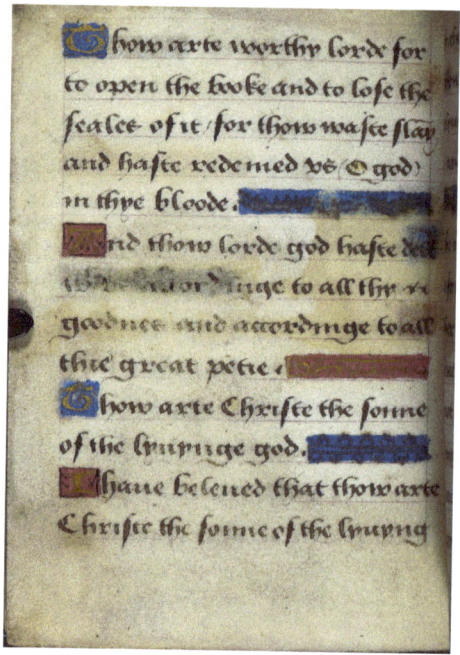

Thow arte worthy lorde for to open the booke and to loſe the ſeales of it/ for thow waſte flaỹ and haſte redemed vs (O god) in thye bloode.
And thow lorde god haſte delt w^t vs accordinge to all thy xx goodnes and accordinge to all thie great petie.
Thow arte Chriſte the ſonne of the lyuynge god.
I haue beleued that thow arte Chriſte the ſonne of the lyuyng

Thou are worthy, Lord, for to open the book and to loose the seals of it, for Thou was slain and have redeemed us, oh God, in Thy blood.
And Thou, Lord God, have dealt with us according to all Thy goodness and according to all Thy great pity.
Thou are Christ, the Son of the living God.
I have believed that Thou are Christ, the Son of the Living

Folio 135r

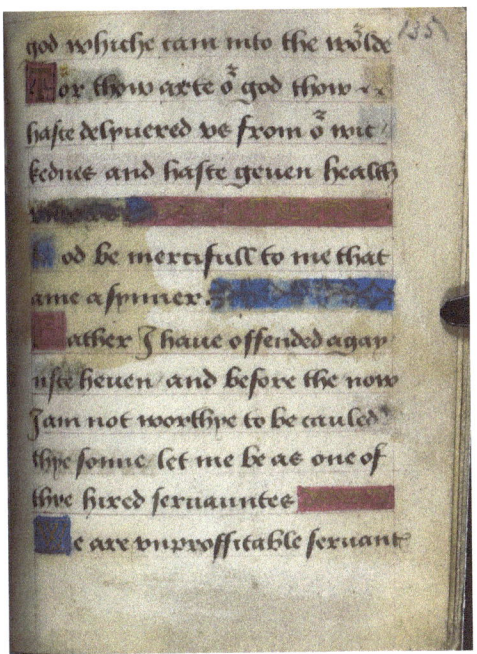

god/ whiche cam into the worlde
[T]or thow arte or god thow xx
haſte deluyered vs from or wic//
kednes/ and haſte geuen health
vnto vs.
[G]od be mercifull to me that
ame a ſynner.
[F]ather J haue offended agay/
nſte heuen/ and before the now
J am not worthye to be cauled
thye ſonne/ let me be as one of
thye hired ſeruauntes.
[W]e are vnproffitable ſeruant℮

God, which came into the world,
[F]*or Thou are our God. Thou
have delivered us from our wic-
kedness and have given health
unto us.
[G]od be merciful to me that
am a sinner.
[F]ather, I have offended agai-
nst Heaven, and before Thee now
I am not worthy to be called
Thy son. Let me be as one of
Thy hired servants.
[W]e are unprofitable servants.

* The decorator mistakenly created a T where an F was indicated instead.

Folio 135v

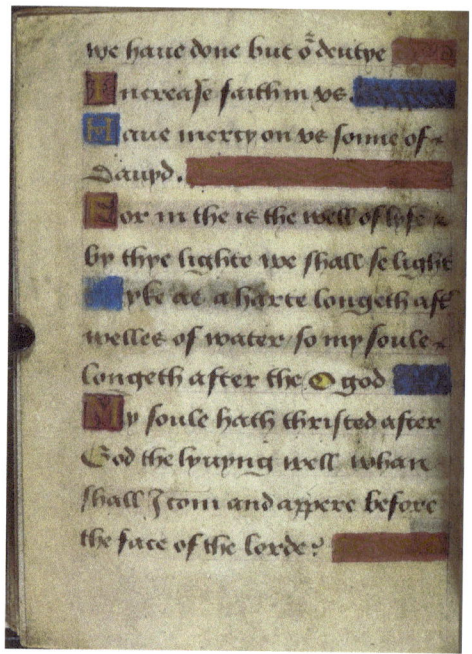

we haue done but oʳ deutye
I ncreaſe faith in vs.
H aue mercy on vs ſonne of ₓ Dauyd.
F or in the is the well of lyfe & by thye lighte we ſhall ſe light
L yke as a harte longeth aftʳ welles of water/ ſo my ſoule ₓ longeth after the (O god)
M y ſoule hath thirſted after God the lyuyng well whan ſhall I cõm and appere before the face of the lorde?

we have done but our duty.
I ncrease faith in us.
H ave mercy on us, son of David,
F or in Thee is the well of life, and by Thy light we shall see light.
L ike as a hart* longs after wells of water, so my soul longs after Thee, oh God.
M y soul has thirsted after God the living well. When shall I come and appear before the face of the Lord?

---

* archaic term for a male deer after its fifth year

Folio 136r

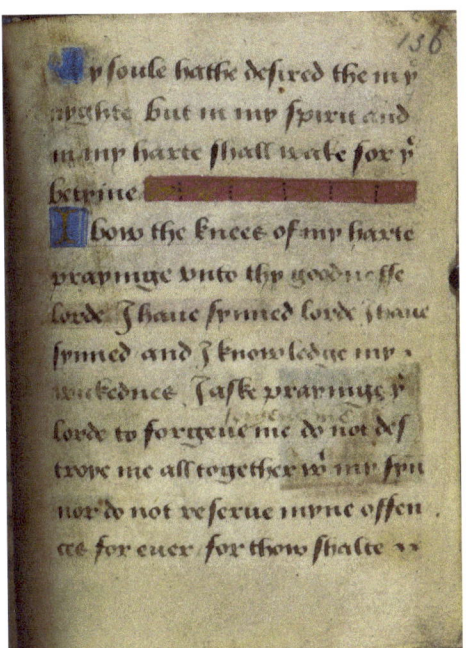

My foule hathe defired the in yᵉ nyghte/ but in my fpirit and in my harte fhall wake for yᵉ betyme.
I bow the knees of my harte prayinge vnto thy goodneffe lorde/ J haue fynned lorde J haue fynned/ and J knowledge my x wickednes J afke prayinge yᵉ lorde to forgeue me do not def troye me all together wᵗ my fyn nor do not referue myne offen/ ces for euer/ for thow fhalte xx

My soul has desired Thee in the night, but in my spirit and in my heart [I] shall wake for Thee betime.*
I bow the knees of my heart praying unto Thy goodness, Lord. I have sinned, Lord, I have sinned, and I acknowledge my wickedness. I ask praying Thee, Lord, to forgive me, forgive me, do not destroy me altogether with my sin nor do not reserve my offenses forever, for Thou shall

* early

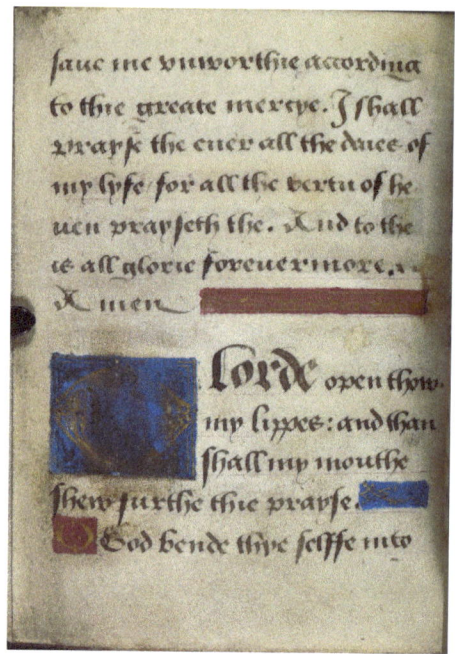

ſaue me vnworthie according to thie greate mercye. J ſhall prayſe the euer all the daies of my lyfe/ for all the vertu of he/ ven prayſeth the. And to the is all glorie foreuermore. xx Amen

save me, unworthy, according to Thy great mercy. I shall praise Thee ever all the days of my life, for all the virtue of Heaven praises Thee. And to Thee is all glory forevermore. Amen.

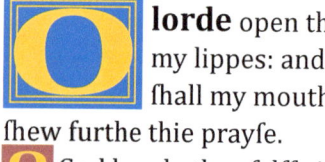**lorde** open thow my lippes: and than ſhall my mouthe ſhew furthe thie prayſe. God bende thye ſelffe into

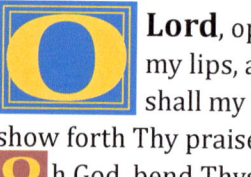**Lord**, open Thou my lips, and then shall my mouth show forth Thy praise. Oh God, bend Thyself into

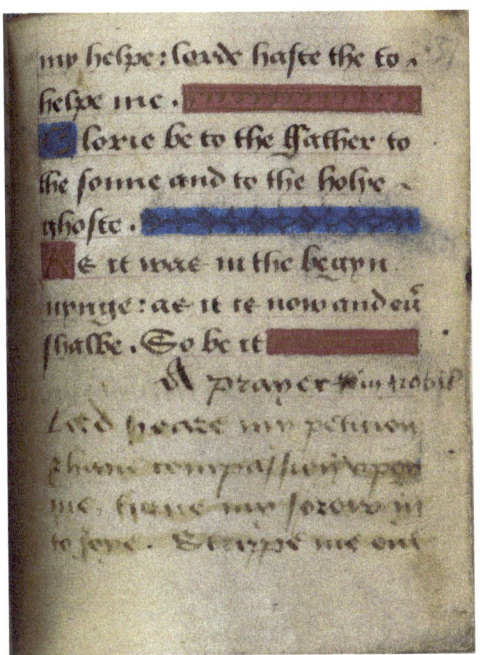

my helpe: lorde haſte the to x
helpe me.
Glorie be to the ffather to
the ſonne and to the holye x
ghoſte.
As it was in the begyn//
nynge: as it is now & euʳ
shalbe. So be it.

      A Prayer in trobil
Lord heare my peticion
& haue compaſſion vpon
me, turne my ſorow in
to ɉoye. Strippe me oute

my help. Lord, hasten Thee to
help me.
Glory be to the Father, to
the Son, and to the Holy
Ghost.
As it was in the begin-
ning, as it is now and ever
shall be. So be it.

      A prayer in trouble.
Lord hear my petition
and have compassion upon
me. Turn my sorrow in-
to joy. Strip me out

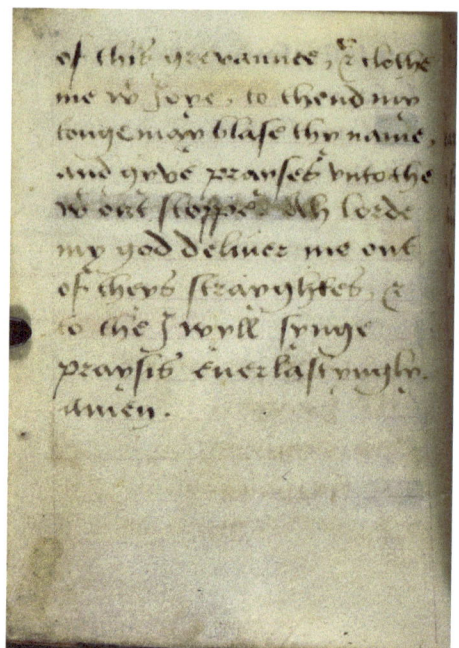

of this greuaunces, & clothe
me wt Joye, to thend my
tonge may blaſe thy name,
and gyue prayſes vnto the
wt out ſtoppe. Ah lorde
my god deliuer me out
of theys strayghtes, &
to the I wyll synge
prayſis euerlasſtyngly.
amen.

of these greivances, and clothe
me with joy, to the end [that] my
tongue may bless Thy name
and give praises unto Thee
without stop[ping].
My God, deliver me out
of these straights, and
to Thee will I sing
praises everlastingly.
Amen.

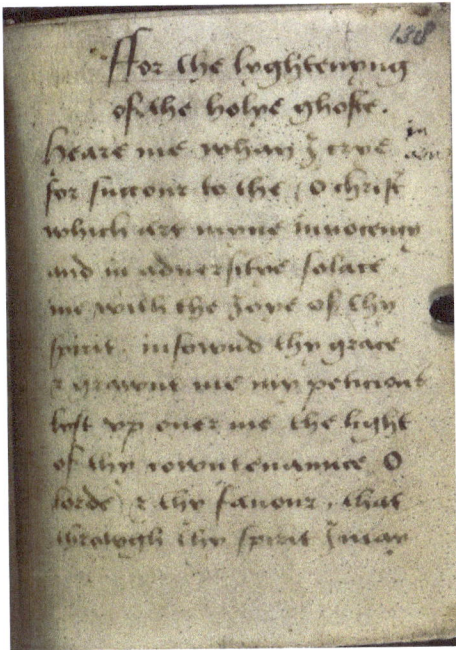

ffor the lyghtenyng
  of the holye ghoſte.
heare me whan J crye
for ſuccour to the (o chriſt
which art myne innocency
and in aduerſtiye ſolace
me with the Joye of thy
ſpirit. infownd thy grace
& grawnt me my peticions
lyft vp ouer me the light
of thy cowntenaunce (O
lord) & thy fauour, that
thrawgh thy ſpirit J may

For the lightening*
  of the Holy Ghost.
Hear me when I cry
for succor to Thee, oh Christ,
which are my innocency,
and in adversity solace
me with the joy of Thy
spirit. Infound† Thy grace
and grant me my petitions.
Lift up over me the light
of Thy countenance, oh
Lord, and Thy favor, that
through Thy spirit I may

* comforting, cheering

† pour into, infuse

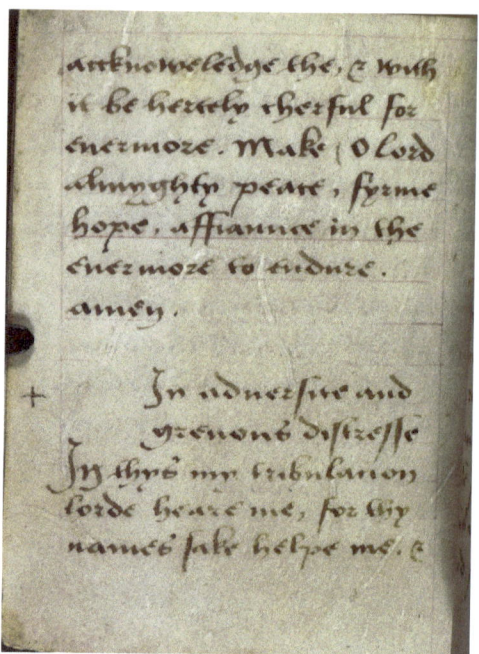

accknoweledge the, & with
it be heretely cherful for
euermore. Make (O lord
almyghty peace, fyrme
hope, affiaunce in the
euermore to endure.
amen.

    Jn aduerfite and
    greuous diftreffe
Jn thys my tribulacion
lorde heare me, for thy
names sake helpe me. &

acknowledge Thee, and with
it be cheerful for-
evermore. Make, oh Lord
Almighty, peace, firm
hope, affiance* in Thee
evermore to endure.
Amen.

    In adversity and
    grievous distress.
In this my tribulation,
Lord hear me, for Thy
name's sake help me, and

* faith or trust

Folio 139r

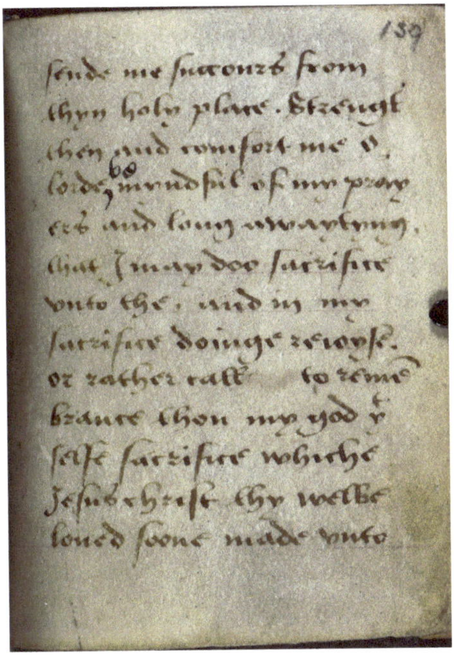

ſende me ſuccours from
thy holy place. Strengt
then and comfort me O
lorde, be myndful of my pray
ers and long awaytyng,
that J may doo ſacrifice
vnto the, and in my
ſacrifice doinge reioyſe.
or rather calle to remẽ
brance thou my god y^{t}
ſelfe ſacrifice whiche
Jeſus christ thy welbe
loued ſoone made vnto

Send me succors from
Thy holy place. Strenght-
hen and comfort me, oh
Lord. Be mindful of my prayers and long awaiting,
that I may do sacrifice
unto Thee, and in my
sacrifice-doing rejoice.
Or rather call to remem-
brance Thou my God that
self-sacrifice which
Jesus Christ Thy well-be-
loved Son made unto

Folio 139v

the his moſt louyng father
for me vpon the croſſe,
who prayed for me in the
dayes of his lyfe,   and for
his humilite and reuerence
was herd for his ſake.
J ſaye, be merciful vnto
me, and helpe me. Out
of thy heauenly towre
graunt that J ones an
noynted w^t thy ſoden &
perpatual Joye, may

Thee, his most loving Father,
for me upon the Cross,
who prayed for me in the
days of His life, and for
His humility and reverence
was heard for His sake.
I say be merciful unto
me, and help me. Out
of Thy heavenly tower
grant that I, once an-
ointed with Thy sudden and
perpetual joy, may

Folio 140r

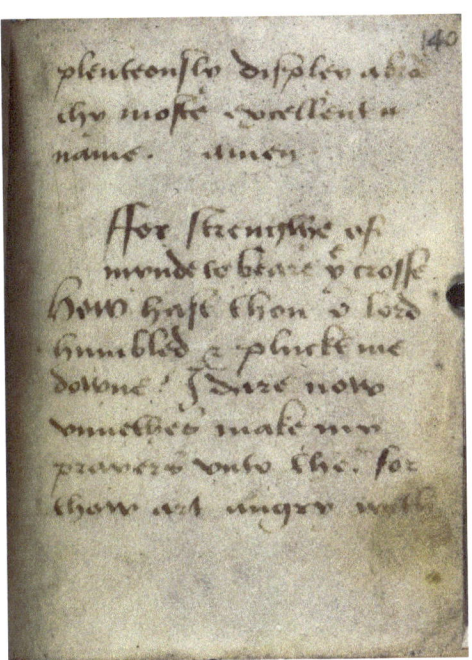

plenteoufly difpley abrod
thy mofte excellent xx
name.   amen.

   ffor ftrengthe of
  mynde to beare ye croffe
how haft thou o lord
humbled & plucke me
downe? J dare now
vnuethes make my
prayers vnto the. for
thow art angry with

plenteously display abroad
Thy most excellent
name.   Amen

   For strength of
  mind to bear the Cross.
How have Thou, oh Lord,
humbled and plucke[d] me
down? I dare now
nonetheless make my
prayers unto Thee, for
Thou are angry with

Folio 140v

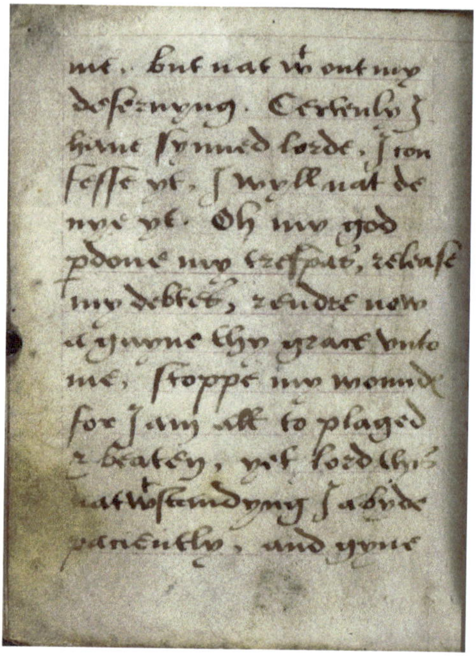

me, but nat wt out my
deſeruyng. Certenly J
haue ſynned lorde, I con
feſſe it, J wyll nat de
nye yt. Oh my god
pdone my treſpas, releaſe
my debtes, rendre now
agayne thy grace vnto
me, ſtoppe my wound{e}
for J am all to plaged
& beaten, yet lord this
nat w{t}ſtandyng J abyde
paciently, and gyue

me, but not without my
deserving. Certainly I
have sinned, Lord, I con-
fess it. I will not de-
ny it. Oh my God,
pardon my trespass, release
my debts; render now
again Thy grace unto
me. Stop my wounds,
for I am all plagued
and beaten. Yet Lord, this
notwithstanding, I abide
patiently and give

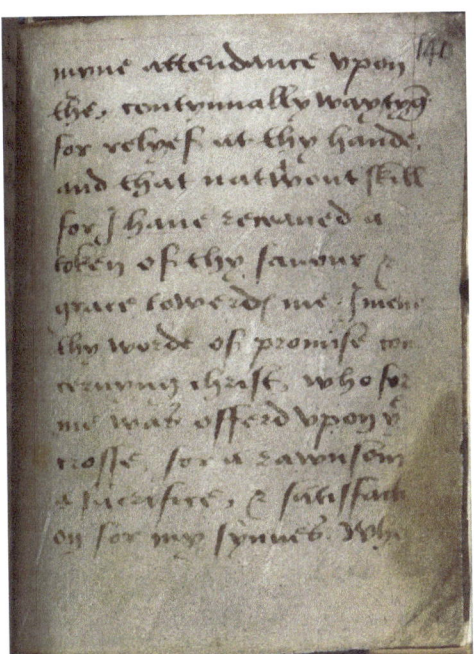

myne attendance vpon
the, contynually waytỹg
for relyef at thy hande
and that nat w^tout ſkill
for J haue remaned a
token of thy fauour &
grace towerd_ℓ me. J mene
thy worde of promiſe con
cernyng chriſt, who for
me was offred vpon y^e
croſſe, for a rawnſom
a ſacrifice, & ſatiſfacti
on for my ſynnes. Whe

my attendance upon
Thee, continually waiting
for relief at Thy hand,
and that not without skill,
for I have remained a
token of Thy favor and
grace towards me. I mean
Thy word of promise con-
cerning Christ, who for
me was offered upon the
Cross for a ransom,
a sacrifice and satisfacti-
on for my sins. The[re]-

Folio 141v

fore acordyng to that thy promys, defende me lorde by thy right hande, and gyue a gracious ere to my steye in pell*e* for all humane stayes are but vayne. beate downe ther fore myne enemyes thyne awen selfe w^t thy power, wch art myne only aydour and protectour O lord	for according to that Thy promise, defend me, Lord, by Thy right hand and give a gracious ear to my stey* in perils, for all human steys are but vain. Beat down therefore my enemies Thine own self with Thy power, which are my only aider and protector, oh Lord

* haughtiness

Folio 142r

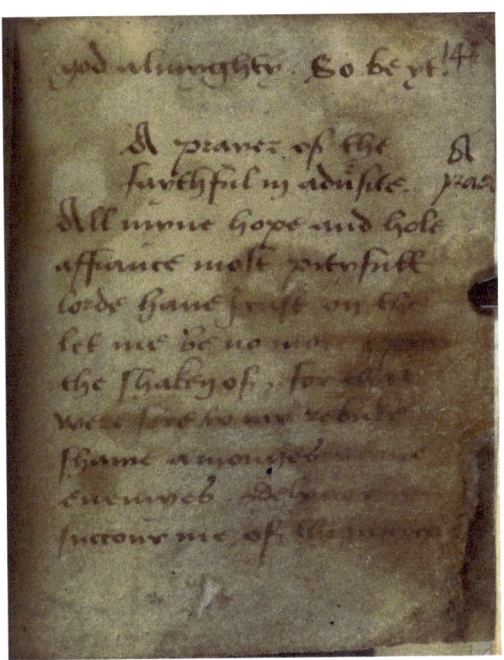

god almyghty . So be yt.

 A prayer of the
 faythful in aduʳſite.
All myne hope and hole
affiance moſt pityfull
lorde haue J caſt on the
let me be no more I praye
the ſhaken of, for that
were ſore to my rebuke
ſhame amonges myne
enemyes. Delyuer and
ſuccour me of thi

[blank]

Bibliography

Primary Sources

Chaloner, Thomas. *De rep. Anglorum instauranda libri decem*.... London: Vautrollerius, 1579.

Coverdale, Miles. *Biblia the Byble, that is, the holy Scrypture of the Olde and New Testament, faithfully translated in to Englyshe*. Southwark?: J. Nycolson, 1535. (STC 2063.3)

Commendone, Giovanni Francesco. "Il Successi d'Inghilterra." In *The Accession, Coronation, and Marriage of Mary Tudor, as related in four manuscripts of the Escorial*, trans. Cesare V. Malfatti. Barcelona, 1956.

The fountayne or well of life ... translated out of latyn in to Englysshe. London: Thomas Godfray, 1534. (STC:11211)

Here in this booke ye haue a godly epistle made by a faithful Christian A comunication betwene Feckna[sic] and the Lady Iane Dudley. A letter that she wrote to her syster Lady Katherin. The ende of the Ladye Iane vpon the scaffolde. Ye shal haue also herein a godly prayer made by maister Iohn Knokes. London: Successor of A. Scoloker, 1554.

Marshall, William. *A primer in English with certain prayers & godly meditations, very necessary for all people that understand not the Latin tongue*. London: John Byddell, 1534.

National Archives (UK). State Papers.
1/190, f.220.
10/15/79, ff. 1787–1789.

A Necessary Doctrine and Erudition for any Christen Man. London: Thomas Berthelet, 1543.

Nichols, John Gough, ed. *The Chronicle of Queen Jane and of Two Years of Queen Mary*. London: J.B. Nichols and Son for the Camden Society, 1850.

Richard Taverner, *An epitome of the Psalmes, or briefe meditacons upon the same, with diverse other moste Christian prayers, translated by Richard Taverner*. London: Printed by R. Bankes for A. Clerke, 1539.

A very proper treatise, wherein is briefly sett forthe the arte of limming.... London: Richard Tottill, 1571.

Secondary Sources

Carley, James. "Italic Ambitions: The Works of Henry VIII's last queen and the problem of identifying exactly what Katherine wrote." In *Times Literary Supplement* 5644 (3 June 2011): 3–5.

Cressy, David. *Education in Tudor and Stuart England*. London: E. Arnold, 1975.

------------------. *Literacy and the Social Order: Reading and Writing in Tudor and Stuart England*. Cambridge: University of Cambridge Press, 1980.

Cumming, Valerie, C.W. Cunnington, and P.E. Cunnington. *The Dictionary of Fashion History*. New York: Berg, 2010.

Davey, Richard. *The Nine Days Queen: Lady Jane Grey and Her Times*, ed. and intro. Martin Hume. New York: G.P. Putnam's Sons and London: Metheun, 1909.

de Hamel, Christopher. *British Library Guide to Manuscript Illumination*. Toronto: University of Toronto Press, 2001.

Edwards, J. Stephan. "A Further Note on the Date of Birth of Lady Jane Grey." *Notes and Queries* 55, no. 2 (June 2008): 146–148.

------------------. "'Jane the Quene': A New Consideration of Lady Jane Grey, England's Nine Days Queen." Unpub. PhD dissertation. University of Colorado–Boulder, 2007.

------------------. "On the Birth Date of Lady Jane Grey." *Notes and Queries* 54, no. 3 (Sept. 2007): 240–242.

------------------. *A Queen of a New Invention: Portraits of Lady Jane Grey Dudley, England's Nine Days Queen*. Palm Springs: Old John Publishing, 2015.

James, Susan E. *Catherine Parr: Henry VIII's Last Love*. Stroud: Tempus Publishing, 2008.

Loades, David. *The Wyatt Rebellion*. Oxford: Davenant Press, 2000.

------------------. *Two Tudor Conspiracies*. Cambridge: Cambridge University Press, 1965.

Morgan, Nigel. "Books for the liturgy and private prayer." In *Cambridge History of the Book in Britain*, II:219-316. Cambridge: Cambridge University Press, 1999–2012.

Mueller, Janel, ed. *Katherine Parr: Complete Works and Correspondence*. Chicago: University of Chicago Press, 2011.

Murphy, Beverley A. *Bastard Prince: Henry VIII's Lost Son*. Stroud: Sutton, 2001.

Nuvoloni, Laura. "The Harleian Medical Manuscripts." *The Electronic British Library Journal* 2008: Article 7. http://www.bl.uk/eblj/2008articles/article7.html. Accessed 2 October 2015.

Smith, Margit, and Jim Bloxam. "The Medieval Girdle Book Project." *The International Journal of the Book* 3:4 (2006): 15–24.

Tait, Hugh. "The girdle-prayerbook or 'tablett': An important class of Renaissance jewellery at the court of Henry VIII." *Jewellery Studies* 2 (1985), 29–57.

Index

Act of Settlement (1701), 6
Act of Six Articles (1539), 16
Act of Ten Articles (1536), 15
Anne I (1665–1714), Queen of England (1702–1714), 6
Aylmer, John (1521–1594), 22, 23 and n.6

Bentinck, Margaret Cavendish Harley (1715–1785), Duchess of Portland, 6
Boleyn, Queen Anne (c.1501–1536), 21
Book of Common Prayer, 17 and n.44
  First Book of Common Prayer, 16, 23 n.11
  Second Book of Common Prayer, 16
books of hours, 12, 17
Brandon, Katherine Willoughby (1519–1580), Dowager Duchess of Suffolk, 12
Brandon, Mary Tudor (1496–1533), 22
British Library, foundation of, 7
British Museum, 6
Brydges, Sir John (1492–1557), Lieuteant of the Tower of London, 1, 3, 4, 5, 19, 20
Brydges, Thomas (d.1599), 4–5
Bucer, Martin (1491–1551), 24 and n.12
Bullinger, Heinrich (1504–1575), 24 and n.12
Burscough, Rev. Robert (1651–1709), 5

Capito, Wolfgang (c.1478–1541), 18

Carew, Peter, Sir (c.1514–1575), 25
Cecil, Mildred (1526–1589), 11
Cecil, William (1520–1598), 11
Chapel of St. Peter-ad-Vincula, *see*: Tower of London
Convocation of Bishops, 15
Cotton, Robert, Sir (1571–1631), 6
Court of King's Bench, 2
Cranmer, Thomas (1489–1556), Archbishop of Canterbury (1533–1555), 16

Denny, Joan Champernowne (d.1553), 12
Douglas, Margaret Tudor Stuart (1489–1541), 22 and n.4
Dudley, Guildford, Lord (1536?–1554), 2, 3 and n.9, 24, 25, 26
Dudley, Jane Grey, Lady (1536/7–1554),
  birth, 21
  education, 23
  execution, 3–4, 26–27
  eye-witness description of, 3–4
  gives prayer book to Thomas Brydges, 4
  handwriting, 19
  imprisonment, 1, 25
  inscription to John Brydges, 19
  marriage, 24
  optimism in face of death, 20
  portraits of, 15
  proclaimed Queen of England, 25
  public popular fascination with, 4–5
  receiving gifts of books, 11
  reign as Queen of England, 2
  religious beliefs, 23–24

theological debate with Feckenham, 26
trial for treason, 2
upbringing, 22–23
written messages to father Henry Grey, 3, 26
Dudley, John (1504–1553), Duke of Northumberland, 24, 25 and *n*.15
Dudley, Katherine (*d*.1620), 25

Edward VI (1537–1553), King of England (1547–1553), 2, 16, 24, 25
Elizabeth I (1533–1603), Queen of England (1558–1603), 10 *n*.29, 11, 17, 21, 24
English Reformation, 16

Feckenham, John Howman de (*c*.1515–1584), 4, 26
First Act of Uniformity (1548/9), 16
Fitzalan, Mary (1540–1557), Duchess of Norfolk, 12
Fitzroy, Henry (1519–1536), 21, 22 and *n*.3
Foxe, John (1516/17–1587), 26

girdle book or tablet, 12
Godfray, Thomas, 18
Grey, Arthur (1536–1593), Baron Grey de Wilton, 25
Grey, Frances Brandon (1517–1559), 21, 22, 26
Grey, Henry, Duke of Suffolk (1517–1554), 2, 3, 21, 25
Grey, Katherine, Lady (1540–1568), 25, 26
Grey, Mary, Lady (c.1545–1578), 25

Harley, Henrietta Cavendish Holles (1694–1755), Countess of Oxford, 6
Harley, Robert (1661–1724), 1st Earl of Oxford, 5
Hastings, Henry (*c*.1535–1595), 3rd Earl of Huntingdon (1560–1595), 25
Henry VII (1457–1509), King of England (1485–1509), 21
Henry VIII (1491–1547), King of England (1509–1547), 15, 16, 18, 21
Herbert, Henry (c.1538–1601), 2nd Earl of Pembroke (1570–1601), 25
Herbert, William (c.1501–1570), 1st Earl of Pembroke, (1551–1570) 25
Hoby, Elizabeth Stoner, 24

illumination of manuscripts, 10

James II and VII (1633–1701), King of England and Scotland (1685–1688), 5

limner, 10, 11

Marshall, William, 17
Mary I (1516–1558), Queen of England (1553–1558), 2, 21, 24, 25
Mass, Roman Catholic, 16
More, Thomas, Sir (1478–1535), 18

Parr, Elizabeth Brooke (1526–1565), 24
Parr, Queen Katherine (1512–1548), 5, 8, 10, 11, 12, 19, 24
Partridge, Nathaniel, Gentleman Gaoler, 1
pendant prayer books, 12
Philip of Spain (1527–1598), King of England (1554–1558), King of Spain (1556–1598), 2, 25
primers, 17, 18
Protestantism, 15, 23
psalters, 12
purgatory, 15, 16, 18

Reformation, in England, 16, 24, 25
Roman Catholic, 5, 6 *n*.16 and 18, 15,

16 *n*.41, 17, 18, 19, 20, 21, 23, 24, 25, 26
Rowe, Nicholas (1674–1718), 6

Sarum Use, 16
scribes, professional, 8, 10
Second Act for the Succession (1536), 21
Seymour, Anne Stanhope (1497–1587), Duchess of Somerset, 24
Seymour, Queen Jane (*c*.1508–1537), 21, 22
Shaxton, Nicholas (*c*.1485–1556), Bishop of Salisbury (1535–1539), 18, 19 and *n*.51
Sloane, Hans, Sir (1660–1753), 6
Stuart, James (1688–1766), 5

Taverner, Richard (1505–1575), 18 and *n*.48
Tower Hill, 2
Tower of London, 1, 2, 3, 25, 26, 27
 Chapel of St Peter-ad-Vincula, 2, 27
Tudor, Margaret Stuart Douglas, *see*: Douglas, Mary Tudor Stuart
Tylney, Mistress, 4

Wyatt, Thomas, Sir (1521–1554), 2, 5, 25
Wyatt's Rebellion, 5, 25

www.ingramcontent.com/pod-product-compliance
Lightning Source LLC
Chambersburg PA
CBHW042059290426
44113CB00005B/101